Under God

I pledge allegiance
to the flag of the United States of America
and to the Republic for which it stands,
one Nation under God,
indivisible,
with liberty and justice for all.

Everyone must submit himself to the governing authorities, for there is no authority except that which God has established. The authorities that exist have been established by God. Consequently, he who rebels against the authority is rebelling against what God has instituted, and those who do so will bring judgment on themselves. For rulers hold no terror for those who do right, but for those who do wrong. Do you want to be free from fear of the one in authority? Then do what is right and he will commend you. For he is God's servant to do you good. But if you do wrong, be afraid, for he does not bear the sword for nothing. He is God's servant, an agent of wrath to bring punishment on the wrongdoer. Therefore, it is necessary to submit to the authorities, not only because of possible punishment but also because of conscience.

This is also why you pay taxes, for the authorities are God's servants, who give their full time to governing. Give everyone what you owe him: If you owe taxes, pay taxes; if revenue, then revenue; if respect, then respect; if honor, then honor.

Romans 13:1-7 (NIV)

Under God

Seventh edition

William C. Hendricks

Mott Media
1130 Fenway Circle
Fenton, Michigan 48430

© 1966, 1972, 1976, 1981 by The National Union of Christian Schools
(now Christian Schools International)
Fifth edition © 1984 by Christian Schools International
Sixth edition © 1998 by Mott Media
Seventh edition © 2013 by Mott Media

All Scriptures are from the NIV Bible.

Printed by: Dickinson Press, Inc., Grand Rapids, Michigan, USA
Batch # , February, 2013

For more information about other Mott Media publications,
visit our website at www.mottmedia.com.

Lori Horton Coeman and Joyce Bohn, editors

ISBN-10: 0-88062-292-X
ISBN-13: 978-0-88062-292-9

Preface

The goal of **Under God** is to develop effective citizens within the framework of the Christian faith and Christian principles. To help students attain this goal, **Under God** includes sound ideas about the foundations of constitutional government and the historical background of United States government.

The starting point in teaching government is the basic conviction that God ordains it. He is the source of authority. That concept is the root of good government. The fear of the Lord is not only the basis, but also the motivation for good citizenship.

The author is deeply conscious of each student's need to develop a wholesome regard for government and a sense of personal responsibility for its proper functioning.

Christian citizenship leaves no room for apathy. After students have considered the ideas presented in this book, we hope they will choose to do some of the suggested activities and to express their concerns through citizen action groups in their communities. Such action will help them to make a lifelong commitment to Christian citizenship.

The *Teacher's Resource Booklet* which includes pertinent teaching suggestions, answer key and unit tests is available to help the teacher or homeschool parent maximize the effectivness of this textbook.

We trust these materials will help Christian students realize their potential for effective citizenship under God.

This textbook follows the standard of using the masculine pronouns when referring to a person or persons of common gender.

Acknowledgments

William C. Hendricks, formerly Associate Professor and Coordinator of Elementary Education at Calvin College, also wrote *God's Temples* and *Toward Christian Maturity*.

The original development of the *Under God* manuscript was made possible with grants from Christian Schools International Foundation and Canadian Christian Education Foundation, Inc.

Before the publication of the first edition in 1966 and since that time, many classroom teachers have made valuable suggestions and contributions to this volume.

Cover design by William P. Hoetger. Background art c grounder—Fotolia.com #34690412.

Credits

Acknowledgment is made to the following for permission to reproduce photographs:

i, ii, v, vii (top), viii (top), ix (top), x (right), xiii, xvi (right), xviii, 15, 19 (bottom), 24, 29, 37, 107, 146, 161 (left), 167 (bottom left), 220, H. Armstrong Roberts; vii (middle), 4, Milford Presbyterian Church, Milford, MI; vii (bottom), 9, Canadian Parliament; viii (top), 49, JVT, stock 2105005; viii (bottom), x (left), xi (top), 27, 28, 33, 34, 35, 39, 51, 61, 64, 71, 94, 103, 123, 158, 179, 180, 203, 217 (bottom), 219, 225, 251, Library of Congress; ix, (bottom), 53 (left), 55, 99, c bbourdages—Fotolia,com; xi (bottom), 95, 205, Ronald Reagan Library; xii (left), 89 (left), 93, 224, Lyndon Johnson Library; xii (right), xvii, 66, 96, 127 (bottom), 161 (right), 227, 232, 249 (top, bottom) Wide World Photos; xiv, J Bryson, stock 724544; xv, xvi (left), 43, 46, 47, 111, 129, The National Archives; 1, 14, Eigene Fotografie, Adrian Sule; 3, Snap Photo, Inc.; 13, EdStock2 #19677331; 19, 23, Ancient Art and Architecture Collection, Ltd.; 21, Corbis-Bettmann; 25, UPI/Corbis-Bettmann; 40, Rogers Cantel, Inc.; 53 (right), SKLA, stock 3965649; 75, JD Jana, stock 3865368; 77 (left), York Foto, stock 19995891; 77 (right), Matthias Haas, stock 13471715; 79 (right), Navy photo 110831-N-IC111-165.ppg by Mass Communication Specialist 2nd Class Kevin B. Gray; 83, U. S. Mint; 89 (right), Gerald Ford Library; 92, The White House; 106, Joe Bob Bubba, stock 299261; 114, c LE image—Fotolia.com #39662572; 116, Milford Police Department, Milford, MI; 122, 188, 208, 213, Edstock, #18966071, #18920679, #18946960, #18966526; 127 (top), Bowden Images, stock #20599495; 127 (center), 155, Bureau of Alcohol, Tobacco and Firearms; 137, 144, Oregon State Highway Travel Division; 141, Eric Guinther, Eikipedia; 143, David R. Frazier; 145, c Jamie Wilson—Fotolia.com #275792; 147, Michigan Dept. of Agriculture; 149, Michigan Dept. of Corrections; 159, 247, Christmas in April®, Oakland County; 160, K. Shabu/CCSD; 166 (top left), 167 (bottom left), White Lake Township Fire Dept.; 166 (top right), 4774344 Sean, stock #13818359; 166 (bottom left), AVTG, stock #20788090; 166 (bottom right), Kurhan #18084463; 167 (top left), Seattle Police Dept.; 167 (top right), Chicago Park District; 167 (center left), Village of Milford DPS, Milford, MI; 169, 172 c moodboard—Fotolia.com #28128483; 174, Bill Bullard, Jr.; 175, Bultman Studios; 181 (top, bottom left, bottom right), U. S. Secret Service; 182, 183, U. S. Air Force; 186, hkuchera, stock #21524183; 190, National Labor Relations Board; 192, spxChrome, stock #4430255; 195, Fermi 2 Power Plant; 211, Casch, stock # 17287189; 235, bonneij, stock #830600; 238, Mari, stock # 14016786; 241, sjlocke, stock #20506127.

Contents

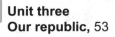

Unit five
Liberty and Justice, 169

Introduction

How often have you said the pledge to the flag of the United States of America? It used to be much more common—in classrooms and at sporting events, club meetings, and public gatherings. Is it difficult for you to remember or count all the times you have placed your hand over your heart and made the pledge, or is it easier because it hasn't been done so often?

What is a pledge? A pledge is a solemn promise. What do you promise when you pledge *allegiance?* Our dictionary says that *allegiance* means **loyalty, faithfulness,** and **obedience**. Because you are a citizen of God's kingdom as well as of the United States, you need to know what Christian citizenship means before you can keep the solemn promise of allegiance you have made so often. You must understand what government is, where its authority comes from, and how your allegiance is to be put into practice.

When you think about it, you may discover many ways in which citizenship could be improved. Are you concerned about this need for improved citizenship? Many students may think seriously and sincerely about this problem. This is important, but it is not enough.

The pledge of allegiance follows you wherever you go. After you graduate from school, will you remember that you have solemnly promised loyalty, faithfulness, and obedience to a nation that is **under God?**

To understand the importance of citizenship, you must realize that the nation to which you pledge your allegiance is under God. The government of our nation is under God in two ways. First, it is under God's rule because He

Understanding the importance of citizenship begins at an early age.

ordained it; our laws must reflect His law. Second, our government is under God's care because He watches over it and provides for it. Perhaps the diagram on this page will help to make this relationship clearer.

While we are called to Christian citizenship, to loyalty, faithfulness, and obedience to our nation under God, people in other lands under other governments have the same responsibilities to the governments God has established there.

God's Word says, "Everyone must submit . . . to the governing authorities . . ." Romans 13:1). It is hoped that this study may help us honor the King of kings as we keep our pledge of allegiance to our nation.

Government under God	
Under His Rule	Under His Care
God ordains or establishes government. God rules the people through the government He establishes.	God cares for the nations through the ages of history. He provides for the needs of individual citizens.

The bombardment of Fort McHenry inspired the "Star-Spangled Banner."

Respecting our flag and national anthem

The flag is displayed in so many places that you see it almost every day. In fact, you may often see it several times a day. The flag is usually hung in such plain view that you can hardly miss seeing it.

But do you really see it? When you look at the flag, do you have the feeling that it is your flag, that it represents your country? Or has the flag become such a common sight that it no longer causes you to be thankful you are an American?

On the evening of September 13, 1814, the American-held Fort McHenry was under the fire of the British fleet which lay anchored in Chesapeake Bay. Throughout the night Francis Scott Key was able to get only a few glimpses of the flag in the light of exploding shells. The questions he asked as the next

morning slowly drew near are found in the first verse of the "Star-Spangled Banner."

> Oh, say! can you see,
>   by the dawn's early light,
> What so proudly we hailed
>   at the twilight's last gleaming,
> Whose broad stripes and bright stars,
>   through the perilous fight,
> O'er the ramparts we watched
>   were so gallantly streaming?
> And the rockets' red glare,
>   the bombs bursting in air,
> Gave proof through the night
>   that our flag was still there.
> Oh, say, does that Star-spangled Banner
>   yet wave
> O'er the land of the free
>   and the home of the brave?

In spite of the attack made during the

Francis Scott Key

The Marine Corps War Memorial in Arlington, Virginia, commemorates the raising of the U.S. flag over Iwo Jima during World War II.

night, the star-spangled banner was waving over that fort the next morning. It was tattered and torn, but it was still there. How happy Mr. Key must have been to see it. He must have been thankful, too, for the song he wrote ends with a verse that contains a prayer.

Oh, thus be it ever when free men shall stand
Between their loved homes
    and the war's desolation!
Blest with vict'ry and peace,
    may the heav'n-rescued land
Praise the Pow'r
    that hath made and preserved us a nation!
Then conquer we must,
    when our cause it is just,
And this be our motto:
    "In God is our trust."
And the Star-spangled Banner
    in triumph shall wave
O'er the land of the free
    and the home of the brave!

"In God is our trust," "Praise the Pow'r that hath made and preserved us a nation!" These are thoughts that came to the mind of Francis Scott Key when he saw the flag as the sun began to rise the morning after the battle. Seeing the flag surely meant a great deal to him.

The pledge to the flag was first written in August, 1892, by Francis Bellamy, a newspaperman on the staff of the *Youth's Companion* magazine. This popular magazine was then published for young people in Boston, Massachusetts. The pledge was first used in public at a Columbus Day program on October 12, 1892.

Later the words "of the United States of America" were added after "flag" so that the pledge might mean more to immigrants and their children.

In 1954 Congress passed an act to add the words, "under God." When President Eisenhower signed this act, he said,

From this day forward, the millions of school children will daily proclaim in every city and town, every village and rural school house, the dedication of our nation and our people to the Almighty.

To anyone who truly loves America, nothing could be more inspiring than to contemplate this rededication of our youth, on each school morning, to our country's true meaning.

Especially is this meaningful as we regard today's world. Over the globe, mankind has been cruelly torn by violence and brutality and, by millions, deadened in mind and soul by a materialistic philosophy of life. Man everywhere is appalled by the prospect of atomic war.

In this somber setting, this law and its effects today have profound meaning. In this way we are reaffirming the *transcendence* of religious faith in America's *heritage* and future; in this way we shall constantly strengthen those spiritual weapons which forever will be our country's most powerful resource in peace and in war.

"Under God," the words most recently added to the flag pledge, form the title of this textbook about citizenship and government. As you read these pages, may you clearly see how our government is under God's watchful care and under the authority of His law.

President Dwight D. Eisenhower

Symbol only

Respect is shown to our flag because it is a symbol. We do not honor the flag because the cloth from which it is made is different from other cloth, nor do we salute it because it is hung in a high or prominent place. We respect the flag because it is a symbol of our nation. When we pledge our allegiance to the flag of the United States of America, we promise to be loyal, faithful, and obedient to the republic, the nation under God, for which it stands.

A 2004 Supreme Court decision implies that the words "under God" in the flag pledge are only an expression honoring the historic tradition of our nation. For a large part of our nation's people, this is undoubtedly so. Yet, as Christians, we may give these words real meaning in our lives.

How to respect and display our flag

We should respect our flag and display it according to the present-day rules of the United States flag code. Here are a few of the most common regulations.

1. The flag may be displayed out-of-doors from sunrise to sunset on buildings and stationary flagstaffs. However, the flag is to be lighted at all times, whether by sunlight or by an appropriate light source if displayed after sunset.
2. The flag should not be displayed out-of-doors when the weather is inclement.
3. The flag should be hoisted briskly and lowered ceremoniously.
4. Do not let the flag touch anything beneath it, such as the ground, floor, or water.
5. The flag should not be used for holding, carrying, or delivering anything.
6. When carried in a procession with other flags, the United States flag should be on the marching right, or in front of the center of a line of flags in the parade.
7. Do not display the flag with the union down except as a signal of dire distress.
8. When the flag is displayed on a speaker's platform, it should be on the speaker's right as he faces the audience if it is on a staff. If it is displayed flat on the wall, the flag should be behind and above the speaker with the union on his right.
9. Do not place lettering of any kind on the flag or attach these to it.
10. The flag may be flown at half-staff as a sign of mourning. On such occasions it must first be hoisted to the peak and then lowered to the half-staff position. The flag should be raised to the peak before it is lowered for the day.
11. If other flags are displayed on the same flagstaff, the United States flag should be uppermost.

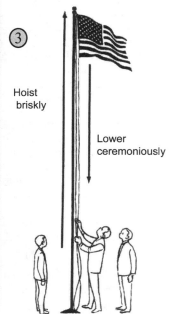

Hoist briskly

Lower ceremoniously

12   When a flag is in such condition that it is no longer a fitting emblem for display, it should be destroyed in a dignified way, preferably by burning.

The salute to the flag, and the national anthem

When the flag is raised or lowered, all those present should stand at attention and salute with the right hand over the heart. Men not in military uniform should remove their hats. Non-citizens are expected to stand at attention.

If the flag is carried in a parade, men should remove their hats and spectators should give the salute at the moment the flag passes.

When the national anthem is played and the flag is not displayed, everyone should rise and stand at attention, facing toward the music. If the flag is present, the audience should face the flag and salute with their right hands over their hearts. This honor should always be shown to the national anthem when it is played by a band, orchestra, or other musical instruments. However, when the "Star-spangled Banner" is played on a recording over a radio or other sound system in a public place, such as a restaurant, the Office of the National Americanism Commission believes that it would seem forced and unnatural to pay special respect. The national anthem should not be applauded, nor should it be played as some other song would be, but should be played at places of ceremony and good order where proper respect can be displayed by those present.

Hoist to peak   Lower to half-staff

Do you remember what you have read?

1. In what two ways is our nation under God?
2. What do you promise when you say, "I pledge allegiance"?

For further thought

1. Why should we stand at attention when the national anthem is played?
2. Some religious groups refuse to salute the flag because they believe that it makes the flag an object of worship. What do you think of this belief?

Things to do

1. Plan a patriotic assembly for your school.
2. Read and report on the story *A Man Without a Country,* by Edward Everett Hale. A motion picture film with this title is available for classroom use.
3. Create an artistic display of the pledge of allegiance and post it near the flag in your classroom or other appropriate area.
4. Sponsor an all-school creative writing and poster contest using the theme, RESPECTING THE FLAG. As a class, set up the rules. Then divide into groups to introduce the idea to the other classes and serve as the contest judges.
5. Do a random survey to see how many prople can recite the pledge of allegiance. If the respondent cannot do so, ask if they can remember how long it has been since they recited it.

Words to study

allegiance	ordain
ceremoniously	transcendence
heritage	

Francis Bellamy's pledge to the flag was first recited at services marking the 400th anniversary of Columbus' discovery of America.

Have you ever watched a construction
crew as they built the foundation
for a high building?
Usually, a bulldozer and a power shovel
are used to dig a large hole.
The loose surface dirt is removed,
and a concrete footing
is placed deep into the ground
to provide a solid foundation.
If you look carefully,
you can see the many steel rods
that are placed in the concrete
to keep it from cracking or crumbling.
The construction engineer knows that
if the building is to be high and solid,
the foundation must be deep and strong.
Then, though storms come and years
pass, the building will stand.
Governments also
are built on foundations.
Loyal, faithful, obedient citizens
form the solid foundations

Unit one
The foundations
of government

of strong governments.
Good citizenship
cannot be built on ignorance
because unlearned people
can be swayed easily.
Citizenship cannot be stable and enduring
if citizens quickly change
from one ideal to another.
To learn more about our own government
and those of other nations we must first
examine some of the basic ideas
about all government.
We must know what government is
and where it gets its authority.
We should seek to understand
the purpose of government
as well as its different *spheres*
of authority.
Gaining a thorough knowledge
of these ideas
can strengthen our own convictions
and ideals.
As our citizenship grows stronger
through a more complete knowledge
of the basic ideas of government,
we will be better able to fill our place
in the foundation of our government.
We and all members of our generation
must work willingly
with courage and conviction
so that the foundations of our government
will not crumble.

1

Government and authority

Important ideas to look for:
- God has the supreme right to authority.
- Everyone is under authority.
- The home, school, church, and state are spheres of authority.
- The spheres of authority change in influence as you grow and mature.

Authority, a basic idea of government

We read in Romans 13:1,* "Everyone must submit . . . to the governing authorities, for there is no authority except that which God has established. The authorities that exist have been established by God."

This text says that God establishes governments, and that everyone must be obedient to them. When God *institutes* or *ordains* a government, He gives *authority* to it. **Authority is the right to be heard, to direct, to command, and to be obeyed.**

God, as Creator and Guide of all things, has this right of *supreme* authority for two reasons. First, it is *inherently* a part of His divinity. Because He is God, He has the right to be heard, to direct, to command, and to be obeyed. Authority is one of the *attributes* of His being. Without the right of supreme authority, God could not be God. Second, God has authority over the world because He made it. It is His. Psalm 24:1 tells us, "The earth is the Lord's, and everything in it, the world, and all who live in it." All people are God's creatures whether they admit it or not. When you invent something, you patent it and control your invention. In a similar way God has the right to ordain governments among people because He created them.

Spheres of authority

Everyone is under authority. You, too, are under government. During your lifetime you are affected by government in several spheres: the home, the school, the church, and the state. To each sphere you are to grant your loyalty, your faithfulness, and your obedience as they are expected and required.

For each of us government begins in the **home.** God gave the fifth commandment, "Honor your father and your mother, so that you may live long in the land the Lord your God is giving you" (Exod. 20:12). By this commandment God ordered that children must respect the authority of their parents. This authority is also under God. Parents have the responsibility to "Train a child in the way he should go . . ." (Prov. 22:6). We know from the story of Eli and his sons that

---

*All Scripture references are taken from the New International Version unless otherwise noted.

God is not pleased with parents who fail to do so. This responsibility includes helping children to build habits of personal devotion and prayer as well as teaching them how to live among their fellow human beings in a Christian way.

We see, then, that children must obey their parents because God directed that parents should exercise authority in the home. Parents in turn must be very careful how they use this authority, for they must do so according to God's will.

In early childhood you knew only the authority of your parents in the home. As you grew older, you had more freedom from parental authority and more personal responsibility toward God and your fellow men. This responsibility increases until finally you become the authority in a new home, one of your own, which also must be dedicated to God's praise.

When you were about four or five years old, you met a new authority, the **school.** We say that the school is a sphere of authority because as a pupil you are under its rule. You must give your loyalty, your faithfulness, and your obedience to your school because it also is under God. Teachers must use authority not for their personal wishes, but rather in obedience to God. Teachers receive their authority from God, and He will hold them responsible for the way in which they use that authority.

God has entrusted the training of children to their parents. Some parents who wish their children to receive a Christian education form societies and build Christian schools. Such parents share some of their parental authority and responsibility with the Christian teachers they hire. Several other kinds of private schools are also in operation in our nation.

Many churches in our nation maintain *parochial* schools for the education of the children and the young people in their membership. In these schools the church assumes the primary responsibility for the type of education given.

Parents who do not desire or cannot obtain a Christian school education for their children and do not send them to some other type of parochial or private school allow the state to educate their children in public schools.

A Christian school represents the authority of both the home and the state.

Public education, as all education, is very necessary if the state is to have citizens who are able to vote intelligently and to carry out the duties of citizenship.

Government in a Christian school represents the authority of both the home and the state because the state makes laws for all schools.

Although the influence of the school continues through life, the sphere of authority of the school ends upon graduation.

We are also under the authority of the **church.** This sphere of authority is the greatest in the life of the Christian. The authority that God ordains in the home, the school, and the state concerns us only for this life or a part of it. But the authority of Christ, as it is represented in the church, continues through this life and into eternity. In a special way Christ is the source of authority in this sphere of government because He is King of the church: ". . . All authority in heaven and on earth has been given to me" (Matt. 28:18).

According to Scripture, the state may

*The church exercises authority
in spiritual matters.*

not make laws that prevent people from worshiping and serving God according to their consciences. **God has kept the heart of man for Himself; He has not turned it over to earthly governments.** This does not mean that the thoughts of the heart are outside of law; no, it is exactly here that the authority of the church in our lives may be seen.

The church is the earthly manifestation of the Lord's heavenly kingdom. The church on earth proclaims God's Word and celebrates the sacraments ordained by Christ. As we grow older and become professing members of the church, its authority in our lives increases.

We do not have a vote in making the laws

of God's kingdom, for He has made them Himself. He has the power to do this, for He is *sovereign*; He has absolute authority, for He is God. No one can say to God ". . . What have you done?" (Dan. 4:35). Here, too, we must pledge our loyalty, faithfulness, and obedience, not out of fear but out of love for Him.

Besides the home, the school, and the church, the one other large area of authority that governs us is the **state,** or *civil,* government. Just as God provides for the authority of parents in the home, the authority of the teacher in the school, and the authority of the consistory or council in the church, so He also establishes civil governments among men to promote law and order.

It is true that people have misused the authority that God has entrusted to them. You will remember the story of Jezebel when she asked Ahab, "Is this how you act as king over Israel?" (I Kings 21:7). She thought that because Ahab was king, he could do anything he wanted to do. But the rulers of the past were not free to do just as they pleased; nor are the rulers of today, for the authority that God has entrusted to the state or civil governments of the earth must also be used according to His laws.

As you grow up and *mature*, the authority of the home diminishes, and *political* authority increases in your life. For example, when you obtain a driver's license, a whole new area of civil authority, the traffic laws for automobile drivers, enters your life. Remember, then, to be loyal, faithful, and obedient to the governing authorities. When you grow older, you may enter military service, some type of business, or a profession. Perhaps you will buy property or build a house. In all of these activities you will be expected to assume the full responsibility of adult citizenship in the sphere of civil government.

These four spheres of authority—the home, the school, the church, and the state—all

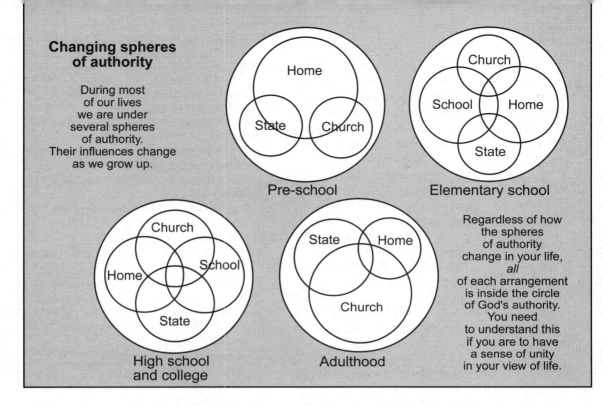

Changing spheres of authority

During most of our lives we are under several spheres of authority. Their influences change as we grow up.

Pre-school

Elementary school

High school and college

Adulthood

Regardless of how the spheres of authority change in your life, *all* of each arrangement is inside the circle of God's authority. You need to understand this if you are to have a sense of unity in your view of life.

reflect God's sovereign authority. The authority that God gives to one sphere necessarily limits the authority of the others. The home may not do whatever it pleases because the authority of the school, the church, and the state do not permit it to do so. The school may not do whatever it wishes because the home, the church, and the state limit its authority. We see, then, that although these four spheres of authority are partly independent or sovereign, they are in many ways *interdependent*. All are ordained by God, and are under His rule and care.

It is not always easy to determine the point at which the authority of one sphere ends and the authority of another begins. This point is difficult to determine because the spheres of authority often overlap. For example, the home influences the school. The church and the state, to some degree, control both the home and the school. Even though lines of authority are not always clear, we must remember that the basis for all authority is

the same—the spheres of authority all rest inside the circle of God's authority. There are no blank spaces.

Some citizens act as though there were blank spaces among the four spheres of authority, where there is no government. These people may be well-behaved in their homes and also in their schools. They may be sincere and well-mannered in church, and they may drive carefully when a patrol car is following them. But when persons in authority are temporarily absent—parents away from home, teacher out of the room, church service not yet begun, or patrol car nowhere in sight—they display very poor citizenship. These people prove that they do not really understand what *allegiance* means.

The Bible commands us to "submit to the governing authorities," that is, to obey authority in every sphere that God has placed over us. This is not always easy for us to do because we are rebellious by nature, and we would rather not obey anyone.

There is, however, one condition under which we may justly disobey the governing authorities that God has appointed for us. We may disobey a law of our earthly authorities or rulers if in obeying it, we would break the law of God. Then, regardless of the punishment we might receive, we must say, as Peter did, ". . . We must obey God rather than men!" (Acts 5:29).

Our obedience to the authorities that God has placed over us must not be a blind and thoughtless response. Rather, we must consider the requirements carefully. We must remember that by obeying the governing authorities we are first of all obeying God, who appointed them to rule over us. True citizenship can only be Christian citizenship, for every earthly authority is always under God.

Do you remember what you have read?
1. What is authority?
2. Give two reasons why God has the right of supreme authority.
3. List the four main spheres of authority.
4. How do the spheres of authority change for you as you grow older?

For further thought
1. In what way does the authority of the school and the state overlap in your life today?
2. If the laws of the Bible and the laws of our nation disagree, where must your allegiance be placed?
3. Why are there no blank spaces where there is no authority over us?
4. If we believe that all governing powers are of God (Rom. 13:1), how do we explain that some governments limit religious freedom or forbid their people to worship God? What should Christians do in such countries?
5. Are demonstrations, such as anti-abortion marches, proper means for a Christian to protest injustice?
6. If you believe a law is wrong, do you have the right to break the law? Why?
7. Tell which sphere of authority should govern these situations:
   a. A person disobeys a speed law on the highway.
   b. A girl talks back to her mother.
   c. Two children are fighting on the school playground during recess.
   d. A boy who is too young to obtain a driver's license drives a car on the highway.
   e. A man insults his neighbor.
   f. A person borrows a hymnbook from church and never returns it.
   g. A woman parks her car in a "no parking" zone before attending church.
   h. A boy throws a ball through the living room window of his own home.
   i. Breaking fire regulations, the ushers fill the church aisles with chairs.
   j. A person uses obscene language in a public place of business.

Words to study

allegiance	mature
attribute	ordain
authority	parochial
civil	political
inherent	sovereign
institute	sphere
interdependent	supreme

The nature of government

Important ideas to look for:
- Government is God's agency for governing human beings.
- Government gives order to human relations.
- God uses various means to appoint government leaders.
- Government must serve the people and administer justice.

What is government?

The word *government* comes from the Latin term *gubernare.* It means to guide, to steer, to manage, or to pilot. **Government is, therefore, that authority which manages or controls the people.**

Government is an agency God uses to carry out His will among human beings. In some nations God uses many people to rule; in others He uses only a few. Sometimes God uses only one person to carry out His plan for a nation.

God governs the nations by means of people. However, all of the people of a nation cannot always be involved in running their government, so the government must usually be operated by a small number of leaders. In some nations these leaders are selected by all of the people; in others, the people have very little to say about who their leaders will be.

The leaders use their authority to enforce laws that were made in the past, and to formulate policies or decide upon the things that need to be done. The leaders also *execute* or carry out their plans and purposes. As they formulate and execute their plans, these leaders are governing—they are serving as the government of the nation.

Some governments decide upon and carry out their plans according to the wishes of the people. Other governments do not ask the people, but make the decisions themselves. In either case, the government manages or controls the people.

Although the governments of the earth are *constituted* of sinful humans who are free to make their own decisions, behind this earthly picture is the controlling power of our God. It is He who ordains governments to rule the people. He gives the rulers the daily strength and wisdom to do so. He holds the nations of the earth in His almighty hand. Every earthly government, even one that wickedly rebels against God's will, performs its purpose in His plan for history.

"There are four testaments," said Joseph Cook, a nineteenth-century philosopher, when he was talking about the foundations of the Christian religion, "the oldest, the Old, the New, and the newest. The Old Testament and the New are written. The oldest testament is the way God reveals Himself in the creation, in the nature of things. The newest is the present action of God in human history.

"I interpret the oldest and the newest by the Old and the New. Our surest guide beyond all doubt is the written Word; but God wrote the oldest testament in the creation and nature of things, and God still writes the newest current

The four Testaments

Oldest	God reveals Himself to us through the universe that He has created —through nature, the nature of things. In school our geography, science, and mathematics help us to understand this oldest testament that God has given to us about Himself.
Old/New	This is the written Word of God where we can read most clearly the story of sin and salvation. We must use the Old and New Testaments to interpret the oldest and the newest.
Newest	Since the Bible has been completed, God continues to reveal Himself to us through the newest current history. As we study the languages and literature, music, art, and all the inventions of mankind, we may also see some of the beauty and wisdom of God, for man was made to reflect God's image.

history, the last unrolling chapter . . . whether in church, in science, or in politics. He is here with us today in the oldest testament and here in the newest, although He is not as easily seen in them as He is in the written Word, but the four testaments are His and therefore one."

The governments of the nations of the earth will continue to serve as His instruments until each has played its part and the curtain is drawn at the end of time. The earthly governments we know will not be needed when Christ returns, for the kingdom of the world will become the kingdom of our Lord and Christ, Who "shall reign for ever and ever" (Rev. 11:15).

Why government?

Have you ever wondered why we must have governments? Have you ever wondered what the world would be like if there were no laws, no taxes, no police officers, no government of any kind?

Sin came upon the human race when our first parents disobeyed the law that God had made for them. Since that time, humanity has been a race of lawbreakers; we have set ourselves not only against God but also against our fellow humans.

During the time of the Judges we read that ". . . everyone did as he saw fit" (Judges 17:6). What confusion such behavior must have caused! Since the population of the earth has increased a great deal, how much more confused the world would be if people did what they wanted to do today!

We know that our God is a God of order and not of confusion. We see God's order reflected in the way He has made the universe. He has given each planet an orbit of its own; He has given each star its place to shine. To help preserve order among people, God has established governments.

God created humans as *social* beings, and, in His divine wisdom, made them members of *society.* God said, "It is not good for the man to be alone" (Gen. 2: 18). Because of this need for other human beings, implanted in them by God, there exists a *fundamental* need and desire for fellowship and association with others. You know from your own life that this is true in adults and children alike. You like to be with other people; it is a part of your nature.

The purpose of government, then, is to guide and control human relationships. What would life be like without laws to regulate it? Undoubtedly, it would be *chaotic*. But God did not create the world to be chaotic. God

8   *The foundations of government*

established laws to govern social life. These laws were originally written in the human heart, and Adam obeyed them because his will was in harmony with God's will. But when humanity fell into sin, the will was changed so that it was no longer in harmony with the will of the Creator. Natural or sinful humanity does not care for the principles established by God for the regulation of social relationships. The Christian should not forget, however, that the government God ordains to restrain evil is itself made up of sinful people who may often do wrong as they attempt to maintain right.

Governments must seek to bring social and civil relationships into harmony with God's will. Restraining evil deeds is one way in which the government fulfills this purpose. Laws of our government which restrain evil are not a heavy burden upon an unhappy people; they are good gifts of God to bring social relationships into God's order.

The business of governing Canada is carried out in the House of Commons Chamber in the Parliament Building, Ottawa, Ontario.

How is government established under God?

After God created the world, He did not leave it to care for itself. He has kept it in His care every moment since He made it. We call His care for the earth and for each of His creatures *providence.* Although God's providence is also shown in special ways, such as direct answers to our prayers and unusual blessings, most of the time God provides for us through the use of natural forces or laws which He has created. The law of gravity, the orderliness of the seasons, the rain cycle—all of these are of God and under God, for He ". . . works out everything in conformity with the purpose of his will" (Eph. 1:11).

God uses natural and human means to bring the people He appoints to positions of leadership in government. In some of the nations of the world, the leaders are ordained through inheritance of a throne; others are established in power by means of influence or special ability. In our nation God uses the votes cast by the people to establish govern-

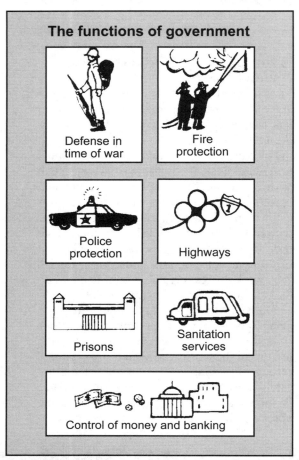

The functions of government

Defense in time of war

Fire protection

Police protection

Highways

Prisons

Sanitation services

Control of money and banking

Governments provide many services as God's servants for our good.

ment leaders. Therefore, we must vote intelligently and prayerfully as we seek to elect the people God would have to lead us.

But government officials do not always use fair and honest ways to gain power. Often *treachery,* cheating, and force are used. Yet, we know that even such *unscrupulous* leaders hold their positions only by God's providence. God's appointment involves more than good leaders for our happiness and prosperity. He also judges the nations of the earth by sending corrupt leaders for the punishment of those who do not fear and obey His laws and for the *chastisement* of those He wishes to draw nearer to Himself. Even godless rulers are the servants of God, for He is the Lord of lords and King of kings.

What is the function of government under God?

After the Bible tells us in Romans 13:1-3 that governments are instituted by God and that we are to be obedient to them, we read in verse 4: "for he is God's servant to do you good. But if you do wrong, be afraid, for he does not bear the sword for nothing." In this verse God gives two very important tasks to the governments that He has established. First, God expects governments to do good for the people they rule, and second, God gives these governments the responsibility to punish evil. These two tasks are so important that they become the very nature of the government itself.

The responsibility to do good

"For he is God's servant to do you good" (Rom. 13:4a). Here we are told that these "higher powers," or governing authorities ordained by God, must not only be rulers, but also servants to do good. The various nations may not all agree on what is good. They may seek to do this good for their subjects in widely different ways. Yet one of the functions of government is that it seeks to provide good services for the people of the land. These services are blessings from our God.

Government must function as the organization for solving the problems of society; its laws must be based upon God's law if it is to function as God's servant for good.

As the governments of the earth carry out their tasks, they do so in a world filled with sin. In our nation, as in all other nations, the government often oversteps its bounds and fails to serve as a servant of God for good.

The responsibility to punish evil

"But if you do wrong, be afraid, for he does not bear the sword for nothing. He is God's servant, an agent of wrath to bring punishment on the wrongdoer" (Rom. 13:4b). Here we have an expression of the second function of government—the responsibility to punish those who do evil.

Shortly after the flood, in the days of Noah, God stated: "Whoever sheds the blood of man, by man shall his blood be shed" (Gen. 9:6). Early in history, even before the Ten Commandments were given on Mt. Sinai, God had commanded society (the organization of humankind) to punish those who tried to destroy that society or any member of that society. At the time the Apostle Paul wrote the book of Romans, the sword of the Roman soldier was the symbol of authority in the Roman Empire. Roman soldiers were often *ruthless* as they punished those who dared to break the Roman law.

The governments on the earth today must still bear the sword to control those who would do evil. Although the nations may differ in the way they make their laws and in their methods of law enforcement, they all have the same responsibility to punish those who do wrong. Earthly governments must be very careful as they bear the sword, as servants of God. One day all people involved in government will have to give account to God for the use of the power entrusted to them.

As we study the government of our nation, we will learn that it has many laws for controlling evil. Law enforcement agencies, such as the FBI, the Secret Service, the state patrol, the border patrol, as well as local police officers, daily bring lawbreakers to trial. Our system of courts and prisons also helps to bear the sword as it administers justice. Our President, our senators, our judges, our law enforcement officers—all government officials must remember that their authority comes from God. He calls them not only to be His servants for good, but also to bear the sword for the punishment of those who do wrong.

Do you remember what you have read?
1. What is government?
2. Why is government necessary?

3. What do we mean when we say that humans are social beings?
4. What are the two functions of government?
5. Name five services that our government provides for her citizens as a servant of God for good.
6. In what way does our government bear a sword?

For further thought
1. Are we losing some of our individual freedoms today because of the expanding services of government?
2. How are people brought to positions of government leadership in our country? In other countries?
3. Make a list of the services that the government provides for you in your community.
4. How can you determine if a service should be provided by the government or left to some other aspect of society, such as the home or private business?
5. Do you know of any government law that provides a good service for some people and causes hardship for others? How should lawmakers decide if a government service is good?
6. Review the Book of Judges and make a list of times that God used foreign governments to punish His people Israel.
7. God sometimes uses evil rulers to fulfill His will. Does this excuse them for their evil deeds? Why or why not?
8. Controlling evil consumes much of the government's time and money. Why is this such a difficult task?

Memory work
Romans 13:1-7

Words to study

chaotic	providence
chastisement	ruthless
constitute	social
execute	society
fundamental	treachery
government	unscrupulous

Chapter 3

Civil governments compared

Important ideas to look for:
- Our type of government is one of many.
- God may use one man or many to control government.
- Some countries may not be ready for democracy.
- Democracy demands an educated, responsible citizenry.

Types of civil government

Throughout the ages many types of civil government have existed. There have been areas of the world where there was *anarchy* (lawlessness or lack of government). In the absence of government each person would do as he pleased. Other countries have had governments that believed in the concept of *laissez-faire* (leh'-say-fair'). This term literally means "let be" or "hands off" and refers to government policies of noninterference in certain affairs of the country, such as economics. In nations or in times of little or no government, chaos and confusion could often be found. In contrast, some areas have also been under the complete control of cruel leaders who ruthlessly demanded that everyone *conform* to their will. Are either of these extremes good? No, for one disregards God's desire for an orderly society, and the other ignores the basic civil rights of each individual to life, liberty, and the pursuit of happiness. Let us look briefly at the main types of government.

Theocracy This type of government is directly under the rule of God. When God led the children of Israel out of the land of Egypt, He showed them the way to go. He led them with a pillar of cloud by day and a pillar of fire by night.

The people neither voted on the route they were to take nor decided when a battle should be fought. They were directly under the government of the Lord. He spoke directly to Moses and continued to reveal His will to the people through the prophets. Although some countries have state religions, there are no theocracies on earth today.

Monarchy We know this is an old type of government because, when the Israelites wanted a king, they said to Samuel ". . . now appoint a king to lead us, such as all the other nations have" (I Sam. 8:5). God consented to the request of the people, but He warned them at that time that they could expect their king to make heavy demands for their goods and work. History is filled with the stories of monarchs, both wise and foolish, kind and cruel. Some were chosen by the people they would rule; others came to the throne by inheritance. The doctrine of the "divine right of kings," most clearly stated by James I of

England, held that the king was appointed by God to rule the people. Although this doctrine was often misused by kings to excuse their wrongdoings and strengthen their positions, history shows us that God has long used the office of monarch for the government of people. Monarchies have existed in two different forms: absolute and limited.

In an *absolute monarchy* the king has complete power over his subjects. King Nebuchadnezzar was such a king. He ordered the astrologers killed or he spared them as he wished. Although the absolute form of monarchy was quite general in early civilizations, it is almost out of existence today.

A *limited monarchy* is a form of monarchy in which the power of the king or queen is controlled, or limited, through laws that have been passed by representatives of the people. Today, the Queen of England, for example, has no real power; she is only a formal ruler. The prime minister, leader of a majority of the elected representatives, is the head of government.

Oligarchy An oligarchy is a type of government controlled by a small group of leaders. They may be leaders of the armed forces, of politics, or of finance. Often such governments are short-lived because disagreements and jealousies usually arise between the members. No one has complete authority. There is no system of checks and balances, such as the system that exists between the branches of government in a democracy. You will remember that Caesar was stabbed because others within the small group of Roman leaders thought that he was trying to make himself an emperor.

An *aristocracy* is one form of the oligarchic type of government. The upper class of people in a nation are called its aristocracy. In many nations in the past and in several today the upper class people are also the rulers of the nation. In a government controlled by the aristocracy, those people who have the most

In a limited monarchy like Great Britain, Elizabeth II (shown with the Duke of Edinburgh), rules as queen, but the prime minister is elected by the citizens.

property, the most education, or the most influence generally make the laws to govern the lower classes of people. Sometimes the aristocrats assume their leadership through force and deceit, but often they become leaders because of their position and abilities. The oligarchic type of government can serve a nation very well, if qualified leaders seek the welfare of the people in a way that is pleasing to God.

Democracy A democratic type of government is one in which the people of a nation have the power to govern themselves either directly or through their elected representatives. Democracy literally means "rule by the people."

A *pure democracy* is a government in which every adult citizen has an equal voice in the operation of the country. Such pure democracy was possible in some of the early Greek states whose populations were rather small. Every free person took part in the election of officers, in voting for taxes, and in passing laws. Slaves, however, were not allowed to participate. The pure form of democracy was also used for some time in local government of the early towns in

Pure democracy is possible when the population is rather small. At this outdoor meeting a canton in Glarus, Switzerland discusses its problems.

New England; everyone was given an equal voice in the town meeting. A few cantons in Switzerland still use the Citizens Assembly for deciding matters of public business.

A *republic* is the form of democracy that is most commonly used today. In a republic the nation is governed by officials who have been elected by the people. Many nations are so large and their population so great that all

their citizens could not possibly have a common meeting place for everyone to discuss the problems of government and make laws. Therefore, a representative democracy, or republic, is the form of government closest to a pure democracy that large nations can have. In a republic, as in a democracy, the highest authority, under God, is with the people.

Although many nations of today are republics, they use different systems of governing themselves through their elected representatives. Our United States government uses the *presidential system.* Under this system, the elected officials remain in office a specific length of time regardless of whether they have the support of Congress. Under the *parliamentary system*, however, government leaders depend upon the constant support of the elected assemblies for their positions in office.

Dictatorship A dictatorship, like an absolute monarchy, is governed by just one individual who has complete authority over his people. The position of a king is usually *inherited*, but the position of a dictator is generally gained with the aid of influential friends or by force.

Whenever any government allows no other political groups to exist, the government is said to be *totalitarian*. We must recognize, however, that it is almost as impossible for an absolute monarch, or dictator, to rule completely alone as it is for all citizens in a democracy to have rights that are absolutely equal.

Comparison of governments

After discussing these types and forms of government we should ask, "Which do you like best?" Or perhaps a better question would be, "Which one actually is the best?" To answer this, we would have to say, "The one that governs best—the one that is the best servant of God for good and best bears the sword to punish evildoers." We believe that, for us, the democracy or the republic, which is a representative democracy, is best able to do this. Our form of government is based upon the value of each individual citizen. The Declaration of Independence states that each citizen has received the inalienable rights of life, liberty, and the pursuit of happiness from the Creator. We believe that our Constitution gives to our people the *dignity* and the rights, the freedom, and the opportunity that God intended them to have.

However, before a republic can provide liberty and justice for all its people, it must have a high rate of *literacy*, the ability to read and write. Because people are expected to vote intelligently in a republic, they should be literate and well-educated.

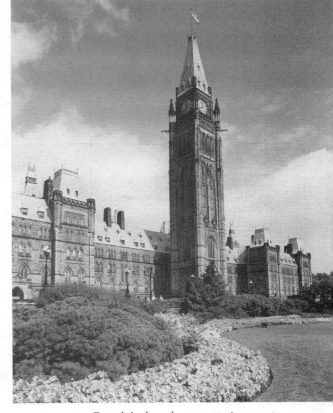

Canada's elected representatives meet in the Parliament Building in Ottawa. Government leaders must have the constant support of the members of parliament.

Most important of all, before a nation can govern itself successfully in a republic, the people must be able to assume responsibility. Unless the citizens of a nation are willing to be loyal, faithful, obedient, and able to keep themselves informed, the government is soon subject to corruption and revolution. Not all countries that have tried democracy have found it to be successful. Under such conditions, God may ordain an oligarchy, a

Types of government and their differences

Type of government	Number who rule	Chief executive	Characteristics and examples
None— anarchy	None	None	Chaos, often war, reigns as in Israel during the times between the various judges.
Absolute monarchy Totalitarian or Dictatorship	**One person**	King Dictator	King holds complete authority. Self-assumed throne and elected monarchs preceded the hereditary types of today. Dictator has complete authority; gets office by force or through political friends.
Oligarchy Aristocracy	**Few people**	Small group of leaders Best qualified	Efficient when led by able men. Jealousy and distrust may arise between leaders. Government controlled by most able persons. Common people have little or no voice in government.
Limited monarchy Republic	**Many people**	King or Queen and Prime Minister (monarch under law) President (elected representatives)	These governments are of two types: 1 Parliamentary—government executives are dependent upon the constant support of the elected assemblies. Most of these are limited monarchies (Canada, Great Britain, The Netherlands, Sweden) while a few are republics (France, Italy). 2 Presidential—government executives remain in office for a specific length of time regardless of whether or not they have the support of the elected assemblies (United States).
Pure democracy	**All people**	Elected leaders	Usually a small, well-educated society with great concern for government on the part of all.

monarchy, or even a dictatorship. God can use a few people, or even just one person, to fulfill His will as well as He can use all.

The best form of government for one period of history is not necessarily the best for another. Nor is the best form of government necessarily the best form when conditions change. If a nation is overcome by corruption in government office, or by disorder, disobedience, indifference, or *apathy* among the citizenry, another type of government may be more suitable.

Governments of all types and forms are gifts of God, but the gift of a democratic society composed of a well-ordered, responsible body of citizens is the greatest of such benefits. In the sixteenth century governments ruled with a *rod of iron* and discipline was harsh. Even then John Calvin believed that the republican form of government was a choice gift of God to man. In his commentary on Samuel he writes, "And ye, O peoples, to whom God gave the liberty to choose your own magistrates, see to it that ye do not forfeit this favor by electing to the positions of highest honor, rascals and enemies of God."

God has made us in America stewards of a representative form of government. We are guardians of this gift. If you want a republic to continue to be the best form of government for our land, keep, and urge others to keep, the pledge of loyalty, faithfulness, and obedience to our nation. Do your share as a citizen to see that our nation provides liberty and justice under God.

Do you remember what you have read?

1. Give a historical example of each of the five types of governments. Also try to cite examples from today's world.
2. Under what conditions do we say that a country has too little government?
3. When does a country have too much government?
4. What are the advantages of a republic?
5. Why would it be impossible for our national government to be a pure democracy?
6. What is the difference between the parliamentary and presidential systems of a republic?

Matching exercise

1. _____ Government having both a king and elected representatives
2. _____ Government whose total authority is in the hands of a king
3. _____ Government whose total authority is in the hands of one person who has gained this position with the aid of political friends or by force
4. _____ Government operated by the highly educated, the upper class of the people
5. _____ Government administered by a small group of people
6. _____ Government in which all the people have equal voice
7. _____ Government administered by elected representatives of the people
8. _____ Ability to read and write; educated
9. _____ Indifference; lack of interest
10. _____ To be obedient; to act according to the wishes or law of another
11. _____ Worthiness, nobleness, honor
12. _____ Receive from one's ancestors
13. _____ Do as one chooses; noninterference

a. laissez-faire	h. republic
b. conform	i. dignity
c. absolute monarchy	j. literacy
d. limited monarchy	k. dictatorship
e. oligarchy	l. apathy
f. aristocracy	m. inherit
g. pure democracy	

For further thought

1. Discuss why many of the newly independent countries of the world do not have democratic forms of government.
2. What signs of corruption in our government and apathy among our citizens are evident today? What can Christian citizens do to help overcome these problems?
3. Why are there no real theocracies in the world today?
4. Why might an absolute monarchy, or a dictatorship, be better than a republic in an uneducated or a corrupt nation?
5. Totalitarian governments are sometimes controlled by one person, such as Germany under Hitler. They can also be controlled by a small political party, such as Russia under Communism. Of these two types of totalitarian government, which is likely to remain in existence longer? Give a reason for your answer.
6. Some early European monarchs believed in the "divine right of kings." They believed
   a) that God had made them kings
   b) that all the people should therefore give them unquestioned obedience
   c) that they could do anything they wished with little regard for their subjects.

What was right and what was wrong with their beliefs?

Words to study

anarchy
democracy
monarchy
parliamentary system

presidential system
rod of iron
theocracy
totalitarian

UNIT RESEARCH PROJECTS

1 As a daily project, let the members of the class take turns giving a brief summary of daily news related to the role of government in our nation or other nations. The report can be on an important international, national, or local event.

2 Have a bulletin-board committee responsible for displaying pictures, news items, and other materials of interest related to the unit.

3 Organize the class by electing a president, vice-president, and secretary, and draw up a constitution. Conduct an occasional class meeting, using parliamentary procedure, to discuss some possible projects in citizenship; for example, a project to improve some aspect of your school or your community.

4 Begin a semester project of keeping a notebook with pictures, clippings, articles, or other illustrative materials related to the classwork. Newspapers, magazines, books, lectures, radio and television programs, and materials (which you can send for) can be used as sources.

5 Make a current events notebook, compiling political cartoons that relate to important international and national events. Try to place the subjects of the cartoons in their historical sequence.

6 Compare the type and structure of any two governments chosen from the following list: Great Britain, Switzerland, Egypt, Japan, Argentina, Mexico and the U.S.

7 As our government carries out its responsibility to function as a "servant of God for good" and as it "bears the sword," it employs many people to provide services and enforce laws. It is estimated that approximately 20 percent of our population is government employed. Such government employees work as local, state, or federal workers of all kinds. Choose one of the services that government provides for you or for your family and make a study of the number of persons required to make that service possible.

"O God, our help in ages past,
Our hope for years to come,
Our shelter from the stormy blast,
And our eternal home."

The government
to which we owe our allegiance today
has its roots in history.
It did not grow
as the vine of Jonah
in a single night.
No, our government
has been under God's providential care
and guidance in the past.
To better understand
our government today, we must consider
its broad background.

In CONGRESS, July 4, 1776.

The unanimous Declaration of the thirteen united States of America.

When in the Course of human events it becomes necessary for one people to dissolve the political bands which have connected them with another, and to assume among the powers of the earth, the separate and equal station to which the Laws of Nature and of Nature's God entitle them, a decent respect to the opinions of mankind requires that they should declare the causes which impel them to the separation. — We hold these truths to be self-evident, that all men are created equal, that they are endowed by their Creator with certain unalienable Rights, that among these are Life, Liberty and the pursuit of Happiness — That to secure these rights, Governments are instituted among Men, deriving their just powers from the consent of the governed, — That whenever any Form of Government becomes destructive of these ends, it is the Right of the People to alter or to abolish it, and to institute new Government, laying its foundation on such principles and organizing its powers in such form, as to them shall seem most likely to effect their Safety and Happiness. Prudence, indeed, will dictate that Governments long established should not be changed for light and transient causes; and accordingly all experience hath shewn, that mankind are more disposed to suffer, while evils are sufferable, than to right themselves by abolishing the forms to which they are accustomed. But when a long train of abuses and usurpations, pursuing invariably the same Object evinces a design to reduce them under absolute Despotism, it is their right, it is their duty, to throw off such Government, and to provide new Guards for their future security. — Such has been the patient sufferance of these Colonies; and such is now the necessity which constrains them to alter their former Systems of Government. The history of the present King of Great Britain is a history of repeated injuries and usurpations, all having in direct object the establishment of an absolute Tyranny over these States. To prove this, let Facts be submitted to a candid world. — He has refused his Assent to Laws, the most wholesome and necessary for the public good. — He has forbidden his Governors to pass Laws of immediate and pressing importance, unless suspended in their operation till his Assent should be obtained; and when so suspended, he has utterly neglected to attend to them. — He has refused to pass other Laws for the accommodation of large districts of people, unless those people would relinquish the right of Representation in the Legislature, a right inestimable to them and formidable to tyrants only. — He has called together legislative bodies at places unusual, uncomfortable, and distant from the depository of their Public Records, for the sole purpose of fatiguing them into compliance with his measures. — He has dissolved Representative Houses repeatedly, for opposing with manly firmness his invasions on the rights of the people. — He has refused

Chapter 4

The development of government

Important ideas to look for:
- Government began with the family.
- The thread of representative government is woven throughout history.
- The background of our American government is basically British.
- Important English documents granted freedoms that were brought to America.

Origins of government generally

The earliest form of government is unknown to us, but it is fairly safe to assume that the family formed the starting point in the administration of the affairs of society. When God created Adam and Eve, He started the family through the institution of marriage. The family has always been the strongest building block in the structure of any society. Even today the strength of a society, or nation, depends largely on the families within it. If the homes are orderly with harmony and love, the nation will be strong; if the rate of divorce and broken homes increases the society will become weak and unstable.

You will remember that after the confusion of tongues at the Tower of Babel, people moved into new areas. Hardships and dangers likely forced families with similar problems to join together, thus forming a larger group. This larger community gave obedience to a recognized leader, or chief, who was generally chosen for some outstanding personal quality, such as physical strength, good judgment, or the ability to lead in time of war or natural disaster. Through this leader, the group acted together in matters that applied to more than one individual or family.

The way of life of the Old Testament *patriarchal* Jews is an example of an early type of family government. The family (really a combination of families in the modern sense) worshiped together, organized its own defense against enemies, arranged for hunting grounds and pasture lands, and looked after needed shelter and supplies.

We can learn something about these early forms of government from history. People used different systems for controlling their community life. In New Guinea tribes were loosely organized. A council, with one member selected as spokesman, generally served as the governing authority. In Australia a group of tribal elders served as judges as well as lawmakers. In many parts of Africa a chief ruled with the advice and agreement of the wise men.

Although there were many different forms of government organization in the early days of history, there does not seem to have been too much of what we would call absolute dictatorship. The chief apparently had to rule according to the unwritten law and custom of the tribe. When a serious decision had to be made, the chief called his council of wise men or consulted the tribal elders for their opinions. This strong tone of representative government found among early tribes and among uneducated peoples of today has caused many history scholars to claim that governmental *tyranny* runs against a deep-seated human instinct.

We recognize this desire and need for freedom to be a reflection of the image of God in humanity. People were created to rule the earth, and given the ability to choose right from wrong. Although God's image bearers have fallen into sin, they still reflect traces of God's image, and this gives people the desire to be free.

Many of these ancient tribal governments, however, became absolute monarchies. The kings had full power over the people and inherited their right to rule from their *ancestors*. Such absolute monarchies exercised the power of life and death over their subjects. Their word was law. The people had no voice in the government. In some early kingdoms nobles and other groups wrested power away from the king and formed an oligarchy.

In Greece and Rome more representative forms of government appeared. In the city-state of Athens a form of democracy existed before the birth of Christ. In Rome a republican form of government developed at about the same time or soon afterward.

The period of history that followed the breaking up of the Roman Empire has often been referred to as the Dark Ages. During this time the disunited parts of the Empire were faced with the problems of governing themselves. In some areas this was done with little change as leaders continued in power much the same as before. In others, anarchy and chaos existed. In still other districts, church authorities began to take over many of the responsibilities of civil government, and church officials regulated some of the civil affairs of the people living in the region of their church.

Gradually, however, a new social order known as *feudalism* came into being. Here and there throughout Europe, a man arose and gathered around him a group of men to protect his land. Other, weaker landowners of the *vicinity* came to him and asked for protection; these lesser *nobles* were required to transfer the ownership of their land to the feudal *lord.* The lesser nobles, or *vassals,* then received their land back as *fiefs.* The land now belonged to the feudal lord, but could be ruled and cultivated by the vassal. The vassal and his helpers, or serfs, could now perform their farming tasks in reasonable safety.

The agreements or contracts between the feudal lord and his vassals were generally based on personal relationships and tradition rather than on written law and legal procedure.

Although there were constant petty wars for the possession of land, the feudal lord and

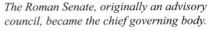

The Roman Senate, originally an advisory council, became the chief governing body.

The development of government 21

his vassals stood together for their common defense. Civil affairs within some *manors,* or estates, were conducted with order and fairness for the standards of that day. In others justice was unheard of, and affairs were conducted according to the pleasure of those who ruled.

From these feudal kingdoms grew the modern nations of Europe. This process involved much war and bloodshed as well as a variety of alliances and even marriages of family members in adjoining kingdoms. Again absolute monarchies and oligarchies developed in the various countries. As time went on, new forms of government arose. In England the idea of a limited monarchy grew, that is, a king under law. In other countries a more democratic type in the form of a republic began. Dictatorships which often held a totalitarian or complete-control idea of government also appeared. All these types of government are listed in the chart on page 16.

Origins of American government

We have seen that there were many types of government in the past; there are many varieties of these types in the world today. Each type has been and still is **under God** to meet the needs of His people throughout all ages. The government of a country and the everyday events within that country will be used by God to fulfill His purposes until that day when Christ will return and the pages of history will be closed. Out of the broad background of government in the past, we find that the ideas of American government today have grown.

The story of democracy did not begin in our United States of America. It began with the basic, God-given desire to be free. The Egyptian slaves who rebelled against their cruel taskmasters were a part of that story. The Greeks and Romans who started plans for self-government were another part. But the people who really surveyed and cleared the pathway for American freedom were the people of England.

British background of American government

The background of the American government is basically British. England is our mother country even though we revolted against its rule. Our government is patterned after England's government, our customs follow after its customs, and our ideas of freedom are built upon the English struggle for self-rule.

Though it is true that we have changed, developed, and added to the ideas and customs that came to us from England, there is much in the American system of government that bears the trademark of Great Britain. Does this seem strange when we think of the United States as a country made up of immigrants from many lands? Perhaps, but we must remember that the thirteen English colonies were under royal rule from 1607 to 1775, a span of 168 years—almost as long as the United States has been a nation! In fact, most of the important principles of government that are in use in the United States today were in existence long before the colonies declared their independence from England.

The Magna Carta or Great Charter

Over 700 years ago King Henry II began to strengthen the monarchy in England. Although he was forced to destroy some of the personal power of the leading nobles, he introduced many judicial reforms and strengthened royal law, thereby ensuring fairer treatment to all English subjects. He was succeeded by his crafty son, King John, who proved to be selfish and cruel. King John did not care for the welfare of the people nor for the laws made by his father. He increased taxes and ignored the right of trial by jury. Often the rich who committed crimes were allowed to go free if they paid money to the King. Because King John had trouble with the Pope, there could be no church services.

Life was fast becoming unbearable under King John's rule. In 1213 a group of important bishops and barons met to discuss what could be done to reestablish the rights they had previously held. At this meeting Stephen Langton, Archbishop of Canterbury, made a list of the rights and liberties given to the church leaders and nobles by Henry II and other kings. The group then asked King John to observe them also. But King John paid no attention to their request.

The barons and bishops, however, were determined not to be refused. They gathered a great army in 1215 and marched against King John near London. Although the King was furious, he was forced to sign his name to the list and to attach the Great Seal of England. Thus the first written "bill of rights" in English history came into being. It was one of the first steps made by Englishmen to change absolute monarchy into limited monarchy. John Richard Green in the *History of the English People* stated that ". . . the Great Charter marks the transition from the age of traditional rights, preserved in the nation's memory . . . to the age of written legislation. . . ."

Among the important provisions of the Magna Carta were the following:

Clause XII No scutage [tax for military purposes] nor aid [tax or payment paid by a vassal to a feudal lord] shall be imposed in our kingdom, unless by the common council of our kingdom . . .

New tax laws therefore needed to be approved by the King's Great Council before they could be put into effect. At that time this clause had meaning only for the barons or

King John is depicted in this sculpture from his tomb in the cathedral of Worcester.

feudal lords. However, it deals with the basic rights of an individual to own property.

This right later became an issue in the American Revolution when the colonies protested "taxation without representation." In the January 9, 1769 copy of the *Boston Gazette* Samuel Adams wrote, ". . . no man can take another's property from him without his consent."

Clause XXXIX No free man shall be seized, imprisoned, dispossessed [deprived of his land], outlawed, or exiled, or in any way destroyed; nor will we proceed against or prosecute him except by the lawful judgment of his peers [equals] or by the law of the land.

King John signed the Magna Carta in June 1215.

the Magna Carta was largely ignored and nearly forgotten in the years that followed. But when the system of feudalism finally disappeared and serfs became freemen, many of the rights in the Magna Carta became the rights of all Englishmen.

Other rights gained by Englishmen

About 400 years after the Magna Carta was signed, Charles I became King of England. Parliament at that time was eager to extend its rights and so refused to Charles I the privileges and powers that earlier kings had enjoyed. The King then dissolved the Parliament and ordered people to lend him money. Some rich people who refused to pay were thrown into prison, while people of lower rank who opposed the King were forced into the army. During the winter of 1627-1628 thousands of families were ordered to feed and lodge the King's soldiers in their homes without pay. Many of these soldiers were rough and disorderly and did not respect the rights of the people with whom they lived.

The people of England were angry with King Charles, and when Parliament next met it forced the King to sign a *Petition of Right.* The petition said that: (1) the King could not force anyone to lend him money (all gifts, loans, and taxes required by the government of the people must be approved by Parliament); (2) the King could not put any citizen into prison without just cause; (3) no soldier could be housed in a private home without the consent of the owner (this right became important many years later when American colonists protested against the Billeting Act, which forced the colonists to keep British soldiers in their homes); and (4) during the time of peace, the laws of the army could not be forced upon the general population. This Petition of Right added to the freedoms already gained under the Magna Carta.

Although this clause protested against the type of jury trials held under the rule of King John and against the royal courts' use of royal law, the later misinterpretation of these words is very important. Centuries afterward it was assumed to be an early expression of our present-day right of trial by jury.

Clause XL To none will we sell, to none will we deny, to none will we delay right or justice.

In 1215 the rights provided by the Magna Carta applied only to the powerful freemen of that day, that is, the clergy and the barons. Very little or nothing was said about the rights of the other five-sixths of the population who were serfs on the land of the barons. History seems to indicate that

In 1679 another milestone was reached along the road to freedom when the *Habeas Corpus* Act was passed. This act said that a person could not be put into prison and kept there without a charge being made against him or without a trial. He had to be brought before a judge within a certain length of time. The judge would then decide whether the prisoner should be held for trial or set free.

The *Bill of Rights* passed in 1689 gave freedom of speech to the members of Parliament during its sessions. The Bill of Rights kept the judges from levying fines that were too heavy and prevented cruel and unusual punishments. The people were given the right to petition the King freely if they felt they were being unjustly treated. The Bill of Rights also made it illegal to keep a standing army in time of peace without the consent of Parliament.

These four—the Magna Carta, the Petition of Right, the Habeas Corpus Act, and the Bill of Rights—are the most important documents of the English Constitution. They are the result of violence and revolution. The freedoms they include were forcefully extracted from unwilling kings by those who often sought only their own interests. How much sin is evident in the lives of those who ruled and those who rebelled against that rule!

Yet we may be thankful that the freedoms of the people of England were carried, under God's providential care, by the colonists to the New World as they sought new homes and greater opportunities. Here they found the greatest freedom of all—freedom to worship God as they pleased.

Do you remember what you have read?

1. Define the following terms:
   feudalism   patriarch
   vassal   ancestor

This is the final reissue of the Magna Carta. Only one other copy of this document exists.

    fief   manor
    tyranny   vicinity

2. What was the first form of government?
3. Give an example of patriarchal government.
4. Why were the "Dark Ages" called by that name?
5. How did the feudal lord increase the size of his land holdings?
6. What group of people led the rebellion against King John?
7. How did the Magna Carta help to change the absolute monarchy of England to a more limited one?
8. List two rights granted in the Magna Carta that we still enjoy.
9. Why did Parliament pass the Petition of Right?
10. What practice did the Habeas Corpus Act stop?

For further thought

1. Although the Magna Carta benefited only one-sixth of the English people, why was its signing such an important moment in history?

2. The freedoms of the Magna Carta did not apply to all the people of thirteenth century England. Do you think that the freedoms of our Constitution apply to all people of twenty-first century America? Why of why not?

3. When do you think people generally appreciate things more—when they are given to them, or when they have to work and sacrifice to get them?

4. How can we learn to appreciate more the blessings we have today because of the efforts of our ancestors?

5. Our country is well into the third century of its existence. What challenges and problems face us today that were unknown to the people living at the time the Magna Carta was signed? Can we solve our problems in the same way they did? Why or why not?

6. Do Christians and non-Christians view history in the same way? If not, what differences would you expect to find in the way they study a historical event or in the conclusions they reach?

Words to study

banish	Magna Carta
Bill of Rights	noble
custom	Parliament
document	peer
Habeas Corpus	petition
levy	serf
lord	

Chapter 5

Independent government acquired

British ideas of self-government are brought to America

Now thank we all our God
With hearts and hands and voices,
Who wondrous things hath done,
In whom His world rejoices;
Who, from our mothers' arms,
Hath blessed us on our way
With countless gifts of love,
And still is ours today.

The crops of their first year in America had been harvested. The Pilgrims, under the leadership of Governor William Bradford, had proclaimed a day of Thanksgiving. The table was spread with what was to them a bounteous meal. Fresh venison and wild turkey were supplied by the friendly Indians who lived in the nearby forest. Cornbread, freshly baked, was made from maize that had recently been gathered from the fields. Before the meal was begun, the voice of the elder of Plymouth was raised in a prayer of thanksgiving to God.

We might well ask, "For what blessings did these Pilgrims feel thankful?" They had suffered the cold and hardship of a New England winter without adequate housing or supplies. Many had died from an illness that had plagued the colony. Yet, under God, the settlement was successful. The Indians had been helpful. The needed homes had been built. The crops planted in the spring had provided sufficient food for the coming

The Pilgrims crossed the ocean in the Mayflower, *bringing English ideas of government with them.*

The Pilgrims signed the Mayflower Compact on board the Mayflower *in Cape Cod harbor.*

winter. But above all the Pilgrims were thankful for the freedom they had discovered in America—the freedom to worship God in the way that they felt was right and true to the teachings of the Bible.

The leaders of the colony were not only concerned about their religious freedom; they also carried to America the ideals of political freedom that had developed in England. These ideals of self-government had been written in the Magna Carta, the Petition of Right, the Habeas Corpus Act, and the Bill of Rights. These English ideals were dear to the hearts of the Pilgrims. During their short stay in Holland, the Pilgrims saw their children growing up in the customs of the people there. The Pilgrims wanted their boys and girls to remain English in speech and custom, so they soon left the Netherlands. When they came to America, they faced this question: "How could these ideals of self-government best be carried out in the new colony?"

Before the Pilgrims left the *Mayflower,* while it lay anchored in the harbor now named Cape Cod Bay, the Pilgrim men met in a cabin of the ship. They discussed the problems that faced them, such as the building of houses and the need for protection from unfriendly Indians and from the dangers of the unknown wilderness. They realized that they would all perish unless they worked together for the welfare of one another. They decided that they must all work together to make laws and abide by them if they were to survive.

This agreement was written in the form of a document that was called the Mayflower Compact. Under the terms of this *compact* the people recognized their obligation and pledged their allegiance to the King. They also provided for a way in which they could make laws for their colony and elect officers to enforce them.

Read carefully this part of the Mayflower Compact to see how the ideas of a democracy were stated in it.

In ye name of god, Amenn. We, whose names are underwriten, the loyall subjects of our dread soveraigne . . . King James . . . Haveing undertaken for ye Glorie of God, and advancements of ye Christian Faith, and Honour of our King and countrie . . . to plant ye first Colonie in ye Northerne parts of Virginia, Doe . . . solemnly & mutually in ye Presence of God and of one another, covenant & combine ourselves togeather into a Civill body Politick; for our better ordering & preservation & furtherance of ye ends aforesaid; and by Vertue hereof to enacte . . . such just and equall Lawes . . . from time to time, as shall be thought most meete & convenient for ye Generall Good of ye Colonie, unto which we promise all due submission and obedience . . ."

On their first Thanksgiving Day the Pilgrims were thankful that this form of government had provided liberty and justice, good order, adequate protection, and freedom in civil government, as well as religious freedom.

We may admire the courage of the Pilgrims in the face of hardship. We should realize that the Mayflower Compact gives us a view of self-government in action by means of a written agreement. But we must not overlook the fact that the Plymouth settlement was small compared to the total population and size of the Massachusetts Bay Colony and the other American settlements. To obtain a clear view of colonial government, we must look carefully at the others as well.

Government in the original colonies

Among the thirteen English colonies at the time of the Revolution there were three forms of government: *royal, proprietary,* and *charter.* The chief difference was the way in which the governor was chosen.

Royal colonies The royal colonies were New Hampshire, New York, New Jersey, Virginia, North Carolina, South Carolina, Georgia, and (after 1691) Massachusetts. For the government of these colonies the King

James Fort (Jamestown, Virginia) was built soon after the settlers landed. It was triangular with the river side 120 yards long and the other two sides 100 yards each.

appointed a royal governor and usually a council, or "upper house." The "lower house," or colonial *assembly,* was elected by the eligible voters of the colony. In Virginia the assembly was called the House of Burgesses; Massachusetts called their assembly the House of Representatives; the people of South Carolina called theirs the House of Commons. In the royal colonies the governor enforced the rules given him by the King while smaller colonial matters were handled by the assembly. The royal governors often ruled sternly. However, most of them were very able men and fulfilled the duties of their office very well. Nevertheless, much of the bitterness that later led to the Revolution began in the royal colonies when disagreements arose between the governor appointed by the King and the assembly elected by the people.

Proprietary colonies There were three proprietary colonies: Pennsylvania, Delaware, and Maryland. Government in these colonies was largely controlled by the owner, or *proprietor,* who had received the grant of land from the King. The proprietor appointed the governors, provided for the courts, and usually established local governments as well. He was responsible to the King in only a very general way. The proprietors provided written *frames of government* or simple constitutions that allowed for a large degree of self-government on the local level.

Charter colonies The charter colonies, Rhode Island and Connecticut, had the largest measure of official self-rule. The charters were written documents listing the privileges of self-rule granted to the colonies by the King. They could be withdrawn by him at any time, for the King's authority gave him power to change the type of government of any colony when he felt it was wise. Among the privileges granted to charter colonies was the right to elect the governor of the colony. The council and colonial assembly were also elected by the eligible voters.

The chart on the opposite page compares the voting rights of people in the three types of colonies.

In New England, where the farms were small, the people lived close together in *townships.* At the *town meeting* the people gathered to vote upon proposed taxes for schools, roads, and the support of the poor. All matters of community concern were discussed and settled in a democratic way.

In the South, where farming was done on large plantations, the people lived much farther apart. Here people came to the county meetings on horseback, on foot, or in boats. After the local assemblymen were elected, local business was transacted. Court was held. When the business was finished, the remainder of the day was usually devoted to speeches, athletic contests, horse trading, storytelling, and various other social events.

The Middle Colonies usually adopted either the township or the county system, depending upon the density of population and the local custom.

Voting privilege, or *franchise*, was generally controlled closely and was related to the purpose of the colony. In New England, where church life was the central purpose, franchise was generally given with church membership. In the Middle and Southern colonies where land ownership was the most important factor, the voting privilege was given with a deed of property. No colony in America at that time granted voting rights to all men. In fact, no one then even considered such broad franchise to be desirable. The ideal of universal *suffrage* or franchise was to come much later in our country's history.

Colonial conditions that affected government

The colonists were mainly Englishmen. Others who arrived from foreign nations also became British subjects. They owed

Voting rights in the colonies

Type of colony	Govenor	Upper house	Lower house
Royal	appointed by the king	appointed by the king or royal governor	elected by the eligible voters
Proprietary	appointed by the proprietor	elected by the eligible voters	elected by the eligible voters
Charter	elected by the people and subject to approval of the king	elected by the eligible voters	elected by the eligible voters

their allegiance to the land, the laws, and the King of England. But the headquarters of the British Empire was some 3000 miles from the practical problems faced by the pioneer in America. Although the governor in every colony spoke for the King, a protest against any of a governor's acts involved a great deal of delay. The struggles for existence on the frontier could not wait six months for an answer from the Crown. The Eastern colonial settlements, particularly those along the Atlantic Coast, kept in rather constant touch with England, and the tendency of a wilderness environment to change the ideas and habits of the colonists was held in check to some degree by this contact with the homeland. On the fringes of the coastal settlements, however, and in the western zone, with few navigable streams to form an outlet to the Atlantic Ocean, there was very little communication with the Old World, or for that matter, with the government of the colony. Thus many of the colonists became quite used to doing things in the way that suited them best. Only in times of extreme danger, such as Indian wars and struggles with Spain and France for land rights, did the colonists recognize the need for help from the mother country. Even then, they were more concerned with local conditions than they were with the problems of the British Empire. They willingly accepted the protection of England as colonists, but the feeling of responsibility for the total Empire was very small. The Englishmen in America were beginning to think and act more independently. The mother country's apron strings were wearing thin.

At this time many government leaders in England did not understand the feelings and problems of the colonists in America. They regarded the thirteen colonies merely as a source of raw materials and a market for the excess finished products of England —a territory that should be happy to provide for the good of the Empire. These English leaders forgot that men and women who were willing to endure the hardship of colonial life for the freedom they desired would not easily give up the freedom they had found.

Do you remember what you have read?

1. Why were the Pilgrims perhaps more thankful than we are for the same type of blessings?
2. Why did the Pilgrims leave Holland?

3. Why was the Mayflower Compact written?
4. In what ways did the Englishmen in America become different from the Englishmen in England?
5. How did the colonies depend upon the mother country?
6. What names did the different colonies have for their assemblies?
7. Which of the types of colonial government was the most democratic? Why?

Words to study

assembly	proprietor
charter	royal
compact	suffrage
frame of government	township
franchise	town meeting

Early attempts at colonial union

As time moved forward and the colonies grew in size, the colonies became more aware of each others' existence. In times of danger they were better able to work together. This increased concern for one another in time of special need grew into a desire for closer union; we may see in this another step in the unfolding of God's plan for the government of our nation today.

During a large part of early American history each of the colonies had its own relations with the government of England, but the colonies had very little to do with one another. Communications were poor; distances were great; and travel was difficult and often dangerous.

In spite of these problems, the leaders of the settlements in Massachusetts Bay, Plymouth, Connecticut, and New Haven joined in a "league of friendship" as early as 1643. The purpose of this New England Confederation was to form a united defense against the Indians. This union lasted only a few years. In 1696 William Penn proposed a plan for improving commerce or trade among the colonies. He was also concerned because a criminal in one colony could escape punishment simply by moving to another. His plan would have provided a better system of justice for all. Although his plan was well organized, nothing came of it.

Almost sixty years later, in 1754, at the insistence of the British Board of Trade, a meeting was held in Albany, New York. Delegates of seven of the northern colonies attended to consider the danger of Indian attacks and methods of improving colonial trade. Benjamin Franklin made a proposal that a meeting of delegates, one from each of the thirteen colonies, be held once each year. These representatives would have power to levy taxes; to make war, peace, or trade treaties with the Indians; and to deal with other problems that affected all of the colonies.

The **Albany Plan of Union,** as Franklin's ideas came to be called, was rejected by all of the colonies. They were not yet ready to surrender part of their power as individual colonies to a larger, more distant government. The Albany Plan of Union was, however, a forerunner of the United States Constitution, for it made people think in terms of a strong central government.

Stamp Act Congress, 1765

A common problem, however, drew the colonies together more solidly. Just as a common danger from Indian attack had caused the early settlements to band together in the New England Confederation, so now the Stamp Act passed by the English Parliament in 1765 was the cause of the first significant cooperation among colonies. They strongly resented the tax being placed upon them by the mother country, and they used the now well-known cry, "No taxation without representation," as the basis for their protest. The colonists felt that the freedom guaranteed by the Magna Carta was being violated, for Parliament was placing this direct tax upon the colonies without allowing them to have membership in that lawmaking body.

Protesting taxes, an angry mob dressed as Indians dumped tea into Boston Harbor.

Feeling against the Stamp Act was immediate. In the Virginia House of Burgesses Patrick Henry made a fiery speech, condemning the act. At the invitation of Massachusetts a **Stamp Act Congress** met in New York. Delegates from nine states attended and drew up a Declaration of Rights and Grievances, which was sent to the King.

As we consider the Stamp Act passed by the British government, we must first of all recognize that Parliament had every legal right to tax the colonies as it wished. The colonial actions of resistance and defiance were wrongful forms of disobedience and rebellion against their governing authorities. Although the Stamp Act was repealed and judged to be unwise, this does not excuse the colonies for their lack of obedience.

However, the meeting of delegates from various colonies was another means that drew the colonists into a closer union. This flame of freedom that was being kindled in a more closely united America was soon fanned by more actions of the English Parliament—the Townshend Acts, the Intolerable Acts, and many others.

Just as many colonists had refused to buy the stamps of England, many now refused to buy English goods. Others wrongly bought smuggled goods to avoid paying the taxes required by England. Because the trade between England and America was lagging badly, Parliament removed most of the taxes. She left only the one on tea. But now the colonists would not be satisfied until all of the taxes had been removed. In Boston, an angry mob boarded three British tea ships and dumped 340 chests of tea into the harbor. They dressed as Indians to avoid detection and were never punished. This was open rebellion against the authority of the British government, as well as destruction of the property of others.

In Exodus 23:2 God tells us that we are not to go with a crowd to do evil. We also know that God holds each person responsible for his or her actions. So, too, He holds the persons who were members of the Boston Tea Party individually responsible for their actions.

Moderate men in America at that time, such as Benjamin Franklin, condemned the Boston Tea Party as an entirely wrong, unlawful display of mob spirit. Friends of America in England, such as William Pitt, also denounced "the late illegal and violent proceedings at Boston." It would be nice to believe that all the things done by our ancestors were done according to God's laws. But we know that at the Boston Tea Party, as well as on many other occasions, they openly defied the legal authority that God had ordained to rule them. However, God sometimes uses people's evil actions to carry out His plans, and He cares for us in spite of the wrong that we do. This does not excuse anyone. Mob rule and violence toward the governing authorities which God has established does not promote Christian citizenship.

This London print is titled "The Bostonians paying the excise man or tarring & feathering."

After the Boston Tea Party, Parliament immediately passed the act that stopped Boston's trade with the outside world. The Massachusetts Government Act took away the charter of the colony and placed Boston under the military rule of General Gage, commander of British troops there.

The First Continental Congress, 1774

Many early calls for colonial union had gone unheeded, and others had been answered halfheartedly. But now one of the American cities was being severely punished. The people of Boston were in need of food and supplies. As a result, the other colonies soon responded with offers of help and provisions.

On September 5, 1774, the First Continental Congress met in Philadelphia to consider the tense relations between the colonies and England. The delegates traveled long distances at their own expense in order to attend. They were hoping that they could find a solution to the problems that faced them.

The First Continental Congress restated the loyalty of the colonies to the King and at the same time again asked him to reconsider the rights of the colonists as Englishmen. Agreements were made to refuse imported goods from England unless its trade laws were changed. Before adjourning, the Congress set a date for the meeting of a second Congress in May, 1775, if England should fail to respond to the colonial demands for better treatment.

Do you remember what you have read?

1. Name three early attempts for union of the colonies.
2. What were the purposes of these early attempts?
3. Why was the Boston Tea Party an unlawful action by the colonists?
4. Why is mob rule dangerous and wrong?
5. How was the city of Boston punished for the Boston Tea Party?

6. Why were the colonies more ready to send delegates to the First Continental Congress than to agree to the Albany Plan of Union?

Memory work
Exodus 23:2

The demand for independence grows in America

During the days of the First Continental Congress the colonies spoke of loyalty to England; they demanded their rights as Englishmen. Their request for more favorable treatment had again been sent to the King. But conditions became even worse. Some leaders in America began urging the people to revolt and to become independent of the rule of England. Patrick Henry, one of the leaders in the royal colony of Virginia, stood before the House of Burgesses and asked, "Why stand we here idle? . . . Is life so dear, or peace so sweet, as to be purchased at the price of slavery?" Thomas Paine said it was only "Common Sense" that a continent should not be governed by a small island. People everywhere began to talk guardedly and later more openly of freedom from England. Then in April, 1775, Paul Revere sounded the alarm, "The British are coming!" American blood was shed at the Battles of Lexington and Concord. The revolution, the fight for independence, had begun.

The Second Continental Congress, 1775

In May *delegates* of all the states assembled in Philadelphia at Carpenters' Hall. Among them were some of the most able men America has ever known: George Washington, John Adams, Benjamin Franklin, and Thomas Jefferson. John Hancock was chosen as president of the Congress.

In 1776 this Second Continental Congress became the first government of the "United States." At first it had no constitution, yet it formulated and carried out the policies of

Patrick Henry concludes his famous speech with the words "Give me liberty or give me death!"

the colonies for six years; that is, until the Articles of Confederation went into effect in March, 1781. During this time it set up a postal system and printed money; it carried out the normal functions of government as best it could.

This Second Congress appointed George Washington as commander-in-chief of the Continental Army that had grown up around Boston, and it made arrangements to enlist additional troops. The delegates again sent a message, called the Olive Branch Petition, to King George III saying that the colonists were still loyal, but demanding that they be given the right to carry on their own local government. When the King again rejected their appeal, the feeling for independence grew even more rapidly. On June 7, 1776, Richard Henry Lee, delegate from Virginia, arose in the Congress to read a resolution of independence:

Resolved that these United Colonies are, and of a right ought to be, free and independent states; that they are *absolved* from all allegiance to the British Crown, and that all political connexion between them, and the state of Great Britain is, and ought to be, totally *dissolved.*

The Declaration of Independence

"Proclaim Liberty throughout all the Land to all the Inhabitants thereof. Lev. XXV Vs X." This is the inscription on the Liberty Bell.

It was a solemn occasion in the history of the United States when Lee read his resolution for independence. The step about to be taken could not easily be retraced. After the resolution had been debated at length, a Committee of Five, consisting of Thomas Jefferson from Virginia, Benjamin Franklin from Pennsylvania, John Adams from Massachusetts, Robert Livingston from New York, and Roger Sherman from Connecticut, was appointed to prepare the final *draft*. While this was being done, many of the delegates wrote letters to their home colonies, and others went home themselves to make sure of the way that the people felt about the resolution for independence.

On July 4, 1776, the Declaration of Independence, written mainly by Thomas Jefferson, was passed and signed after a few minor changes had been made.

Church bells were rung, parades were held, and general celebration was everywhere. One of the letters of John Adams shows how the people of that time felt about independence when Lee's resolution was passed:

It ought to be commemorated, as the Day of Deliverance by solemn Acts of Devotion to God Almighty. It ought to be solemnized with Pomp and Parade, with Shews, Games, Sports, Guns, Bells, Bonfires and Illuminations from one End of this Continent to the other, from this Time forward forever more.

The Fourth of July is still one of our most honored national holidays.

What did this Document declare?

The Declaration of Independence has been called the "birth certificate" of our nation. Its main purpose was, of course, to declare that our country was no longer a colony of England but rather was now a nation by itself. We were independent. We would govern ourselves. We would stand alone, under God.

In addition to this leading purpose, the Declaration includes many basic ideas about government. When Jefferson states, "We hold these truths to be self-evident . . ." he expresses some fundamental human rights. The Declaration of Independence is a great document because these basic ideas apply not only to the American colonists; ideally, they apply to all people everywhere. The Declaration lists eight of these *"self-evident truths"*:

1. That all people are created equal.
2. That the Creator has given to all certain *inalienable* rights.
3. That among these rights are life, liberty, and the pursuit of happiness.
4. That governments are instituted or ordained among human beings to preserve these rights.
5. That the government gets its just powers from the consent of those who are governed.
6. That if a government does not preserve, but rather destroys, these rights, it is the duty of the people to change it or abolish it.
7. That people then have the responsibility to establish a new government—one that will provide these basic rights for them.
8. That governments are not to be changed for light and *transient* causes but only when there are deep and enduring wrongs against God-given human rights.

Reasons given

The Declaration of Independence is given on pages 251-253. When you read it carefully, you will notice that a large part of it lists the many reasons why the colonies were rebelling and declaring their political independence.

The original copy of the Declaration of Independence is on display at the National Archives Building in Washington, D.C.

IN CONGRESS, JULY 4, 1776.

The unanimous Declaration of the thirteen united States of America.

Many of the reasons are written as accusations against the King of England. As you study these reasons, you must remember that the Declaration of Independence was written and approved by people who disliked the King very much, and they began to blame all their troubles on him. People often make unjust accusations when their minds are set against someone. Because of this feeling against the King, the Declaration of Independence was written from the colonists' point of view. Let us consider a few of the reasons that have been given to see why the colonists felt that they should declare their independence.

He [the King of England] has refused his *assent* to the laws the most wholesome and necessary for the public good.

He has forbidden his governors to pass laws of immediate and pressing importance, unless suspended in their operation till his assent should be obtained; and, when so suspended, he has utterly neglected to attend to them.

Before laws passed by the colonial assemblies could become effective, they had to be agreed upon by King George III. Sometimes laws that the colonies felt were needed had been passed by the assemblies only to be deliberately ignored or refused by the King. Thus, the power of the people to make their own laws was limited.

He has obstructed the administration of justice, by refusing his assent to laws for establishing judiciary powers.

He has made judges dependent on his will alone for the *tenure* of their offices, and the amount and payment of their salaries.

The King had refused to approve the laws made by the assemblies that would establish colonial courts of justice. The colonists wanted to elect their own judges and operate their own courts. The King decided how much salary judges in the royal courts should receive and how long they should remain in

office. Because the judges depended upon the King for their salaries and positions, they represented the authority of the Throne rather than the wishes of the people.

He has combined with others to subject us to a jurisdiction foreign to our constitutions and unacknowledged by our laws, giving his assent to their acts of pretended legislation.

For quartering large bodies of armed troops among us;

For protecting them [the soldiers] with a mock trial, from punishment for any murders which they should commit on the inhabitants of these states;

For cutting off our trade with all parts of the world;

For depriving us, in many cases, of the benefits of trial by jury;

For transporting us beyond the seas, to be tried for pretended offenses.

The Parliament had made and the King had quickly approved laws that forced the colonies to obey even though they had no share in making the laws. Large armies had been sent to live among the colonists. When soldiers killed some of the people in America, these soldiers had been protected from punishment by a mock trial. Although history has shown that the colonists were at fault in the Boston Massacre, the shootings and the trials that followed were still fresh in their minds. As a result of the Boston Tea Party, Boston Harbor had been closed. The Navigation Act and other similar acts of Parliament kept the colonies from trading freely with other nations.

These reasons and many more are listed in the Declaration of Independence so that all the world might know why the colonies were seeking their political independence.

The Declaration of Independence was passed unanimously by the delegates to the Second Continental Congress. This came as no surprise since the men selected as delegates were chosen because of their sympathy for

The Declaration of Independence was signed July 4, 1776, in Independence Hall, Philadelphia. This famous painting is by the American artist John Trumbull.

breaking away from the political control of England. As the years of the Revolutionary War took their toll, the men who signed the Declaration of Independence suffered heavily from the ravages of the war. Many lost their property and possessions. The suffering of the troops of General Washington at Valley Forge, their hunger and their discouragement, their long marches and short rations, even the sacrifice of their lives in hardfought battles, showed that these hardy people were dedicated to a cause they believed in. The price they had to pay for their convictions was not small.

As is the case in most wars, there were others with equally strong convictions. Some felt it was their duty to remain loyal to England. Their land had been part of the English nation for over 150 years, and although there were aggravating trade restrictions and other things which annoyed them, they felt that these were not important enough to convince them to join a rebellion.

The rebellion grew into a revolution. The colonists were unable to remain neutral. They had to make a choice.

The problem of whether or not to join the revolution became particularly difficult for Christians. Those on both sides of the issue believed in the same God and read the same Bible, which included Romans 13. Both groups knew their first allegiance was to the Kingdom of Heaven, but this did not remove the difficulty and pain of choosing sides in this political struggle.

By the time the war was over and the bitterness following the war began to lessen, an estimated 35,000 persons had left their homes

Thousands of Loyalists fled to Canada following the Declaration of Independence. Shown here is a Loyalist landing at Saint John, New Brunswick.

and possessions to live elsewhere. Most of these went to Canada. The price they had to pay to live according to their convictions was very high.

Which side was right?

Historians are still discussing the question and probably will for some time to come. As Christians we should be aware of the issues that people of the past have faced. We should evaluate their decisions in the light of our Christian convictions in order that we may be able to decide the issues of our day as wisely as possible.

As a result of the Declaration of Independence and the Revolutionary War that followed, a new nation under God had come into existence. Prayer for it and loyalty to it are not only proper but they are required of the Christians who choose to be part of this nation. Christians know, however, that their highest allegiance is to God, for "The Lord is exalted over all the nations, his glory above the heavens" (Ps. 113:4).

Do you remember what you have read?

1. What part did each of the following play in the story of the American Revolution?

    Patrick Henry   George Washington
    Paul Revere   John Adams
    Thomas Jefferson   Richard Henry Lee
    Thomas Paine   Benjamin Franklin

2. What important events happened between the close of the First Continental Congress and the opening of the Second one?

3. Complete the following sentences.
    a. Washington was appointed as commander-in-chief by _____ .
    b. Both the First and Second Continental Congresses met in the city of _____ .
    c. The Committee of Five was given the task of _____ .
    d. Three rights listed as inalieable in the Declaration of Independence are _____ , _____ and _____ .
    e. The reasons the colonies declared their independence were included in the Declaration because _____ .

For further thought

1. Before the delegates voted on the adoption of Lee's resolution, many of them wrote or went home to assemblies of their own colonies to see how the people there felt about independence. Why was this a wise thing to do?

2. Do you feel that the colonies were justified in rebelling against Great Britain? Why?

3. In what ways are the feelings of the colonists evident in the content of the Declaration of Independence?

4. In what ways are people equal and unequal?

5. How can a truth be self-evident? How does a self-evident truth differ from a biblical truth?

6. Can Christians accept all the basic concepts of government that Jefferson included in the Declaration of Independence as "self-evident truths"? Why or why not?

7. Turn to the Declaration of Independence found on page 251 and read the entire document. How many grievances against the King are listed? Imagine you were the King. Select any two grievances and write a brief response to the colonies about them, explaining your side of the situation.

Words to study

absolve	draft	transient
assent	inalienable	unanimously
delegate	self-evident truth	
dissolve	tenure	

Chapter 6

The Constitution is written

Important ideas to look for:
- The states wrote constitutions that established representative democracies.
- The government established by the Articles of Confederation proved to be ineffective.
- The weaknesses of the Articles of Confederation led to the desire for a stronger national government.
- Ideas, compromises, and ideals were blended, under God, into a finished constitution.

Self-rule begins in America

The authority of England's King and Parliament had been set aside through the Declaration of Independence. Royal governors were removed in the states where they had held office.

What authority would now be responsible for providing liberty and justice for the people? The Second Continental Congress recommended that each of the states adopt "such government as shall, in the opinion of the representatives of the people, best conduce to the happiness and safety of their *constituents.*"

State constitutions are drawn up

All of the states formed new, written constitutions for their governments except Rhode Island and Connecticut. These two states simply changed their original charters a bit and used the same documents. Although these new constitutions were different according to the needs of each state, they were much the same in their basic ideas. They all established representative democracies, or republics. Although the

right to vote, or franchise, was generally limited by property ownership or church membership as it had been during the days of the colonies, the final authority belonged to the voters. Elected representatives carried on the work of making and enforcing the laws. Every new constitution limited the power of the governor, perhaps because of recent unhappy experiences with the King and his royal governors. Each provided the rights of life, liberty, and the pursuit of happiness for the people. The powers of government in each new state constitution were divided among those who made the laws (*legislative* branch), those who enforced them (*executive* branch), and the judges who used them in the courts (*judicial* branch). Each state had a complete government with authority and power to rule within its boundaries.

Articles of Confederation are formed

Although each of the states could rule itself under its own constitution, one of the most important issues was the way in which these states should become united into one larger country. The questions that needed to be solved were "To what extent should the government of the United States rule the people of each state, and what authority did the national government have to act for all the states?"

The first national government was the Continental Congress. Because of a national emergency the two congresses had been quickly formed. The delegates had had limited and uncertain authority. They had formed an *extra-legal* government, for there was no constitution to guide or control them. The war was on, however, and the delegates had to act to meet the needs of the situation.

After the signing of the Declaration of Independence, the Congress had realized that some permanent plan was needed. The members had appointed the Committee of Thirteen led by John Dickenson, who had submitted a plan of government called the Articles of Confederation and *Perpetual* Union. This plan was debated, changed, and finally submitted to the states for approval in November, 1777. Some of the states were slow to approve the plan. Maryland was the last to *ratify* it. She did so on March 1, 1781, after disagreements about Western lands had been settled.

By this time the Revolutionary War was nearly over. The Second Continental Congress had served as our national government from 1775 to 1781. Delegates there had borne the burden of most of the needed decisions during the war for independence.

Weaknesses of the Articles of Confederation

Although the Articles of Confederation were a simple form of government, they provided a *legal* basis for the actions of Congress. The Congress was to have delegates from all of the states. These delegates would serve for one-year terms and could be elected in any way chosen by the state. Each state had one vote regardless of its size or population. It was a "firm league of friendship," which assumed

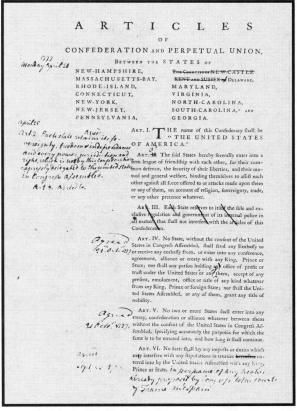

A draft of the Articles of Confederation was printed, and further corrections were made.

that all the states would be in agreement. All real power, or sovereignty, remained with the state governments. Whenever money was needed, Congress asked each of the states to supply its share. If troops were required, some states would be asked to provide them. But in each case the states would have to decide whether or not they wished to comply with the request of the national Congress. The national government under the Articles of Confederation could neither provide services for its citizens as "a servant of God for good" nor "bear a sword" to punish wrongdoers, because it did not have authority. To be effective, a government of any kind must have the right to exercise its authority for the good of the

The Northwest Ordinance

Article 3. Religion, morality, and knowledge being necessary to good government and the happiness of mankind, schools and the means of education shall forever be encouraged. The utmost good faith shall always be observed toward the Indians; their lands and property shall never be taken from them without their consent; and their property, rights, and liberty they shall never be invaded or disturbed unless in just and lawful wars authorized by Congress; but laws founded in justice and humanity shall from time to time be made for preventing wrongs being done to them, and for preserving peace and friendship with them.

The Northwest Ordinance is often called the "Ordinance of 1787."
What important values that government should promote are stated in it?

people under its control or jurisdiction.

The Congress could not compel either the states or the people to obey the law. Congress could only ask and hope that they would feel like obeying. Under the Articles of Confederation each state was allowed to keep its "sovereignty, freedom, and independence." Thus, the sovereign right of a state to govern itself existed before our present-day system of *federalism*. The problem of "states' rights" reappears many times in our nation's history. It was of special importance at the time of the Civil War and is still a key political issue today.

Troubles arise

Soon the states began to quarrel among themselves. They became jealous of one another and refused to pay the money requested by Congress for fear that they were paying more than some other state. The government had many debts because of the Revolutionary War. Supply bills had to be paid, as well as the wages of many soldiers. There was not enough money to pay the operating expenses of the government at that time, to say nothing of paying debts of the past.

Problems of trade arose, for Congress had no power to *regulate* commerce. Some states even made separate agreements with foreign nations as though the states themselves were countries. Quarrels among states over trade led to serious disagreements and distrust.

John Fiske describes one of these:

The city of New York, with a population of 30,000 souls, had long been supplied with firewood from Connecticut, and with butter and cheese, chickens and garden vegetables from the thrifty farms of New Jersey. This trade, it was observed, carried thousands of dollars out of the city and into the pockets of the detested Yankees and despised Jerseymen. "It was ruinous to domestic industry," said the men of New York. "It must be stopped by . . . a navigation act and a protective tariff." Acts were accordingly passed, obliging every Yankee sloop which came down through Hell Gate and every Jerseymen market boat which was rowed across from Paulus Hook to Cortland Street to pay entrance fees and obtain clearances at the custom house, just as was done by ships from London and Hamburg; and not a cart-load of Connecticut firewood could be delivered at the back door of a country home in Beekman Street until it should have paid a heavy duty. Great and just was the wrath of the farmers and lumbermen. The New Jersey legislature made up its mind to retaliate. The city of New York had lately bought a small patch of ground on Sandy Hook, and had built a lighthouse there. This lighthouse was the one weak spot in the heel of Achilles where a hostile arrow could strike, and New Jersey gave vent to her indignation by laying a tax of $1800 a year on it. Connecticut was equally prompt. At a great meeting of business men, held at New London, it was unanimously agreed to suspend all commercial intercourse with New York. Every merchant signed an agreement, under a penalty of $250 for the first offence, not to send any goods whatever into the hated State for twelve months.

The Articles of Confederation formed the basis for our national government from 1781 to 1789. Under God's rule and care, it did accomplish several things in spite of its weaknesses. It succeeded in making a reasonable treaty of peace with England at the close of the war. It provided for wise regulation of the land west of the Appalachian Mountains through the Ordinance of 1787. It held the states together for eight dangerous years when our nation was just beginning.

The Articles served as a forerunner of the Constitution. The weaknesses of the Articles of Confederation led to the desire for a stronger central government. Attempts were made to strengthen the Articles, but this was difficult because any change needed to be ratified by all of the states. The small states feared a change because they distrusted the larger ones. The large states could do very little without the agreement of the small ones. It was even very hard to pass a law because a vote of nine states was required before it could go into effect.

Here is a brief listing of the chief weaknesses of the Articles of Confederation.
1. The government lacked the authority to enforce its laws.
2. Under the Articles of Confederation the United States had no chief executive or president. When a foreign nation wanted to make a trade agreement with our country, it did not know whom to see to do so, and it had no assurance that all the states would follow the agreement if it were made. The government at the time of the Articles of Confederation has been called a "body without a head."
3. No national courts had been set up to settle disputes that arose between states.
4. The national government had no money to pay its debts, for it could not collect taxes.
5. It could not regulate commerce among the states and with foreign nations.
6. Making changes and passing laws were very difficult.

Because of the disorder and difficulty within the nation, people everywhere were thinking more and more about the need for a stronger national government. Responsible leaders began planning for a government that had authority to enforce its laws and that could provide liberty and justice for all.

Do you remember what you have read?
1. Why were the states afraid to give too much authority to the federal government after the Revolutionary War?
2. What role did the Second Continental Congress play during the Revolutionary War?
3. Why did the states work together better between 1776 and 1781 than they did between 1781 and 1789?
4. In spite of its weaknesses, what did the Articles of Confederation accomplish?
5. How did the Articles of Confederation fail to provide for a workable government?

Memory work
I Timothy 2:1-2

For further thought
1. Why is it impossible to have supreme authority in both state and federal governments?
2. If all states had been in agreement on all issues, would the Articles of Confederation have been successful?
3. In what way was the organization of our government under the Articles of Confederation similar to the organization of the United Nations today?

Words to study

constituent	legal
executive	legislative
extra-legal	perpetual
federalism	ratify
judicial	regulate

A new Constitution is written

During the time that the Articles of Confederation were in operation the people of the new nation were gradually becoming dissatisfied with the confusion, the disorder, and the trade and money problems that were growing among the states. In 1785 George Washington invited representatives of Virginia and Maryland to his home in Mt. Vernon to discuss a problem of trade on the nearby Potomac River. These men realized that the problem could better be settled by representatives of all the states.

Maryland, therefore, decided to call delegates from all states to a meeting in Annapolis in 1786. Since only five states responded, little was accomplished. The weaknesses of the national government were felt more strongly than ever by these men. Only one thing could be done. The Annapolis Convention asked Congress to call a meeting for the purpose of improving the Articles of Confederation. Invitations were again sent to all the states. The date set was May, 1787; the place was Philadelphia.

On May 25, 1787, representatives of a majority of the states assembled in Independence Hall, and the Constitutional Convention began its sessions. It has been said, "Never before or since has so remarkable a group of men met under one roof." They were not politicians but statesmen, men of insight and patriotism, men with property and experience, men of ability and personal honor. Under God's providing care these men gathered to blend their experience and wisdom to draw up the Constitution that, with some changes, still serves our nation.

When the meeting opened, George Washington was unanimously elected chairman. Benjamin Franklin, although over eighty years old, added his wisdom and encouragement. James Madison from Virginia is called the "Father of the Constitution"; he probably worked harder than anyone else to give us the Constitution in its present form. Since all of the meetings were kept secret, most of the information we have about the convention comes from the notes of Madison. Other outstanding men who attended the convention were Alexander Hamilton, Edmund Randolph, and Gouverneur Morris.

The *radicals* of the day avoided the meetings; men such as Patrick Henry, Samuel Adams, and John Hancock were afraid that the power of the states would be restricted and so refused to attend. Therefore, the men attending the convention were mainly a *conservative* group who favored a stronger national government. They were concerned about protection of property rights. Also, they did not want to give the states too much power.

When these men gathered, their common purpose was to provide for better national

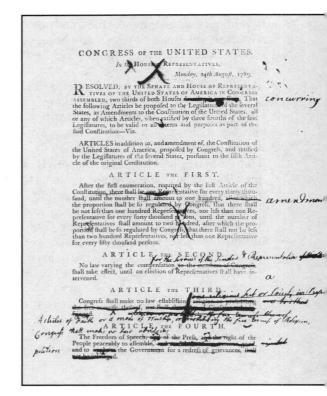

government. Since they believed in inalienable human rights, the only form of government they seriously considered was the republic.

They wanted the government to have authority and power over individuals so that people would listen to it and obey its laws. They wanted a national congress to give voters a voice in lawmaking; they did not want "taxation without representation"; they wanted a system of courts so that quarrels between states could be settled with justice.

The meeting had been called to improve the Articles of Confederation. However, shortly after the meeting began, the delegates saw how impossible this would be, and set about drawing up an entirely new plan for government.

Some of these men had come from large states and some from small states; some had come from the South and some from the North; some had come from agricultural areas and others from areas of trade. These differences of background and interest soon brought differences of opinion and strong debates to the floor of the Convention.

Compromises necessary

The New Jersey, or small state, plan brought by William Paterson suggested that Congress be continued on the *unicameral*, or one house, basis with each state being granted one vote. The Virginia, or large state, plan provided for a *bicameral*, or two house, legislature with representation in both houses being given on the basis of population. This would have given the large states considerably more power than the smaller ones. Debate on this

This working draft of the Bill of Rights was used by the Senate to make further refinements and improvements.

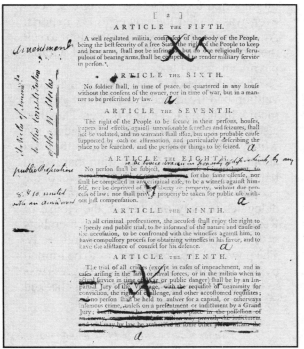

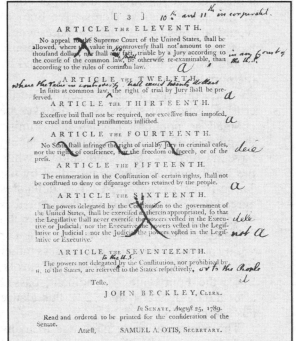

Types of legislatures

Unicameral legislature

One house

=

Bicameral legislature

Senate + House of representatives

The large unicameral legislature of the Articles of Confederation was torn down and rebuilt into the bicameral legislature provided for by the Constitution.

issue went on for weeks with neither the large nor the small states being willing to change their opinions. But this spirit of pride and selfishness was replaced with a willingness to give and take when Roger Sherman of Connecticut suggested the Great Compromise. This plan provided for a bicameral legislature. The smaller house of the new Congress (legislative branch) would be a Senate in which the states would have equal representation; the larger house would have its membership determined by the population of the states.

Next a question arose between the Northern and Southern states. Should slaves be counted as population when determining the number of representatives a state should have in Congress? The South said yes while the North said no. This was settled by the Three-fifths Compromise. The delegates agreed that five slaves should be counted as three white persons. The chief concern of the delegates seemed to be the representation or voting power of the states in Congress rather than the "inalienable rights" of the slaves. Since the Fourteenth Amendment, passed after the Civil War (page 122), this clause has had no effect.

The control of trade gave rise to many problems during the days of the Articles of Confederation. The people from the trading states of the North and East wanted the federal government to be able to control commerce closely. But the people of the agricultural areas of the South and West were afraid that they might be forced to sell their goods at low prices to the New England states instead of to the richer foreign markets. The agreements reached gave the federal government the power to control trade by making laws for interstate commerce and by placing *tariffs* on imported foreign goods. Congress, however, was denied the power to tax exports; Americans were *guaranteed* the right to sell their goods anywhere in the world without paying an export tax.

The delegates to the Constitutional Convention had lived under the British government which had too much power. They had also lived under the Articles of Confederation which had too little power. Now they set about drawing up a Constitution that would balance these two extremes. The power of the people was limited by allowing them to elect delegates to only one house, the House of Representatives; the President and members of the Senate were to be elected indirectly. The power of the President was to be limited by the Congress. The power of Congress was to be balanced by the President and checked by the Supreme Court.

Independence Hall in Philadelphia was the site of the Constitutional Convention.

The finished Constitution was a blend of the ideas from the various state constitutions and the Articles of Confederation, of the compromises reached, and of the ideals of those present.

On September 17, 1787, when the Convention adopted the final draft and the thirty-nine members signed this remarkable document, no bells were rung, and no parades filled the streets. Most of the work had been done behind closed doors. During the warm months of May through September the group of workers had averaged about thirty in number. They had represented all of the states except Rhode Island. The Constitution had been drawn up and signed. To many, it seemed like a "bundle of compromises," and yet God has used it as a means of blessing our nation.

But the writing of the document was only the first step. Now it needed to be adopted, or ratified, by nine states before it could become the law of the land. The delegates realized that the Constitution was not perfect; nevertheless, most of the delegates returned to their own states and urged that it be adopted quickly.

Ratification of the Constitution

People everywhere discussed this new form of government. Those who favored the Constitution began to be called Federalists because some of the power of the states would now be given to the federal, or national, government. They argued that the Articles of Confederation were so weak that they could not be amended but rather needed to be replaced. They pointed to the bad condition of the nation and said that the Union would disappear if a remedy were not found. There might even be war between the states. The Federalists were willing to try the Constitution because they were confident its faults could be corrected by amendments when they were needed.

The Anti-Federalists, as those who did not agree with the Constitution were called, found many faults with it. Although it created authority for the government, it had no Bill of Rights to guarantee the freedom of individuals. The President had too much power; too many powers were taken from the people; the states might no longer print their own money. They felt that the new Constitution was a dangerous experiment because it divided sovereignty between the state and national governments.

These two groups, the Federalists and the Anti-Federalists, became the first two political parties in the United States.

State conventions were held to ratify the new Constitution. Discussion in these conventions revealed that the people insisted on a Bill of Rights. By December 1787, three states—Delaware, Pennsylvania, and New Jersey—had ratified it. Soon others followed, and in June 1788, New Hampshire became the ninth state to adopt it. The new Constitution was now the law of the land. The other states followed, and in May 1790, Rhode Island became the last to join.

The adoption of the Constitution was a peaceful revolution. The Articles of Confederation were to have been a "Perpetual" union until changes were agreed upon by every single state. Now a new form of government adopted by only nine was to go into effect. The Congress of the Confederation, however, prepared the way for the beginning of the new government. The Congress chose New York as the capital; *unanimously* it arranged for the first elections and set March 4, 1789, as the date for the opening meeting of the first Congress under the Constitution.

The new government begins

Since not all of the representatives had arrived by March 4, the electors met to cast their votes on April 6. George Washington, "first in war, first in peace, first in the hearts of his countrymen," was *unanimously* elected to be the first President.

The trip from Mt. Vernon to New York was a memorable one. Crowds of people gathered in every city and town through which the presidential procession passed on the way to the capital. On April 30 the first President of the United States was sworn into office with these words:

I do solemnly swear that I will faithfully execute the office of the President of the United States, and will to the best of my ability preserve, protect, and defend the Constitution of the United States of America.

For over 200 years this Constitution has served as the basis for our government. In spite of many weaknesses and the sinfulness of people in office, it serves our nation well. It seeks to provide liberty and justice for all. Our government can be a servant of God for good through the services it renders to the people of our land. It does not bear the sword in vain, for it has the authority and power to punish evildoers. Although very stable in many ways, it has been flexible enough to face the problems that have arisen throughout our nation's existence.

1976 marked the bicentennial year of our nation's political independence. In celebration, much of our early history was studied in detail. Some little-known acts of heroism, as well as those that were wrong or foolish in the public and private lives of our leaders, were uncovered.

We may well be thankful that God provided for our land during the days of crises when our nation was young. He provided leaders and granted them wisdom and judgment for their tasks. He blessed their labors in spite of their failures and sin. He provided a spirit of unity in a time of disagreement and distrust. Surely our nation has been under God's providential care.

Do you remember what you have read?

1. What two meetings held before the Constitutional Convention tried to solve some of the

George Washington was sworn into office as the first President on April 30, 1789, in New York.

problems caused by the weaknesses of the Articles of Confederation?
2. How did the Virginia plan differ from the New Jersey plan?
3. What compromises were made at the Constitutional Convention?
4. Give two reasons the Anti-Federalists did not like the new Constitution.
5. Name five outstanding members of the Constitutional Convention.

For further thought

1. Why were Constitutional compromises necessary? What can we learn from this?
2. Why was the period 1781—1789 called the critical period in our nation's history?
3. It is often argued that our leaders in government should be older and more experienced; yet, at the Constitutional Convention most of the

delegates were rather young, the average age being only forty-two, and half of them were in their thirties. Taking this into consideration, what do you think of the argument?

Words to study

bicameral	guarantee	unanimously
compromise	radical	unicameral
conservative	tariff	unity

UNIT RESEARCH PROJECTS

1. Find out where the Magna Carta has been kept in the past and where it is today.
2. Write a research paper on one of the following topics:
   Habeas Corpus—What It Means Today
   Conditions in England under the Rule of King John
   The Rise and Fall of Feudalism in Europe
3. Read more about the hardship endured by the Pilgrims during their trip to America and during their first few years in the New World. Report the information you find.
4. Make a report on some of the problems of the people in the United States during the days of the Articles of Confederation.
5. Draw a map of the United States showing the state boundaries and capitals between 1781 and 1789. Shade the national territories that had not yet been divided into states.
6. Describe the money system of the colonies during the time of the Articles of Confederation.
7. Write an essay on the qualities of character that made George Washington a respected leader.
8. Where are the original copies of the Constitution and the Declaration of Independence found today? Report on how these documents have been preserved since they were written.
9. Passing the Northwest Ordinance was one of the major achievements of the United States government under the Articles of Confederation. Investigate its content and report on ways in which its influence is still in evidence.
10. Give a brief biographical sketch about one of the following important framers of the Constitution: George Washington, James Madison, Benjamin Franklin, Alexander Hamilton, Gouverneur Morris, Edmund Randolph, Roger Sherman.
11. The issue of "states' rights" has been important throughout our nation's history and still is today. Make a report on how "states' rights" were related to the Civil War and how they are related to the education standards question today.
12. Imagine that you were living during this period of history and had to choose between being loyal to the King or joining General Washington's army. Write a paper giving the reasons for your choice.

Unit three
Our republic

I pledge allegiance
to the flag of the United States of America
and to the republic for which it stands,
one nation under God . . .

Our nation is a republic
because our form of government
is a *representative democracy.*
Laws are made
for the good of the people
by representatives elected by the people
to regulate the affairs
of our nation for the people.
These lawmakers are guided
in their action
by the Constitution of the United States.

Chapter 7

Our enduring Constitution

Important ideas to look for:
- The Constitution has met the needs of the people in the past.
- Separation of power is a basic principle of our Constitution.
- The Constitution is able to adjust to needs of the future.

Our Constitution has served for many years

The Constitution was instituted under God's rule and care to serve as the basis for our nation's government during the many years of its existence. All nations, including ours, "are like a drop in a bucket . . . as dust on the scales . . ." (Isa. 40:15) before Him. All nations are His, regardless of the form of government He has given them, and they must bring their praises before His throne. As our nation seeks to provide liberty and justice for all, it must first of all reflect the wisdom and justice of God.

For two centuries the Constitution has served as the "supreme law of the land." This is but a short time when compared to the history of the world. Yet, throughout these years enormous changes have taken place in our lives. The men who helped to frame the Constitution had never spoken on a telephone, had never heard a radio or seen a television program. They had never ridden in an automobile or flown in an airplane. Yet, the form of government they prepared works as well for us today as it did for them when it first began.

Why the Constitution is still useful

There are three main reasons why the Constitution has continued to serve our nation so well.

First, the Constitution was aimed at meeting the needs of the people. Because the basic needs have remained nearly the same, the rules that were made long ago are still effective. The way the Constitution intended to meet these needs is stated in the *Preamble:*

We, the people of the United States, in order to form a more perfect union, establish justice, insure *domestic tranquility,* provide for the common defense, promote the general welfare, and secure the blessings of liberty to ourselves and our *posterity,* do ordain and establish this Constitution for the United States of America.

Our needs for unity, for protection from enemies abroad, for justice, for peace at home, for liberty for ourselves and our children, and for general well-being are much the same as the needs of our citizens in 1789. Although the

Congress meets to enact our laws in the Capitol building in Washington, D.C.

method of meeting these needs has changed a great deal, our Constitution is still capable of fulfilling them.

Second, our Constitution has continued to serve our nation well because it is founded on the principle of the separation, or division, of power. These plans were based on the ideas of Aristotle as they were later interpreted by Montesquieu. Montesquieu's chief thought was that "men entrusted with power tend to abuse it." We know that this is true because of man's sinful and selfish nature. The framers of our Constitution acted on this thought when they provided for three branches of our national government: the legislative, the executive, and the judicial.

Each of these three branches can check or balance the other two so that no one person or department can seize all the power. During various periods of our nation's history the relative importance of each of these three branches of government has varied. During time of war, for example, the executive branch may exercise more power than the others.

Our Constitution also provides a division of authority between the national government and the state governments. Certain responsibilities and powers were delegated to the national government while others were reserved by the states. This division of authority affords a balance that has given the Constitution enduring strength. Circumstances today are causing more power to be shifted to the national government.

Third, the Constitution has been able to meet new conditions because it is *flexible*. Our Constitution can adjust to new needs because it can be *amended*, or changed. This has been done repeatedly. Amendments can be added any time a new situation demands such action.

Also, the Constitution has an *elastic clause* which permits Congress to ". . . make all laws necessary and proper for carrying into execution the foregoing powers." This is called the elastic clause because, through a broad interpretation of it, the courts have allowed Congress to stretch its power to make laws that cover situations not specifically mentioned in the Constitution.

Traditions and customs have also helped to make our government flexible. The committee system in Congress, the President's cabinet, the political-party system, and many common procedures have become a part of governmental action simply because they have been used year after year. These customs have no legal basis in the Constitution, yet they are used to meet the demands of the day.

Perhaps the best example of flexibility is found in the standard lawmaking process. New situations demand new regulations, and Congress is on hand to make the new laws as they are needed. This vast accumulation of new laws is also related to our growing Constitution.

BILL OF RIGHTS

1. Freedom of religion, speech, press, assembly, and right to petition.
2. Right to bear arms.
3. Soldiers shall not be quartered in private homes.
4. Protection against unreasonable search and seizure.
5. Judicial protection, including protection against self-incrimination.
6. Criminal trial rights.
7. Right to a trial by jury.
8. Protection against cruel and unusual punishment.
9. Rights not mentioned in the Constitution are retained by the people.
10. Powers not delegated to the Federal government are retained by the states.

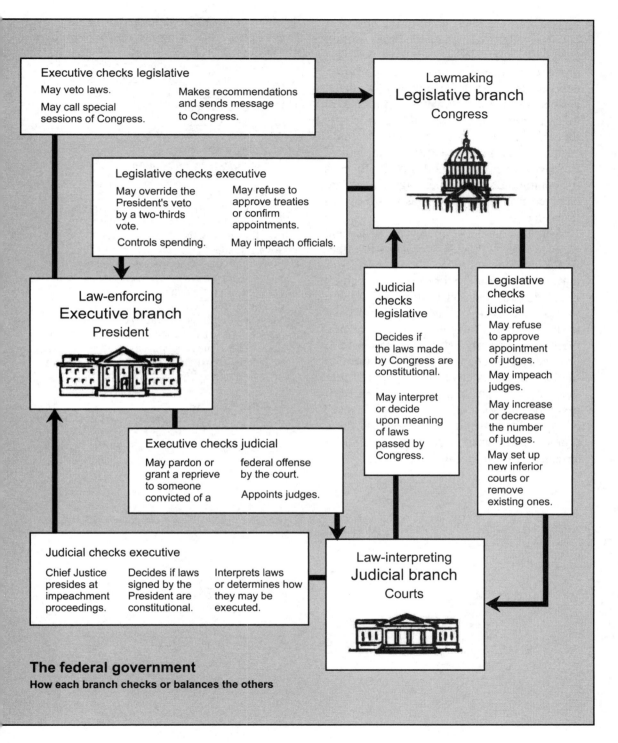

Executive checks legislative

May veto laws.

May call special sessions of Congress.

Makes recommendations and sends message to Congress.

Lawmaking
Legislative branch
Congress

Legislative checks executive

May override the President's veto by a two-thirds vote.

May refuse to approve treaties or confirm appointments.

Controls spending.

May impeach officials.

Law-enforcing
Executive branch
President

Judicial checks legislative

Decides if the laws made by Congress are constitutional.

May interpret or decide upon meaning of laws passed by Congress.

Legislative checks judicial

May refuse to approve appointment of judges.

May impeach judges.

May increase or decrease the number of judges.

May set up new inferior courts or remove existing ones.

Executive checks judicial

May pardon or grant a reprieve to someone convicted of a

federal offense by the court.

Appoints judges.

Judicial checks executive

Chief Justice presides at impeachment proceedings.

Decides if laws signed by the President are constitutional.

Interprets laws or determines how they may be executed.

Law-interpreting
Judicial branch
Courts

The federal government
How each branch checks or balances the others

The laws are interpreted in the courts of law. The judgment made in one case is often used to decide a second similar case. This process called *stare decisis,* using one court decision as the basis for judgment in others, has become a kind of lawmaking process. In this way the use of the Constitution widens its influence in the daily lives of our citizens.

Our nation makes treaties which regulate trade with other nations and provide alliances for common defense. These agreements are changed from time to time as world conditions change.

Although the Constitution was written and adopted over 200 years ago, it is still effective. That does not mean that it's perfect or that citizens should not be concerned about improving it. The Constitution was written to meet the needs of the people as stated in the Preamble, but the government could often be more responsive to these needs. It provides for the separation of power through three branches of government, but at times these branches are somewhat imbalanced. It is flexible, but sometimes the "elastic clause" is stretched to the limit. In spite of these problems, the Constitution provides the stable structure needed for our government.

Do you remember what you have read?
1. What needs of our people are listed in the Preamble to the Constitution?
2. Why is the separation of power among the different branches of government a good plan?
3. In what ways is our Constitution flexible?
4. How long has our country been a republic under the Constitution?

Memory work
Preamble to the Constitution

Research projects
1. Look up the ideas that Montesquieu and John Locke had about government, and try to discover how these ideas are related to our government.
2. Investigate the legal process of *stare decisis.* Try to determine how one court decision has affected the judgment given in similar cases that have followed.
3. Make a study of the methods used to separate power in our government. Try to find illustrations of how one branch has served as a check or balance on the power of another. Report your findings to the class.

Words to study

amend	posterity
domestic	Preamble
elastic clause	*stare decisis*
flexible	tranquility

Chapter 8

Congress— the legislative branch

Important ideas to look for:
- The lawmaking process involves a Congress composed of two houses.
- Many persons and groups influence Congress in the making of laws.
- Most of the work of Congress is done through committees.
- The Constitution clearly limits the legislative branch in what it may or may not do.

The Constitution of the United States*

Preamble

We the people of the United States, in order to form a more perfect union, establish justice, insure domestic tranquillity, provide for the common defense, promote the general welfare, and secure the blessings of liberty to ourselves and our posterity, do ordain and establish this Constitution for the United States of America.

A preamble is an introduction. The Preamble lists the reasons the Constitution was drawn up. "More perfect" means better than the Articles of Confederation. The Constitution is not just a historical document. It is the plan of our government, for we are some of "the people of the United States."

Article 1
Legislative branch

Section 1. Congress

All legislative powers herein granted shall be *vested* in a Congress of the United States, which shall consist of a Senate and House of Representatives.

The legislative branch makes the laws. Only Congress shall have power to make laws for our entire country.

Under the Articles of Confederation Congress had only one house. The Constitution provides for two houses, the House of Representatives and the Senate.

Section 2. The House of Representatives

The House of Representatives shall be composed of members chosen every second year by the people of the several states, and the electors in each state shall have the qualifications requisite for electors of the most numerous branch of the state legislature.

Each state can decide for itself what the requirements for its electors, or voters, will be. Usually the branch of the state legislature

---

* Modern spelling and capitalization are used in the text of the Constitution. Portions that have been changed or set aside by amendments have lines drawn through them.

that had the most members was elected by the most voters. Although states have limited the franchise in various ways, the Constitution guarantees that anyone who may vote in state elections may also vote in national elections.

> No person shall be a representative who shall not have attained to the age of twenty-five years and been seven years a citizen of the United States, and who shall not, when elected, be an inhabitant of that state in which he shall be chosen.

Because a representative must be reelected every two years, he should be especially mindful to carry out the wishes of the people he represents.

Requirements for a **representative:**
1. must be at least twenty-five years of age.
2. must have been a citizen at least seven years.
3. must be a resident of the state from which he or she is elected.

Customarily, voters elect a representative who lives in their district, as he would be more familiar with their problems. In England and Canada, representatives often serve districts other than their own.

> Representatives and direct taxes shall be apportioned among the several states which may be included within this Union, according to their respective numbers, which shall be determined by adding to the whole number of free persons, including those bound to service for a term of years, and excluding Indians not taxed, three fifths of all other persons.

A direct tax is one that must be paid by each citizen directly to the government. Such direct taxes must be divided equally among the people of all of the states.

The number of representatives for a state depends upon its population. "All other persons" refers to slaves. Since the Civil War, this "three-fifths" rule is no longer useful; it was taken away by the Thirteenth and Fourteenth Amendments. Also, Indians are citizens today.

> The actual enumeration shall be made within three years after the first meeting of the Congress of the United States, and within every subsequent term of ten years, in such manner as they shall by law direct.

An enumeration, or *census*, was first taken in 1790 and has been taken in all years ending with zero since that time.

> The number of representatives shall not exceed one for every thirty thousand, but each state shall have at least one representative; and until such enumeration shall be made, the state of New Hampshire shall be entitled to choose three, Massachusetts eight, Rhode Island and Providence Plantations one, Connecticut five, New York six, New Jersey four, Pennsylvania eight, Delaware one, Maryland six, Virginia ten, North Carolina five, South Carolina five, and Georgia three.

There were 65 representatives in the first Congress of the United States. Because the population has increased, the number has grown. In 1929 a law was passed that set the limit at 435 members. Each member must now represent many more people. If each one today represented only 30,000 people, as the Constitution states, there would be over 5000 members in the House of Representatives.

After each census is taken, the 435 seats of the House of Representatives are redivided or "reapportioned" among the states

The first prayer in Congress was offered in Carpenter's Hall, Philadelphia, in 1774.

according to the new population figures. Thus, it is possible for a state to gain or lose seats in the House of Representatives each ten years, depending upon the increase or decrease of its population in proportion to the total population.

When vacancies happen in the representation from any state, the executive authority thereof shall issue writs of election to fill such vacancies.

If a representative dies or resigns, the governor of his state must call a special election to fill the vacant office. This clause keeps the state governor from appointing someone instead of asking the people to vote for their representative.

The House of Representatives shall choose their Speaker and other officers and shall have the sole power of impeachment.

The Speaker of the House is chairman of the meetings. He is elected by the members of the House and is a member of the party in power, or the "majority party." He has many important duties, such as assigning bills to committees. The Speaker would become President if both the President and Vice-President should die.

To impeach means to try an official because of suspected misconduct in office. The House of Representatives must bring the charges; the Senate is the jury. A two-thirds vote is needed before a person can be discharged from office. Impeachment power is to be used when government officials do not carry out the duties of the offices they hold. Congress appoints special "Ethics Committees" to investigate charges of wrongdoing that may lead to removal from office.

Reviewing Sections 1 and 2 of Article I

1. Why is it proper that only Congress may make our laws?
2. How many members are in the House of Representatives? Is this a wise number?
3. Are the requirements for voting set by a state or by Congress?
4. What are the requirements for a representative?
5. Why did the Southern states want to count the slaves as a part of the population?
6. Why is it wise to require members of Congress to be inhabitants of the area that they represent?
7. Why is the census taken every ten years?
8. Why must there sometimes be a change in the number of representatives of a state?

Research projects

1. Learn the name of the person who serves as your representative in Congress. Where in your district does the person reside?
2. Look up the boundary and number of your congressional district.
3. Write a letter to your representative asking about the work done by representatives, his vote on a recent bill, or his opinion on a current national or world problem.
4. Make a study of the work of the Ethics Committees of Congress.

Words to study

apportion	impeach
census	requisite
enumeration	vested

Section 3. The Senate

The Senate of the United States shall be composed of two senators from each state,

chosen ~~by the legislature thereof~~, for six years; and each senator shall have one vote.

Small and large states, new and old states, all have equal voice in making laws in the Senate. This protects the weaker states from the power of the larger ones.

Senators are no longer elected by the state legislatures. The Seventeenth Amendment, passed in 1913, provides that senators shall now be elected by the people just as representatives are. According to this amendment, vacancies in the Senate may be filled by the governor's appointee until an election can be held. The state legislature must give the governor special permission to make a temporary appointment.

Immediately after they shall be assembled in consequence of the first election, they shall be divided as equally as may be into three classes. The seats of the senators of the first class shall be vacated at the expiration of the second year, of the second class at the expiration of the fourth year, and of the third class at the expiration of the sixth year, so that one third may be chosen every second year; ~~and if vacancies happen by resignation, or otherwise, during the recess of the legislature of any state, the executive thereof may make temporary appointments until the next meeting of the legislature which shall then fill such vacancies.~~

Two-thirds of the Senate is always made up of experienced members. One-third has recently been in touch with the voters. In theory, this gives us a continuing and balanced Senate. It is sometimes called "the house that never dies."

No person shall be a senator who shall not have attained to the age of thirty years and been nine years a citizen of the United States, and who shall not, when elected, be an inhabitant of that state for which he shall be chosen.

Each state makes its own laws about being an "inhabitant" by deciding what a legal residence is.

> The Vice-President of the United States shall be president of the Senate
> but shall have no vote,
> unless they be equally divided.

Requirements for a **senator:**
1. must be at least thirty years of age.
2. must have been a citizen at least nine years.
3. must be a resident of the state he or she represents.

The Vice-President has often been required to break a tie vote in the Senate. For example, John Adams in 1789, as Vice-President, cast the vote that gave the President the right to remove a Cabinet member without approval of the Senate. Also, Vice-President Garret Hobart in 1899 broke the tie on the peace *treaty* after the Spanish-American War and voted to accept the treaty.

As president of the Senate, the Vice-President knows about new laws and treaties. This information would help him if he should suddenly become the President of the nation.

> The Senate shall choose their other officers, and also a president pro tempore, in the absence of the Vice-President, or when he shall exercise the office of President of the United States.

Pro tempore is a Latin phrase meaning for the time being.

> The Senate shall have the sole power to try all impeachments. When sitting for that purpose, they shall be on oath or affirmation. When the President of the United States is tried, the Chief Justice shall preside: And no person shall be convicted without the concurrence of two-thirds of the members present.

Before a government official can be tried for some crime or misbehavior in office, the House of Representatives must vote to impeach. The accusations are heard by the Senate. Unless two-thirds of the senators present agree that he is guilty, he is declared innocent.

The Chief Justice, rather than the Vice-President must preside over the Senate when the President of the United States is on trial. This must be done because the Vice-President would be affected by the results. If the President were convicted, the Vice-President would become President in his place.

> Judgment in cases of impeachment shall not extend further than to removal from office and disqualification to hold and enjoy any office of honor, trust, or profit under the United States: but the party convicted shall nevertheless be liable and subject to

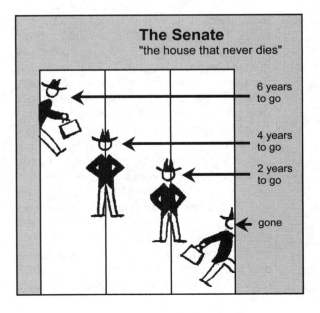

The Senate
"the house that never dies"

6 years to go

4 years to go

2 years to go

gone

Congress—the legislative branch 63

In the troubled years after the Civil War the Senate attempted to impeach President Andrew Johnson. The attempt failed by a margin of one vote.

indictment, trial, judgment, and punishment, according to law.

After an official has been impeached by the Senate, he may be tried before a regular court. For example, if he has taken some government money, the regular court may punish him for this crime. In this trial he has the same right of trial by jury that everyone else has. The only punishment the Senate may give is removal from office.

Our congressmen are under God. They should continually study God's Word to see how it is related to the problems that arise in their office of government. The laws they make for our nation must be based on truth and justice. Our senators and representatives have a heavy responsibility both to God and to the citizens of our land. As of 2012, the Senate has conducted 19 impeachment proceedings, resulting in seven acquittals, 8 convictions, 3 dismissals, and one resignation.

The list includes a senator, two presidents, one cabinet secretary, and the rest judges. It does not include those who resigned rather than face impeachment, most notably President Richard Nixon.

Section 4. Elections and meetings of Congress

The times, places, and manner of holding elections for senators and representatives shall be prescribed in each state by the legislature thereof; but the Congress may at any time by law make or alter such regulations, ~~except as to the places of choosing senators.~~

In 1842 Congress passed a law stating that representatives must be elected by districts. This made illegal the election of all representatives "at large," that is, having all the voters of the state choose all the representatives.

More recently redistricting has become important. You will recall that the U.S. House of Representatives reapportions the 435 members among the states after each census because the population of some states grows much faster than that of others. Because the population of some districts within the states also grows much faster than that of others, district boundaries need to be changed as well if all citizens are to have equal voting power. The Constitution leaves this task of *redistricting* to the states.

Elections are to be held on the Tuesday after the first Monday in November in even-numbered years in all of the states.

The election of senators was to be held in the state legislatures. If Congress had told the states where the elections were to be held, it would be telling them where their state capitals should be. Congress could not do this.

Almost all the laws for elections are made by the states themselves. However, Congress may pass certain laws to guarantee honest and fair elections. One such law requires all states to use secret ballots. Another permits the use of voting machines. Another law passed by Congress limits the amount of money a senator or representative may spend on his election campaign.

> The Congress shall assemble at least once in every year, ~~and such meeting shall be on the first Monday in December,~~ unless they shall by law appoint a different day.

The Twentieth Amendment, passed in 1933, has changed the meeting date of Congress to January 3 of odd-numbered years following the regular November election. This first meeting is called the first session of that particular Congress.

Their second session begins on January 3 of the next year. A session lasts as long as there is work to be done. The President may call a special session of Congress in an emergency. This part of the Constitution makes certain that Congress will not be kept from meeting as Charles II kept the Parliament of England from doing its work.

> **Congress meets:**
> 1. beginning each January 3.
> 2. for its first session in odd-number years.
> 3. for its second session in even-numbered years.

Reviewing Sections 3 and 4 of Article I

1. Why is it wise not to have all the senators elected at one time?
2. What are the requirements for the office of senator?
3. Is it fair to have a senator's requirements stricter than those for a representative? Give reasons for your answer.
4. How many sessions does each Congress have?
5. How long does a session usually last?
6. Why is it important that Congress meet at least once a year?

Research projects

1. Learn the names of the senators from your state. How long have they served in Congress? How old are they? Try to find a copy of the Congressional Directory in a local library and look up their biographies.
2. Write a letter to one of your senators for information about the bills he has sponsored and the committees on which he is serving. Ask which part of his education and past experience he feels helped him most as preparation for his present work.
3. Correspond with the secretary of your state government to determine the following:
   a. How often your state adjusts or changes the boundaries of its representative and senatorial districts.
   b. What procedure was used when redistricting last occurred.
4. Look up the U.S. Supreme Court case of Baker vs. Carr and try to discover how this case influenced redistricting.

Words to study

affirmation   concurrence
attain   disqualification

The House of Representatives voted 376-30 to expel Pennsylvania Representative Michael Meyers (second from right) in 1980, after he was convicted in an FBI bribery investigation. He was the first House member since the Civil War to be expelled by his colleagues.

expiration	redistricting
preside	resignation
pro tempore	treaty

Section 5. Rules of order

Each House shall be the judge of the elections, returns, and qualifications of its own members, and a majority of each shall constitute a quorum to do business; but a smaller number may adjourn from day to day, and may be authorized to compel the attendance of absent members, in such manner, and under such penalties as each House may provide.

If members of the Senate or the House of Representatives feel that one of the newly elected members has been dishonestly elected or that he fails to meet the requirements set by the Constitution, they can keep him from taking his chair. Henry Clay was the first Senator to be elected before he was thirty. He had to reach the required age before he could take the oath of office. Albert Gallatin was refused a seat after being elected as a senator from Pennsylvania because he had not been a citizen for nine years. Another senator was refused because "his campaign was colored with fraud and corruption."

Each House may determine the rules of its proceedings, punish its members for disorderly behavior, and, with the concurrence of two-thirds, expel a member.

Either House can do business if a *quorum*, or more than half of its members, is present. Debates and discussions can go on whether more than half are present or not, but a quorum must come in to vote before a law can be passed. If more of the members are needed to get a quorum for an important piece of legislation, the Sergeant at Arms can compel others to attend the session.

Rules for proceedings of the House are strict, with speeches being limited to one hour except when the entire House agrees to allow a member to make a longer speech.

In the Senate, where there are fewer members, the senators may generally debate as long as they wish on any bill. Sometimes, however, if a senator feels that a bill is not good either for our nation as a whole or for the state he represents, and if he is unable to stop the bill from passing by ordinary debate, he may try to stop it by *filibustering*. That is, he may talk on and on about it until the Senate decides to change the bill or drop it altogether. To lengthen his speech, a filibustering senator may read from various documents or books. A few have even read from dictionaries, phone directories,

LOBBYING AND PRESSURE GROUPS

Each new law that is passed by Congress affects the people in one way or another. Some people will like it because it helps them. Others may dislike the new law because it controls their business or places a tax on them. After a bill has been introduced, a committee studies it carefully. If the bill is an important one, the news media will tell everyone about it. Then the people at home have the opportunity and responsibility to contact their members of Congress. If lawmakers get hundreds of contacts asking them to vote against a certain bill, they usually vote against it. It is the responsibility of all citizens to encourage representatives and senators to vote for those bills that will provide good government and against those that are unfair or bad.

The extent of abuse in recent years has led to more calls for lobbying and legislative reform. Occasionally large numbers of people interested in certain laws assemble in public places or march in Washington to impress lawmakers with their causes. But the greatest pressure that comes to a member of Congress is applied by the lobbyists. A *lobby* is a group of persons who go to the Capitol as representatives of some special-interest group. For example, the automobile manufacturers might hire someone to go to the Capitol to ask the members of Congress to pass a tariff on the importation of foreign cars. Several hundred well-paid lobbyists representing various types of businesses, labor organizations,

agricultural interests, and a wide range of other groups work regularly either for or against a bill that would affect the groups they represent.

The lobbyists are often called the members of the "third house" of Congress because of their influence on the bills. Although lobbyists may not speak to a meeting of the Senate or the House of Representatives, they may appear before committees that are studying a bill. They also talk to members of Congress privately, urging them to vote a certain way on a bill that is being considered. The Constitution does not say anything about lobbyists. The practice of lobbying has slowly grown to be recognized as a very real part of the lawmaking process.

Lobbying is partially regulated by federal and state laws. Every lobbyist must register with the Clerk of the House of Representatives or the Secretary of the Senate. Lobbyists must list the organizations they represent. They must tell who pays them and provide other information.

Lobbying may have helpful or harmful effects. It can supply statistics and other information as well as represent opinions of people who are not able to be at the Capitol. However, some lobbyists represent special interests concerned only with their own well-being. Legislators need much wisdom to carefully assess the information and viewpoints lobbyists provide. They must avoid being "used" to promote selfish and unjust legislation.

and mail order catalogs. The *Closure* Rule can be enforced to limit the length of Senate speeches, but it is difficult to pass since it requires a three-fifths majority. The Senate has been studying ways to strengthen its power to control filibustering.

> Each House shall keep a journal of its proceedings, and from time to time publish the same, excepting such parts as may in their judgment require secrecy; and the yeas and nays of the members of either House on any question shall, at the desire of one-fifth of those present, be entered on the journal.

Everything said and done in Congress becomes part of our nation's public record. This material is printed during the night, and when a member of Congress returns to his or her desk each morning, there will be a copy of the proceedings of the day before. *The Congressional Record* prints everything said in the formal meeting of Congress except during executive sessions of the Senate. This *Record* is available to every citizen. Keeping such a record is wise because it reminds the members of Congress that their work, their comments, and their votes are open to the inspection of all.

> Neither House, during the session of Congress, shall, without the consent of the other, adjourn for more than three days, nor to any other place than that in which the two Houses shall be sitting.

If one House should move to a distant place, communications between the two Houses may become difficult. If one House should adjourn before the other, important bills which need the vote of both Houses may lie incomplete or unfinished.

Section 6. Pay, privileges, and restrictions
The senators and representatives shall

(turn to p.70)

THE COMMITTEE SYSTEM

Much of the work of studying the advantages and disadvantages of a bill is done by committees of Congress before congressmen are asked to pass it into a law. The committee system was not established by the Constitution. Instead, it has developed through the years because of the need to study bills thoroughly. Another advantage is that many bills can be studied at the same time. Small committees can do this better than the whole house of delegates.

After the Constitution was ratified and the Congress began its work, a new committee was appointed to study every bill that was introduced. Soon the number of committees grew large and confusing. Both the Senate and the House of Representatives began appointing *standing committees* to study all the bills of a similar nature. The number of such standing committees has varied a great deal in the past.

When a bill is introduced in the House of Representatives, the Speaker of the House must decide which of the House committees would be the best qualified to study it. If the bill is introduced in the Senate, the President of the Senate is expected to refer it to the appropriate committee.

The committee may then deal with the bill in several ways:
1. After studying it, the committee may send it back to the *chamber* with a recommendation that it be passed.
2. The committee may *pigeon-hole* it, that is, put it aside and never return it to the chamber. This usually kills the bill.
3. If the committee does not want the responsibility of killing a bill, it may send it to the chamber with a recommendation not to pass it. In this way the House members rather than the committee are required to decide upon its value.
4. The committee may amend, or change, the bill before sending it back to the floor. Sometimes several similar bills are combined in this way.

In addition to the standing committees of the Senate and the House of Representatives, Congress also needs several special committees to carry on the vast amount of work it is expected to do.

If the two Houses of Congress cannot agree on the way a bill should be written, a *conference committee* made up of an equal number of senators and representatives is appointed to try to work out the differences. After the conference committee has reached an agreement, the compromise bill is presented to both Houses again.

In addition to these temporary conference committees appointed to study certain bills, the Congress has several, more permanent *joint committees*. The joint committees are also made up of members of both Houses. They generally deal with more long-range problems, such as atomic energy, and other matters, such as the Library of Congress. *Select committees* may also be appointed to conduct some type of investigation or do other work that Congress feels necessary.

The political party that has a majority in Congress will also have a majority in each committee. If, for example, the Democrats held 60 percent of the seats in the Senate, they would also hold 60 percent of the seats on each Senate committee. The majority party is also able to select the committee chair. The chair of the standing committees hold very important positions in the lawmaking process, for they must decide when their committees will meet and also whether they should study a bill or lay it aside. Committee chairpersons are generally selected on the basis of *seniority*, that is, those who have served their party for the greatest number of years in Congress are appointed to important chairmanship positions.

Although the committee system has many advantages for the smooth operation of our large Congress and the great amount of work it is expected to do, there are also many disadvantages of this system. Committee work may become very involved and bring needless delay to the lawmaking process. Although it is often advisable for committee members to travel to gather first-hand information about a problem, many times such *junkets* (trips by a subcommittee) cause our government needless expense.

Of the hundreds of bills that are submitted at each session of Congress, most never get through the committee to which they are assigned for study. Many of these bills deserve to be pigeon-holed, or killed. Sometimes, however, they are kept in committee for political or personal reasons instead of being returned for consideration to the House in which they originated.

Current Standing Committees in Congress

Senate Committees
- Agriculture, Nutrition, and Forestry
- Appropriations
- Armed Services
- Banking, Housing, and Urban Affairs
- Budget
- Commerce, Science, and Transportation
- Energy and Natural Resources
- Environment and Public Works
- Finance
- Foreign Relations
- Health, Education, Labor, and Pensions
- Homeland Security and Governmental Affairs
- Judiciary
- Rules and Administration
- Small Business and Entrepreneurship
- Veterans' Affairs

House Committees
- Agriculture; Appropriations
- Armed Forces
- Budget
- Education and the Workforce
- Energy and Commerce
- Ethics
- Financial Services
- Foreign Affairs
- Homeland Security
- House Administration
- Judiciary
- National Resources
- Oversight and Government Reform
- Rules
- Science, Space, and Technology
- Small Business
- Transportation and Infrastructure
- Veterans' Affairs
- Ways and Means

receive a compensation for their services, to be ascertained by law and paid out of the Treasury of the United States. They shall in all cases, except treason, felony and breach of the peace, be privileged from arrest during their attendance at the session of their respective Houses, and in going to and returning from the same; and for any speech or debate in either House, they shall not be questioned in any other place.

Early in our congressional history, congressmen received only a small allowance for the days Congress met. The first salary they received was in 1855; it was $3000 a year. In 2012, the rank-and-file congressional members earned $174,000 per year plus an allowance for travel and office expenses. The Speaker of the House earned $223,500 per year plus an expense allowance. The Vice President, who serves as leader of the Senate, earned $230,000 plus the expense allowance.

Members of Congress also have the right to send official mail free of charge if it bears their name. This is called the *franking privilege.*

In some European countries the ruler could have opposing lawmakers arrested for a short time until laws had been passed by those who were friendly to the ruler. This cannot be done in the United States. Even though our lawmakers are given *political immunity*, or freedom from arrest, while serving in their official capacities, they may not misuse this privilege, for they are always under God.

No senator or representative shall, during the time for which he was elected, be appointed to any civil office under the authority of the United States, which shall have been created, or the emoluments whereof shall have been increased during such time; and no person holding any office under the United States shall be a member of either House during his continuance in office.

Members of Congress may speak freely against or for a matter without fear of being arrested or sued for what they say in the meetings.

Members of Congress may neither work in any position they helped to create nor hold a job that was given a higher salary during their term of office. This keeps legislators from creating highly paid government jobs for their own benefit.

Reviewing Sections 5 and 6 of Article I

1. Why must a quorum be present before business can be done in Congress?
2. Why are filibusters sometimes used in the Senate?
3. Why is it wise for our nation to keep a record of the speeches and proceedings of Congress?
4. Why should one House of Congress not adjourn without the consent of the other?
5. Why is it better for the United States Treasury to pay all congressmen than for each state to pay its own?

For further thought

1. What problems are connected with keeping a congressional record?
2. In 1977 both the Senate and House adopted codes of ethics that require members to make public disclosure of their personal income and assets. Do you think this is wise or unwise? Why or why not?
3. Discuss the good and bad aspects of lobbying.
4. How does the committee system in Congress strengthen the law-making process?

Research projects

1. Make a study of the use of filibustering in the Senate. Try to determine the length, content, and purpose of several filibusters.
2. Obtain a sample copy of *The Congressional Record.* Study its nature and contents; report to your class.

Andrew Jackson, who used the presidential veto frequently, was portrayed as a tyrant by his political enemies.

Section 7. How bills become laws

All bills for raising revenue shall originate in the House of Representatives; but the Senate may propose or concur with amendments as on other bills.

The Revolutionary War had been fought because of "taxation without representation." Since the senators were first elected by the state legislatures, the framers of the Constitution placed the power of taxation in the hands of the House of Representatives. Members there are elected by the people for a short term of two years. Today, however, senators are also elected by the people and have a more important part in making tax laws than senators did when the Constitution was first adopted.

When a congressman introduces a new plan for a law, it is called a *bill* until it is officially passed and signed. Most bills become laws by being passed by both Houses of Congress by a simple majority vote and then being signed by the President.

Every bill which shall have passed the House of Representatives and the Senate, shall, before it becomes a law, be presented to the President of the United States;
if he approves, he shall sign it; but if not, he shall return it with his objections to that House in which it shall have originated, who shall enter the objections at large on their journal and proceed to reconsider it. If after such reconsideration two-thirds of that House shall agree to pass the bill, it shall be sent, together with the objections, to the other House, by which it shall likewise be reconsidered, and if approved by two-thirds of that House, it shall become a law. But in all such cases the votes of both Houses shall be determined by yeas and nays, and the names of the persons voting for and against the bill shall be entered on the journal of each House respectively.

As our congressmen work behind the closed doors of a committee room, they must be as honest and exact as if they were debating on the floor of Congress. Whether they

How a bill becomes a law

1. Most bills can be introduced in either house. The procedure by which a bill becomes a law is much the same regardless of where the bill originates.

In this chart, the bill is first introduced in the Senate. It is given a number and referred to the proper committee.

2. The committee holds public hearings on the bill.

3. The full committee meets to consider the facts. It may kill the bill, approve it with or without amendments, or draft a new bill. Generally these meetings are open to the public news media, but in rare instances the committee may hold an executive (closed) session.

4. The committee recommends the bill for passage. It is then listed on the Senate calendar.

5. The bill comes up for debate. Depending on the degree of controversy, debate may last from a few hours to several weeks. Amendments may or may not be added. The bill is then voted on.

6. If it passes, it goes to the House of Representatives for action. It is referred to the proper committee.

7. Hearings may be held.

8. The committee rejects the bill, prepares a new one, or accepts the bill with or without amendments.

9. The committee recommends the bill for passage. It is listed on the calendar and is sent to the Rules Committee.

10. The Rules Committee is one of the most powerful committees in the House of Representatives. After a bill has been recommended for passage by the committee to which it was referred, the Rules Committee can block it or clear it for debate before the entire House. (If a bill is blocked, a discharge petition, signed by a simple majority of the House, can clear the bill for House consideration. This procedure of obtaining a discharge petition seldom succeeds.)

11. It goes before the entire body, is debated, and is voted on.

Senate

House

12. If the bill is passed by the second body but contains major differences, either house may request a conference committee. The conferees meet and try to settle their differences. Representing both parties, five conferees are usually appointed from each house.

13. Generally, they reach an agreement. They report back to their respective houses. The report is accepted or rejected.

Speaker of the House

President of the Senate

14. If the report is accepted by both houses, the bill is signed by the Speaker of the House and the President of the Senate, and is sent to the President of the United States.

15. The President may sign or veto the bill within ten days. If he doesn't sign within ten days and Congress is still in session, the bill automatically becomes law. If Congress has adjourned before the ten days have elapsed and the President has not signed the bill, it does not become law. This is known as a "pocket veto." If the President returns the bill with a veto message, it may still become law if passed by a two-thirds majority in each house.

are working in the presence of a large group or with just a few others, they must always remember they are responsible to God and the people they represent.

The President can stop Congress from passing a law he considers to be unwise by refusing to sign it, that is, by *vetoing* it. If after reconsidering the bill, Congress still wants to make it a law, the members can do so by a two-thirds majority without the President's signature. This ability to override a veto keeps the President from blocking a good law that most of the Congress wants.

> If any bill shall not be returned by the President within ten days (Sunday excepted) after it shall have been presented to him, the same shall be a law, in like manner as if he had signed it, unless the Congress by their adjournment prevent its return, in which case it shall not be a law.

The ten-day limit keeps a President from putting off laws he doesn't want to sign. King George III often ignored or delayed action on the laws passed by the colonial assemblies and so stopped them from going into effect. If our President refuses to sign or return any bill sent to him by Congress, it becomes a law without his approval.

However, when Congress adjourns before the ten days have passed, the President may stop a bill from becoming a law by a *pocket veto*. If Congress has adjourned, the President doesn't have to sign the bill; he doesn't have to return it either. He may forget about it. If Congress wants such a bill to become a law, the congressmen must introduce it again at the next session.

> Every order, resolution, or vote to which the concurrence of the Senate and House of Representatives may be necessary (except on a question of adjournment) shall be presented to the President of the United States; and before the same shall take effect, shall be approved by him, or being disapproved by him, shall be repassed by two-thirds of the Senate and House of Representatives, according to the rules and limitations prescribed in the case of a bill.

Reviewing Section 7 of Article I

1. Why was the power to write tax bills given to the House of Representatives rather than to the Senate? Is this difference still important today? Give reasons for your answer.
2. Describe the process followed by most bills as they become laws.
3. If the President vetoes a bill, how can it still be made into a law?
4. In what ways are committees very helpful to Congress in the law-making process?

For further thought

1. Why do you think the framers of the Contitution put so many steps into the lawmaking process?
2. Committee chairmen are selected on the basis of seniority (years of service). How can this system be improved?
3. In what way could a junket be very helpful?
4. Do you favor the President's right to exercise the line-item veto? Why or why not?

Words to study

bill	resolution
chamber	revenue
conference committee	select committee
joint committee	seniority
junket	standing committee
pigeon-hole	veto
pocket veto	

Section 8. Powers granted to Congress

The Congress shall have power: To lay and collect taxes, duties, imposts and excises, to pay the debts and provide
for the common defense and general welfare of the United States;

Section 8 lists the powers given to Congress by the Constitution. This section gives to our federal government many of the powers it lacked under the Articles of Confederation.

Congress may gather money by a system of taxes. Duties and imposts, called *tariffs* today, are taxes on imported goods. Manufacturers of goods made and sold within the United States pay *excise* taxes; these taxes are usually added to the cost of the articles and are paid, indirectly, by the purchasers. Congress also collects taxes, such as the Income Tax, directly from the citizens and alien residents of the United States.

Congress also has the right to spend money, not for anything it wishes, but only for three reasons: the payment of debts, the common defense, and the general welfare of all the states. The President sometimes refuses to sign a bill because it favors one state or group of people in the country. The "general welfare" clause has been stretched so that it now allows the government to spend money for nearly any cause that it chooses.

> but all duties, imposts, and excises shall be uniform throughout the United States;

Federal taxes must be the same percent everywhere in the United States. The tax on automobiles, the gasoline tax, the tax on watches, or the tax on a ticket to a ball game must be the same in Chicago as it is in Los Angeles; otherwise our federal government would not be just and fair in its tax program.

> To borrow money on the credit of the United States;

Congress borrows much money from our citizens through the sale of government bonds. When it borrows this money on the "credit of the United States," it promises that the amount borrowed will be paid back with interest according to the terms of the agreement. It cannot change the terms later. The

Each state sets its own gasoline tax, but the federal gasoline tax is the same in all states.

government also borrows money from banks and other privately owned companies, such as insurance companies, that have money to invest.

> To regulate commerce with foreign nations, and among the several states, and with the Indian tribes;

The power to regulate commerce is one of the most important powers of Congress. Under this part of the Constitution, Congress may control trade through tariff laws and trade treaties with other nations. It may stop the shipment of impure or undesirable articles. Congress may also encourage commerce by improving harbors and requiring safety equipment.

When Congress received the power to regulate *interstate* commerce, it stopped many of the disagreements over trade that had risen under the Articles of Confederation. Today, Congress may control the movement of anything that crosses state boundaries—goods, people, and words. The means by which these goods, people, and words are carried across state lines are also controlled by federal laws.

Good trade laws can encourage business and help industry by controlling the shipment of harmful goods and by regulating unfair business practices.

Congress also has a special responsibility to promote the well-being of the Indian tribes in our land.

To establish a uniform rule of naturalization, and uniform laws on the subject of bankruptcies throughout the United States;

Laws for becoming a citizen must be the same in every state. Only Congress may make laws for granting and withdrawing citizenship. *Bankruptcy* laws protect both the person who owes more money than he can pay and also those to whom he owes the bills.

To coin money, regulate the value thereof, and of foreign coin, and fix the standard of weights and measures;

The colonists had used the money of many nations. Besides this, each colony had printed its own money. This was often confusing. Today, only the national government may print and coin money. It may also make laws against the melting, defacement, and exportation of its money.

Our government has set up a standard for weights and measures. Government agents regularly check the scales in the stores and shops of our nation. It is the duty of every citizen to use these standard weights and measures properly, for "Differing weights and differing measures—the Lord detests them both" (Prov. 20:10).

To provide for the punishment of counterfeiting the securities and current coin of the United States;

Persons thought guilty of manufacturing counterfeit money are tried in Federal District Courts and if found guilty are sentenced to not more than $5000, or 15 years in imprisonment, or both. The Secret Service of the United States Treasury Department has been

METRICATION

The metric system was first proposed in France in 1670. In 1790 Thomas Jefferson recommended that the United States use this decimal system of measurement, but Congress rejected the idea. In 1821 John Quincy Adams also proposed such a change, but again Congress rejected the plan. However, in 1866 Congress legalized the use of the metric system, but did not require its use. Manufacturers of photographic equipment, pharmaceuticals, and firearms began using the metric system. Again in 1890 Congress was asked to change the nation to the metric system, but again it refused.

In 1965 Great Britain began a ten-year changeover to metrication, and in 1970 Canada and Australia began conversion to the metric system, leaving the United States as the last major user of the English system.

In 1971, after a report by a metric conversion study committee, the Commerce Secretary recommended a gradual changeover to the metric system in the U.S. The Metric Conversion Act of 1975 established a national policy of increasing metric system use, coordinated by the U.S. Metric Board.

The conversion to metrics started with the automobile, construction, farm equipment, computer and bottling industries. Although the metric system has not caught on completely in the United States today, it is important that young people have a good understanding of it. As the future leaders of our nation in matters of the world trade and business, a thorough knowledge of this universal system of measurement will be very helpful.

The federal government designs and prints money for use in all the states.

made responsible for carrying out this power of Congress.

To establish post offices and post roads;

When the Constitution was written there were only about seventy-five post offices in all of the thirteen colonies. By law Congress has added many, many more; today, we find one in nearly every city and town. Many other services have also been added: post cards, parcel post, registered mail, airmail, and free delivery of mail. At first, Congress only selected the roads over which the mail should be carried. Later, it helped provide roads so mail could be delivered more quickly. Mail in transit has the same protection as "the property of the United States." Recently the Post Office Department was reorganized into what is now known as the United States Postal Service.

To promote the progress of science and useful arts by securing for limited times to authors and inventors the exclusive right to their respective writings and discoveries;

Congress has passed laws that give an inventor the exclusive right "to make, use, and sell" his invention for twenty years without having someone else copy it. A patent may be renewed for seven years only by a special act of Congress. If a person can control the production of his invention and make a profit by selling it, he will try harder to invent worthwhile new products. Copyright laws keep persons from copying writings, photographs, films, maps, art, speeches, and other documents. A copyright stays in effect throughout the life of the composer, artist, or author, and for fifty years after he or she dies. A copyright includes this information: copyright ©, the year in which the copyright was secured, and the name of the copyright holder. (See the copyright page of this book.)

To constitute tribunals inferior to the Supreme Court;

Congress has the power to provide for a system of federal courts. This helps our citizens receive liberty and justice because a court case may be appealed from a district court to higher courts, and in some instances even up to the United States Supreme Court.

> To define and punish piracies and felonies committed on the high seas, and offenses against the law of nations;

When our ships go to sea, they are still protected by the power of the United States. If a United States ship violates an international law, Congress may punish it instead of letting that one ship draw our whole nation into trouble. Congress may also punish any citizen who breaks an international law. While we were colonies of England, the British government was responsible for enforcing the international laws. But when we became an independent nation, our own government became responsible for carrying out the international laws for us.

> To declare war,

It is not for the individual but for the government to decide whether the nation shall at any time enter into war. You already know that war came after the breaking of God's law and that war has its source in sin. War can be caused by feelings of hate, envy, and revenge.

In Genesis 3:15 we read that there would be enmity between the woman's seed and the seed of the serpent. Since then wars have been common. Many times in the Old Testament God used war in His providence for the people of Israel. He allowed the sun to stand still while Joshua fought. War belongs to this world; after this world has passed away, there will be no more war.

Military service and war are not sinful in themselves. They can be used to maintain justice. The Bible does not teach that we should allow the innocent to be oppressed and killed. In a nuclear age, the power to declare war is an awesome responsibility.

Men like Ambrosius, Augustine, Thomas Aquinas, and John Calvin maintained that war has a rightful existence. However, they defended war only when it was just. They saw the following as just reasons for carrying on a war:

1. Not the individual but the government must declare war, as it must guard the welfare of the state in case of invasion and rebellion.
2. War must be carried on in behalf of a just cause, not out of vanity, pride, selfishness, lust for power, or desire for land. It can be used to protect our nation, our homes, and our fireside, or to protect religious worship and other high causes which cannot be maintained in any other way.
3. War must be carried on in the spirit of a just intention and purpose, not for the sake of ruling over or taking revenge on the enemy. It may be used only as a means to obtain peace and justice.
4. The method of carrying on war must be just. There are certain rights that must be respected in time of war, as well as in time of peace. During war, people must not degenerate into animals, for we are always under God whether in time of peace or war.

When the Constitution gives Congress the power to declare war, it also gives Congress the power to pass laws to carry on the war it has declared.

> grant letters of marque and reprisal, and make rules concerning captures on land and water;

Letters of "*marque* and *reprisal*" were given to private boat owners before our nation had a navy of its own. These boat owners could attack enemy ships in the name of the United States. This was especially important

during the War of 1812. Letters of marque and reprisal are not used today.

Sailors and Marines man the rails aboard the aircraft carrier USS Ronald Reagan (CVN 76) while entering Pearl Harbor for a port visit.

To raise and support armies, but no appropriation of money to that use shall be for a longer term than two years;

Congress has often used this power to draft the men necessary to carry on a war.

Since a representative's term is only two years, the citizens may decide every two years if they want to change the size and character of our military defense. However, sudden changes in our country's defense plans are seldom made. Military training of both enlisted men and officers, maintenance of military camps, and research in the development of new weapons and war equipment must be carried on with a long-range plan if our national defense is to be effective. Nevertheless, this clause does give the voters an opportunity every two years to consider carefully the choice of men who are responsible for defense spending.

To provide and maintain a navy;

Because the life of a ship is longer than two years, the limit on the army did not apply to the navy.

To make rules for the government and regulation of the land and naval forces;

Many people thought an amendment should be added to the Constitution to govern the air force when it was added to our military defense. It was decided, however, that the war power given to Congress by the Constitution allowed congressmen to start an air force without adding an amendment.

To provide for calling forth the militia to execute the laws of the Union, suppress insurrections, and repel invasions;

The *militia*, or National Guard, is separate from the army and is usually under the control of the states. However, Congress may call on these soldiers of the states for help to enforce the country's laws, to fight those who rebel against the government, and to fight an enemy that might attack our country.

> To provide for organizing, arming, and disciplining the militia, and for governing such part of them as may be employed in the service of the United States, reserving to the states respectively, the appointment of the officers and the authority of training the militia according to the discipline prescribed by Congress;

The national government pays most of the bills for training and equipping the National Guard. In return for this expense Congress controls a large group of citizens that have military training. These trained citizens may be called into the regular army if they are needed. Also, they are called upon by the governors of the states to meet emergencies within the states.

> To exercise exclusive legislation in all cases whatsoever, over such district (not exceeding ten miles square) as may, by cession of particular states and the acceptance of Congress, become the seat of the government of the United States,

This section gives Congress the responsibility of governing the District of Columbia. For many years Congress did so directly, and the people there had little voice in local government. Today they elect their own mayor and councilmen, and make their own local laws. Congress still has the right to make laws for the District, even if they override local laws.

The people living in the District of Columbia do not live in any state and therefore do not have representatives or senators in Congress. The Twenty-third Amendment, however, gives these people the right to vote in national elections.

> and to exercise like authority over all places purchased by the consent of the legislature of the state in which the same shall be, for the erection of forts, magazines, arsenals, dockyards, and other needful buildings—

Whenever Congress buys from private citizens property for forts, parks, post offices, forests, or other governmental purposes, the state in which the land is found must agree to give up the land. The federal government then makes laws to govern this property. The federal government thus has power to buy the property it needs, but it must use this property as a servant of God for good to serve the people.

> To make all laws which shall be necessary and proper for carrying into execution the foregoing powers and all other powers vested by this Constitution in the government of the United States, or in any department or officer thereof.

The wise leaders of our nation knew they had not thought of everything in the new Constitution. To provide for the things they had overlooked and to meet the needs of an uncertain future, they put this "elastic clause" into the Constitution. It gives Congress the power to make all laws necessary to carry out its specified powers. Congress may make necessary and proper laws to meet the needs of changing times. This clause has helped to give the Constitution lasting power.

**Reviewing Section 8
of Article I**

1. For what three reasons may Congress spend money?

2. Why did the authors of the Constitution limit the spending of money to these three ways?
3. What is the difference between a direct and an indirect tax?
4. How do patents encourage inventors?
5. Name two occasions on which the National Guard has been called into service by the governor of a state or by the President.
6. What is the "elastic clause," and why is it important? Has it been stretched too far?

For further thought
1. When is it proper for a person or company to declare bankruptcy? How are bankruptcy laws sometimes misused?
2. Why is it wise to give Congress the right to control trade and print money rather than to give these powers to the states?
3. In 1973 Congress gave to the President the power to retaliate immediately without a formal declaration of war if we are attacked. Why is this necessary in the age in which we live? Is it wise to entrust one person with this much power?

Research projects
1. Give a report on how the District of Columbia is governed and the debate for congressional representation.
2. Study the Federal Reserve System and explain how it controls the value of money.
3. Give the location of the United States mints. Look at several coins and see if you can determine where they were minted.
4. Gather information about international laws that govern ships at sea. Report your findings to the class.

Words to study

appropriation	interstate
arsenal	marque
bankruptcy	militia
counterfeit	naturalization
excise	reprisal
exclusive	suppress
insurrection	tribunal

We have just finished studying Section 8, which lists the powers given to Congress. Section 9 tells those things that Congress may not do.

Section 9. Powers forbidden to Congress

The migration or importation of such persons as any of the states now existing shall think proper to admit shall not be prohibited by the Congress prior to the year one thousand eight hundred and eight, but a tax or duty may be imposed on such importation, not exceeding ten dollars for each person.

Congress could not stop the states from bringing more slaves into our country for twenty years after the Constitution was written. The clause no longer has any use.

The privilege of the writ of habeas corpus shall not be suspended, unless when in cases of rebellion or invasion the public safety may require it.

A *writ* of habeas corpus gives a prisoner the right to have a trial or to be charged before a judge. A person may not be held in jail without being charged with a crime. Holding someone without charge was often done in absolute monarchies and dictatorships. A ruler could put the people he disliked or who disagreed with him into prison for long periods of time without granting them a trial. The Constitution will not permit our government officials to withhold the right of habeas corpus except in time of extreme national emergency or severe danger. The right returns as soon as the danger is past. This law helps to provide liberty and justice for all.

No bill of attainder

A *bill of attainder* is a legislative act by which a man is deprived of civil rights including access to the courts for justice. Bills of attainder were sometimes passed by the English Parliament. A person condemned with or without trial, jury, or witnesses was declared to have tainted or corrupt blood. His land and belongings were taken from him.

He could not even give his property to his children because the government seized it. Our Congress may not pass a bill of attainder because under God the laws of Congress must be just and fair; children may not be punished for the deeds of their parents.

or ex post facto law shall be passed.

Ex post facto means after the deed. Congress may not pass a law to punish you for something you have done if what you did was not against the law at the time you did it; nor may Congress increase your punishment to a heavier punishment than the one that was set at the time you committed the crime.

No capitation, or other direct tax, shall be laid, unless in proportion to the census or enumeration herein before directed to be taken.

A *capitation* tax must be paid by each person directly to the government. All direct taxes must be shared equally by all the people of the country. The Supreme Court has often been asked to decide whether a tax is direct or indirect (excise). We may be happy that Congress must divide these taxes in proportion to the population so that people in all parts of our country are treated fairly.

No tax or duty shall be laid on articles exported from any state.

This clause removed the tariff barriers that caused trouble between the states under the Articles of Confederation. People who produce goods have the freedom to sell their goods where they wish. This freedom encourages trade with other nations as well as other states.

No preference shall be given by any regulation of commerce or revenue to the ports of one state over those of another; nor shall vessels bound to, or from, one state be obliged to enter, clear, or pay duties in another.

The states were jealous of one another during the time of the Articles of Confederation. Most of the problems were caused by trade. The men who drew up the Constitution wanted Congress to be fair to all the states to avoid trouble. It is difficult to be entirely fair in this way because ports of entry, lighthouses, and harbor improvements seem to favor some cities over others.

No money shall be drawn from the Treasury but in consequence of appropriations made by law; and a regular statement and account of the receipts and expenditures of all public money shall be published from time to time.

United States tax money is collected from the people. It may be spent only when Congress (the representatives of the people) passes laws to do so. Spending tax money wisely and honestly is a heavy responsibility. If you believe your congressman votes to spend money wrongly, you have the duty to vote him out of office and to replace him with someone better. Congress must also make public reports of how tax money is spent.

No title of nobility shall be granted by the United States: And no person holding any office of profit or trust under them shall, without the consent of the Congress, accept of any present, emolument, office, or title of any kind whatever, from any king, prince, or foreign state.

The Constitution reserves to the federal government the power to issue money. The United States Mint now uses a large robotic workforce to produce coins.

When our country declared its political independence from England in 1776, it behaved as do most new nations by going to excess in trying to prove a point. Doing away with titles of nobility was part of an attempt to get away from the Old World. Today a more tolerant attitude exists. Americans who have been honored with titles from foreign nations for special services have been allowed to keep these titles. Several Europeans who kept their titles have been made honorary citizens, among them Marquis de Lafayette and Sir Winston Churchill.

Section 10.
Powers forbidden to the states
No state shall enter into any treaty, alliance, or confederation; grant letters of marque and reprisal; coin money; emit bills of credit; make anything but gold and silver coin a tender in payment of debts; pass any bill of attainder, ex post facto law, or law impairing the obligation of contracts, or grant any title of nobility.

Section 10 lists the things that states may not do. Some of the things listed may not be done by the states because they may be done only by the federal government. Some of them may not be done by any person because they would take away the rights of other people in the country.

The Articles of Confederation were weak and the country was disorderly because each state could do as it pleased. Now the power of the states was limited by the Constitution.

No state shall, without the consent of the

Congress, lay any imposts or duties on imports or exports, except what may be absolutely necessary for executing its inspection laws: and the net produce of all duties and imposts laid by any state on imports or exports, shall be for the use of the Treasury of the United States; and all such laws shall be subject to the revision and control of the Congress.

States may not make import and export laws for their own profit. Any money they receive from this must be turned over to the federal Treasury. They may, however, make such laws for their own protection; for example, California has a border-inspection law to keep out diseased fruit. This law protects the farmers of that state. Such laws must be approved by Congress. They may not hurt other states or cause trouble between the states of our Union.

No state shall, without the consent of Congress, lay any duty of tonnage, keep troops or ships of war in time of peace, enter into any agreement or compact with another state, or with a foreign power,
or engage in war, unless actually invaded, or in such imminent danger as will not admit of delay.

In a republic the national government must be stronger than the state governments. Congress controls all deeds of states that might affect our relationships with foreign nations. Only in a real emergency may a state use its war power without the permission of Congress.

Reviewing Sections 9 and 10 of Article I

1. Where was the right of habeas corpus used before it was written in the United States Constitution? (Refer to page 25.)
2. Why are ex post facto laws unfair? Why are bills of attainder unfair?
3. It is sometimes said that we have a "bill of attainder" attitude toward certain persons. What is meant by this phrase? Do you agree that we have this attitude?
4. Why is it a good thing that money can be spent out of the government Treasury only by the passing of a law to spend it?
5. Why does our government say that no titles of nobility may be given?
6. Why should individual states not be permitted to make treaties with foreign nations?

For further thought

1. What qualifications do you think a congressional representative should have in addition to those stated in the Constitution?
2. If, as a congressional representative, you had to vote on a bill and your opinion differed from that of the majority of the people in the district you represented, how would you vote? Why?
3. Do you think it is wise to have representation according to population in the House of Representatives and to have the same number from each state in the Senate?
4. Under the Articles of Confederation there were many trade problems between the states. (You may wish to refer to pages 44-45 to review one of them.) How does section 10 prevent such problems from arising today?

Words to study

alliance	importation
bill of attainder	migration
capitation	nobility
expenditure	prohibit
ex post facto	writ
imminent	

Chapter 9

The President— executive branch

Important ideas to look for:
- The President is elected by an electoral college system.
- The office of the President is one of the most powerful in the nation.
- The President must act for the United States in our relations with other nations.

Article II
Executive branch
Section 1. President and Vice-President

The executive power shall be vested in a President of the United States of America. He shall hold his office during the term of four years, and, together with the Vice-President, chosen for the same term, be elected as follows.

You will remember that Article I contained the rules for the legislative, or lawmaking, branch of our government. Now we will study Article II which defines the executive branch. The executive branch executes, or enforces, the laws. Our Chief Executive is our President, and under him are all the federal law enforcement agencies. Although thousands of people help him, the President has one of the most difficult jobs in the world. He has the responsibility to lead our nation under God.

Because the office of President is so important, the men who wrote the Constitution did not think it would be wise to let all of the people vote for him. Some of the delegates at the Constitutional Convention thought the President should be elected by the state legislatures; others thought he should be chosen by the governors of the states. Some thought he should be chosen by lot, and some thought he should be elected by *electors*, or persons chosen by the people for this purpose.

Each state shall appoint, in such manner as the legislature thereof may direct, a number of electors, equal to the whole number of senators and representatives to which the state may be entitled in the Congress: but no senator or representative or person holding an office of trust or profit under the United States shall be appointed an elector.

Finally it was decided to let the legislators, who were probably the ablest men in the state, select several men to serve as electors. These electors were to choose the President. You can tell how many electors your state has by adding the number of your senators (always two) and the number of your representatives.

~~The electors shall meet in their respective states and vote by ballot for two persons, of whom one at least shall not be an inhabitant of the same state with themselves. And they shall make a list of all the persons voted for, and of the number of votes for each; which list they shall sign and certify, and transmit sealed to the seat of the~~

~~government of the United States, directed~~
~~to the president of the Senate. The president~~
~~of the Senate shall, in the presence~~
~~of the Senate and House of Representatives,~~
~~open all the certificates, and the votes~~
~~shall then be counted. The person having~~
~~the greatest number of votes shall be the~~
~~President, if such number be a majority~~
~~of the whole number of electors appointed;~~
~~and if there be more than one who~~
~~have such majority and have an equal~~
~~number of votes, then the House of~~
~~Representatives shall immediately choose~~
~~by ballot one of them for President; and if~~
~~no person have a majority, then from the~~
~~five highest on the list the said House~~
~~shall in like manner choose the President.~~
~~But in choosing the President, the votes~~
~~shall be taken by states, the representation~~
~~from each state having one vote; a~~
~~quorum for this purpose shall consist of~~
~~a member or members from two-thirds~~
~~of the states, and a majority of all the states~~
~~shall be necessary to a choice. In every case,~~
~~after the choice of the President, the person~~
~~having the greatest number of votes~~
~~of the electors shall be the Vice-President.~~
~~But if there should remain two or more who~~
~~have equal votes, the Senate shall choose~~
~~from them by ballot the Vice-President.~~

The electors of all the states together would be called the *electoral college*. But they would never meet as a single group; instead, the electors would meet in their own state capitols. These electors would each vote for two men; the votes would be sealed and sent to the United States Senate where the votes from all the states would be counted. The person receiving the greatest number of votes would be the President, the one with the second highest number would be Vice-President.

Under this system it was possible for two men to have a tie. In the election of 1800 all the electors of the Democratic-Republican party voted for Thomas Jefferson and Aaron Burr. The votes were equal. The Congress voted thirty-five times to break the tie before Jefferson was elected President and Burr, Vice-President.

Soon after this, the Twelfth Amendment was passed. Under this amendment the electors still voted for two men, but they had to tell which one they wanted for President and which one they wanted for Vice-President.

The men who drew up the Constitution wanted the electoral college to pick carefully the best man to be President. The electors used free choice when they voted for George Washington as the first President. This free choice for the electors did not last long.

Soon political parties formed. As early as 1830, the political parties began holding conventions every four years to choose men as candidates for the offices of President and Vice-President. Although electors promise to vote for the candidates selected by their party at the national convention, they still have the legal right to vote for anyone they feel is best qualified. In 1948 a Democratic elector from the state of Tennessee refused to vote for Harry Truman, the man selected by the Democratic Party Convention as candidate for President. Instead, he voted for James Strom Thurmond, the "states' rights" candidate. Such action seldom occurs.

At the national convention a political party also decides upon a *party platform*, or statement of policy which will serve as a basis for action if it wins the election. Political parties and national conventions are part of the customs of our government; they are not a part of the Constitution.

When a voter casts a ballot in a presidential election, he does not actually vote for the candidate personally. Instead, according to the Constitution, he votes for an elector who has pledged to vote for the candidate that voter has chosen. In every state each party chooses a *slate* of electors—as many as there are representatives plus senators in that state.

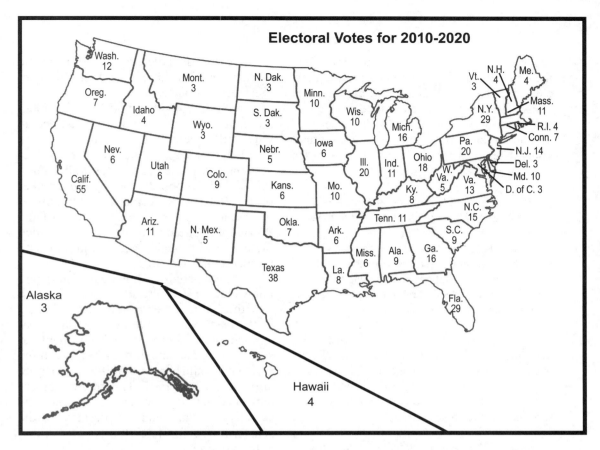

Electoral Votes for 2010-2020

The candidate who receives the greatest number of popular votes in each state receives all (the total of) the electoral votes of that state. The candidate that receives a *majority* (at least 270 of the 538) of the total electoral votes in the country is elected.

Because the electors today almost always vote for the candidate selected by the political party the electors belong to, many people think that the electoral system should be discontinued. They believe that a *popular vote*, or a vote directly by the people, would be a fairer way. The small states, however, would not quickly agree to a change, for they have relatively more power to elect the President under the electoral college system than they would have under a popular-vote system. For example, New York has about forty-four times as many people as Nevada.

Nevada has three electoral votes, and New York has forty-three; therefore, New York has about fourteen times as many electoral votes as Nevada, even though it has forty-four times as many people. California has fifty-three times as many people as Wyoming, yet it has only thirteen times as many electoral votes. This is the way that the men who drew up the Constitution planned it to be. They wanted to protect the rights of the smaller states against the power of the larger ones. **Guarding the rights of the minority is one of the tasks of the government,** for the majority can be wrong.

The Congress may determine the time of choosing the electors, and the day on which they shall give their votes; which day shall be the same throughout the United States.

Every fourth year on the Tuesday after the first Monday of November a presidential election is held. At this time the electors are chosen. The electors in each state go to their state capitols on the first Monday after the second Wednesday in December to cast their votes. The votes are counted by Congress in January.

No person except a natural born citizen, or a citizen of the United States at the time of the adoption of this Constitution, shall be eligible to the office of President; neither shall any person be eligible to that office who shall not have attained to the age of thirty-five years and been fourteen years a resident within the United States.

The requirements for the offices of President and Vice-President are the same. They need to be the same in case the Vice-President has to take the President's place. These requirements are greater than those for the senators and representatives.

In case of the removal of the President from office, or of his death, resignation, or inability to discharge the powers and duties of the said office, the same shall devolve on the Vice-President, and the Congress may by law provide for the case of removal, death, resignation, or inability, both of the President and Vice-President, declaring what officer shall then act as President, and such officer shall act accordingly, until the disability be removed, or a President shall be elected.

Requirements for the President and the Vice-President:

1. must be at least thirty-five years of age.
2. must be a natural-born citizen.
3. must have been a resident for fourteen years.

If the President dies, resigns, or is unable to carry out his duties, the Vice-President must take his place.

If both the President and Vice-President are unable to serve, Congress must decide who will become President. Congress decided, by means of the Presidential Succession Act, passed in 1947, that the Vice-President is to be followed by the Speaker of the House, the president pro tempore of the Senate, and then the members of the President's Cabinet in the order in which the office was established, beginning with the Secretary of State.

From your study of American history you know that the Vice-President has had to take over the duties of the President several times in the past. Never have both the President and Vice-President died or been unable to serve during any one term of office. But the fact that it could happen was illustrated by an airplane crash in 1947. This tragic accident happened in Oregon when the governor, the secretary of state, and the president of the senate, three of the state's leaders, were killed at the same time.

The President shall, at stated times, receive for his services a compensation, which shall neither be increased nor diminished during the period for which he shall have been elected, and he shall not receive within that period any other emolument from the United States, or any of them.

Until 1873 the President was paid $25,000 per year. In 1873 his pay was raised to $50,000, in 1969 it was raised to $200,000, and in 2001 it was raised to $400,000, along with a $50,000 expense allowance. He lives in the beautiful White House and is given the use of two large jet airplanes and a Marine helicopter, as well as smaller planes and helicopters if they are needed. A fleet of automobiles is provided for his use

Hours after the tragic assassination of President Kennedy, a federal judge gave the oath of office to Vice-President Lyndon Johnson on board a plane heading for Washington.

When President Richard Nixon resigned in disgrace after corruption was revealed in his administration, Vice-President Gerald Ford was sworn into the office of President.

as well. An allowance of $120,000 is supplied to cover his travel and entertainment costs. He is provided the best health care available. Although our President's salary seems to be very high, you must remember that he holds the most responsible position in our government. He surely should be paid as much as some industrial leaders, TV comedians, or professional athletes. The President's salary may not be changed while he is in office. He must be paid by the United States Treasury and may not receive payments from any state.

> Before he enter on the execution of his office, he shall take the following oath or affirmation:
> —"I do solemnly swear (or affirm) that I will faithfully execute the office of President of the United States, and will to the best of my ability, preserve, protect and defend the Constitution of the United States."

The oath of office is given to the President by the Chief Justice of the United States Supreme Court. The inauguration is held on the east steps of the Capitol building at noon on January 20 following the November election. As the President repeats the oath, he usually holds his hand on an open Bible at a text that has been selected.

It is only a custom for the Chief Justice to give the oath to the President. Actually, any judge, clerk, or notary public, who is certified to give an oath to an ordinary citizen, can give the oath of office to the President.

When Washington took the oath of office, it was administered by Chancellor Livingston of New York. The Chancellor read the oath to

*At his inauguration George W. Bush was sworn
into the Office of President.*

him and then asked Washington if he would
swear to it. Washington answered, "I swear,
so help me God."

The practice of adding the words, "so help
me God," has been followed by nearly all the
Presidents. At the time the President makes
this solemn promise, he must be very aware
of his weakness and his need for strength
and wisdom from God to lead our nation.
After taking the oath of office, the President
presents his *inaugural* address.

Reviewing Section 1
of Article II

1. Why is our President called our Chief Executive?

2. Why did the men who drew up the Constitution not want the common people to vote for the President directly?
3. How can you figure out how many electors a state has?
4. How have the political parties taken away the power of the electoral college?
5. Why are the requirements for President stricter than those for senator or representative?
6. Why should the separate states not be allowed to pay bonuses to the President?
7. In what way is our President under God?

For further thought

1. Several times in our history a President won election by a majority of the electoral vote but not by a majority of the popular vote. Can you explain how this could happen?

2. Do you think the electoral college should be abolished? Give reasons for your answer.
3. The requirements for the office of Vice-President are the same as for the President. Why is this wise? Why is the office of Vice-President a very important one? What are the main duties of the Vice-President?
4. Is the four-year term of the President of reasonable length? Should it be changed?
5. Under what conditions might a President not be sworn in on the east steps of the Capitol at noon on January 20? Cite some examples.

Research projects
1. Select a committee from your class to search all available daily newspapers and weekly news magazines for pictures and articles about the President's activities during the next two weeks. Ask the committee to clip these articles and pictures and post them on the bulletin board under appropriate headings. If the President traveled during this time, pin yarn on a large map to follow his route.
2. How were King Nebuchadnezzar and King Herod punished when they thought they were not under God? See Daniel 4 and Acts 12.

Words to study

disability	majority
elector	party platform
electoral college	popular vote
inaugural	slate

Section 2. Powers of the President

The President shall be commander-in-chief of the army and navy of the United States, and of the militia of the several states, when called into the actual service of the United States;

The President of the United States holds one of the most powerful positions in the world. Although the veto power is given to him in Article I, most of his power comes from Section 2 of Article II.

The President is the commander-in-chief of our armed forces. He could lead them personally if he wanted to, but there is no need for it. He is responsible for the armed forces even though he appoints others to lead them.

Safeguards from military rule

We may be happy that our President is commander-in-chief of our armed forces.
1. It means that the leader of our armed forces is a person chosen by the people.
2. It keeps any high military officer from getting so much power that he could become a dictator.
3. It keeps a President from becoming a dictator because he can be commander-in-chief only for the short term of years while he is President.
4. It lessens quarrels between the army, navy, and other branches of service since the commander-in-chief is not presently serving in any one of them.
5. The President could be impeached and removed from office if he used his power to withhold liberty and justice from the people.

---

he may require the opinion, in writing, of the principal officer in each of the executive departments, upon any subject relating to the duties of their respective offices,

The President may have a Cabinet of advisers but he does not have to follow their advice. Many hundreds of thousands of people help the President carry out, or execute, the laws of our nation. In 2012, over 114,000 people worked for the Treasury Department; 670,000 worked for the United States Postal Service; 70,000 worked for the Department of the Interior, caring for public lands, national parks, mines, and conservation agencies; 106,000 worked for the Department of Agriculture; and 3.2

million servicemen and women worked for the Defense Department to defend our country. Our President has authority over all who work for the government. He may ask the heads of departments for a report on their work at any time.

and he shall have power to grant reprieves and pardons for offenses against the United States, except in cases of impeachment.

The President may pardon individuals or groups who have been found guilty of breaking a law of the United States. A *pardon* is an act of grace that says a guilty person is not to be punished for his crime. It must be accepted by the person who is pardoned before it can become effective.

In 1915 World War I had already begun in Europe, but the United States had not yet entered the war. A man named Burdick was found guilty of refusing to testify before a grand jury when his loyalty to our country was questioned. When President Wilson gave

him a "full and unconditional pardon for all offenses against these United States," Burdick refused the pardon, and it did not become effective. However, in 1927 the President received the right to change a death sentence to one of life imprisonment even if it was against the will of the prisoner.

Complete pardon in the world of government depends on the prisoner's acceptance of that pardon. God's pardon to sinners likewise depends upon a sinner's acceptance of God's forgiveness. In its system of pardons, our government is under God.

He shall have power, by and with the advice and consent of the Senate, to make treaties, provided two-thirds of the senators present concur;

When the Constitution was written, the President received power to make treaties with other countries, and the Senate received power to approve or reject these treaties. In this way, the Senate acted as a check on the actions of the President. Treaties made by the

This Air Force plane is assigned to the President. Note the presidential seal.

President Johnson signs the Chamizal Treaty, which clarifies the boundary between the United States and Mexico. Just to the right of the President is Secretary of State Rusk.

President today must still be approved by the Senate in the same way.

Since the time that the Constitution was written, however, the number of nations has increased, and our relations with them have grown far more complicated. If we needed to wait for the Senate to pass each agreement made with another nation, our foreign relations would be very limited and would move very slowly.

Our President now carries on most of our relations with other nations by means of the *executive agreement* rather than a treaty. Such an agreement drawn up by our President or someone appointed by him does not have to be approved by the Senate. The use of the executive agreement has the advantage of being faster and more direct. Since it is usually not checked by the Senate, it greatly increases the power and responsibility of the executive department.

and he shall nominate, and by and with
the advice and consent of the Senate,
shall appoint ambassadors, other public
ministers and consuls, judges
of the Supreme Court, and all other officers
of the United States, whose appointments
are not herein otherwise provided for,
and which shall be established by law:
but the Congress may by law vest
the appointment of such inferior officers,
as they think proper,

in the President alone, in the courts of law, or in the heads of departments.

Ambassadors and *envoys* to foreign nations are employed by the State Department and are responsible to the President through the Secretary of State. People appointed to important offices in government by the President must be approved by the Senate.

Appointment of persons to less important offices can be handled by the courts and heads of departments. If the President, today, had to appoint all government employees himself, he would be much too busy.

When Washington became President, he needed to appoint many people to the offices

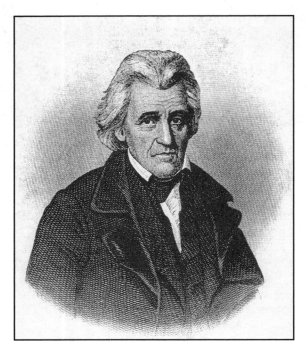

President Andrew Jackson removed from office those who disagreed with him and replaced them with his friends. This turnover of government officials became known as the "spoils system," leading to many abuses.

of government. He realized that people who favored the new government would work hardest to see it succeed. He appointed friends of the Constitution. Later, Jefferson appointed members of his own political party to the offices that became vacant. This was done with very little ceremony or announcement. In 1828 Andrew Jackson used Jefferson's plan more broadly. He not only filled vacant government offices with members of his own political party but also removed many faithful government employees and replaced them with friends who had helped him win the election. During the presidency of Andrew Jackson, Jackson's political enemies began to call this plan of placing the friends of the winning candidate into government office the *spoils system.*

This system continued, and many politicians became greedy for the best positions. Finally, in 1881 President Garfield was shot by an angry office seeker who was not given the job he wanted. Congress then passed the Civil Service Law which states that most government positions may be filled only after the applicant has successfully passed a Civil Service test. He may hold this office as long as his work is done well, regardless of the political party he belongs to.

The President shall have power to fill up
all vacancies that may happen during
the recess of the Senate, by granting
commissions
which shall expire at the end of their next
session.

This clause gives the President power to make temporary appointments if the Senate is not in session to approve them immediately.

Reviewing Section 2
of Article II
1. How does the President carry out his responsibility as commander-in-chief?
2. Why is it wise to have our President as commander-in-chief of all of our armed forces?

At the opening of each session of Congress the President delivers a state of the union message. Here President Ronald Reagan gives his State of the Union Message.

3. Why does our President have a Cabinet?
4. What kind of lawbreakers may the President pardon?
5. Why have executive agreements made by our President frequently replaced treaties?
6. Why is it wise to have ambassadors and judges approved by the Senate?
7. Why was the Civil Service Law needed?

Words to study

ambassador	nominate
consul	pardon
envoy	reprieve
executive agreement	spoils system

Section 3. Duties of the President

He shall from time to time give to the Congress information of the state of the Union and recommend to their consideration such measures as he shall judge necessary and expedient;

When a session of Congress opens in January, the President sends a message telling Congress the state (or condition) of the country. He also asks them to pass the laws he feels are necessary. In the past some Presidents have sent their State of the Union messages as written letters; others have read their messages before the combined Houses of Congress. Because the personal appearance method is more effective, the President, today, comes to Congress himself rather than just sending a letter. It has become a media event.

he may, on extraordinary occasions, convene both Houses, or either of them, and in case of disagreement between them, with respect to the time of adjournment, he may adjourn them to such time as he shall think proper;

Presidents have power to call special sessions of Congress but have rarely done so. No President has ever called one House into session without the other.

Nor has the President ever had to decide the date of the adjournment of Congress. Congress has always been able to agree on this itself.

Egyptian President Sadat, President Carter, and Israeli Prime Minister Manachem Begin (right) clasp hands as they complete a pact promising peace between Egypt and Israel.

he shall receive ambassadors and other public ministers;

The President must treat the leaders of other countries with respect and courtesy. He sometimes personally entertains these foreign officials and shows them points of interest in our country. Because of his busy schedule, however, he usually appoints someone from the State Department to carry out this duty for him. He may also send foreign officials home if he feels their presence is having a harmful effect on our country.

he shall take care that the laws be faithfully executed,

Seeing that the laws are faithfully carried out is one of the President's biggest jobs.

The many departments and agencies of the executive branch assist the President with his task. The more than 4 million people employed by these departments and agencies, including the military, are under the control of the President.

> and shall commission all officers
> of the United States.

When the Constitution was written, this method of commissioning officers was devised to allow the President to control the selection of officers for the armed forces. Today, commissioned officers are usually selected by their branch of service. The certificate of *commission* must, however, be formally signed by the President.

Section 4. Impeachment
The President, Vice-President, and all civil officers of the United States, shall be removed from office on impeachment for, and conviction of, treason, bribery, or other high crimes and misdemeanors.

The power of impeachment insures that even the most powerful person in the United States can lose his job if he does not do it well. Our President is not called a "ruler." He is called a Chief Executive, which means he must carry out laws made by the people. Our President, who holds the highest position of government in our land, is still the servant of all. Primarily, however, he is a servant of God, who in His providence placed the President in that office. As our President works to fill the heavy responsibility of his office from day to day, we are commanded ". . . that requests, prayers, intercession and thanksgiving be made for everyone— for kings and all those in authority . . ." (I Tim. 2: 1, 2)

Reviewing Sections 3 and 4
of Article II
1. The office of President of the United States is considered to be not only the most responsible in our country but also one of the most powerful in the world. Why?
2. For what crimes may a President be impeached?
3. What information should a President include in his State of the Union message to Congress?

For further thought
1. Under what conditions would a President call a special session of the Congress?
2. Why is it important to receive ambassadors of foreign nations politely?

Research projects
1. Make a study of the amount of money spent in a recent presidential election.
2. Report to the class on the attempt to impeach President Richard Nixon or on the role of Special Presecutor Judge Ken Starr as investigator of the actions of President Clinton.
3. Since 1865 four of our Presidents have been assassinated. Have one member of the class report on each assassination. When the pupils have completed their reports, discuss why such incidents happen in our country.

Words to study
bribery   expedient
commission   misdemeanor
convene

Chapter 10

The federal courts— judicial branch

Important ideas to look for:
- Judges receive their authority from God who is Judge of all.
- There are different levels of courts in the judicial branch.
- The right to appeal to a higher court insures justice.
- The Constitution states the kinds of cases to be heard in federal courts.
- Our court system is necessary to achieve liberty and justice for all.

Article III
The judicial branch

Section 1. United States courts
The judicial power of the United States shall be vested in one Supreme Court and in such inferior courts as the Congress may from time to time ordain and establish.

The *judicial* branch of our government, which was established in Article III, is our court system. The courts must interpret the laws made by Congress, determine if the laws themselves are *valid,* that is, constitutional, and decide how the laws should be used to settle a dispute.

The judicial branch of our government is also under God. The Bible tells us that our judges must be just and fair. They may not respect or favor some persons more highly than others; they may not take gifts to blind their eyes to judgment. An earthly judge gets authority from God, who is Judge of all. An earthly judge must try to make decisions honestly and righteously.

The Constitution established only the Supreme Court, but it gave Congress the right and duty to establish lower courts as they are needed. Our modern system of courts has three levels of *jurisdiction.* The first, or lowest, level is made up of the **district courts**, where most cases are tried and settled. The second level is that of the **courts of appeal**, where persons present a case if they believe the lower court was unjust. The third, and highest level is the **Supreme Court**.

Our country was not the first to establish a three-level system of courts. It was used as early as the time of Moses in the Hebrew nation. The elders of each tribe were the lower

The inscription on the Supreme Court building is the goal of all our courts, "equal justice under law."

courts; the priests were the court of appeal; and Moses himself was the supreme court, judging only the hardest cases. Frequently churches have three different levels of government which interpret their laws and policies. They are the church council, or *consistory;* the *classis,* or *presbytery;* and the *synod.* A three-level system is a good system because it has enough lower courts to supply justice for all general purposes. It has higher courts where harder and more complicated problems may be reviewed. Although the courts of appeal must operate within a framework of regulations, they generally have open doors for anyone who wishes to have a second court listen to his case.

When a case is appealed from one court to a higher one, the decision of the higher court is accepted even if its punishments are more severe than those given in the decision of the lower court. For example, when the Apostle Paul was being accused by the Jews, he appealed to Caesar. He said, "I am now standing before Caesar's court" (Acts 25:10). King Agrippa, who was a lower judge, later said, ". . . 'This man could have been set free, if he had not appealed to Caesar' " (Acts 26:32). This right of appeal was a right granted only to Roman citizens in the days of Paul. Today, the right of appeal is enjoyed by all Americans.

> The judges, both of the Supreme
> and inferior courts, shall hold their offices
> during good behavior, and shall,
> at stated times, receive for their services,
> a compensation, which shall not be
> diminished during their continuance in office.

Federal judges are appointed by the President with the approval of the Senate. A federal judgeship is a lifetime appointment. Thus, a judge is independent of new Presidents who might not agree with a judge's decision. Since it is impossible for Congress to lower a judge's pay, Congress cannot force a justice out by lowering the salary. A judge, therefore, is free to make decisions without fear of pressure from Congress or the President. A judge may retire at age 70 if they have served for at least 10 years or at age 65 if they have served for 15 years. In 2012, the Chief Justice received $223,500 per year and Associate Justices received $213,900 per year. Circuit judges received $184,500 per year and district judges received $174,000 per year.

**Reviewing Section 1
of Article III**
1. Name the three main branches of our government.
2. When a President appoints a judge, what kind of person should he look for?
3. Why do we need more lower courts than courts of appeal?
4. What advantages does a three-level system of courts have?

Words to study

classis	presbytery
consistory	synod
jurisdiction	valid

**Section 2.
Jurisdiction of United States courts**
The judicial power shall extend to all cases, in law and equity, arising under this Constitution, the laws of the United States, and treaties made, or which shall be made under their authority;

Section 2 tells what kind of problems may be brought before the Supreme Court and other federal courts for settlement. Judicial power means power to decide, or judge, and settle a quarrel. The proper use of the judicial power of a government is very important. True justice—that which is fair to all people—is the cornerstone of a good system of government.

All problems involving provisions of the

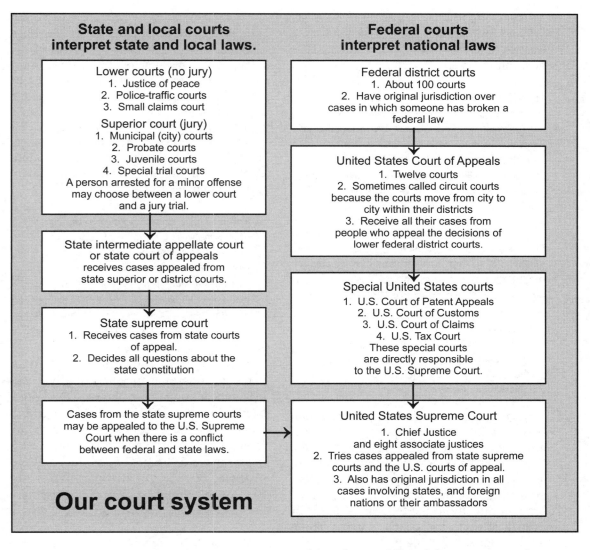

State and local courts interpret state and local laws.

Lower courts (no jury)
1. Justice of peace
2. Police-traffic courts
3. Small claims court
Superior court (jury)
1. Municipal (city) courts
2. Probate courts
3. Juvenile courts
4. Special trial courts
A person arrested for a minor offense may choose between a lower court and a jury trial.

↓

State intermediate appellate court or state court of appeals receives cases appealed from state superior or district courts.

↓

State supreme court
1. Receives cases from state courts of appeal.
2. Decides all questions about the state constitution

↓

Cases from the state supreme courts may be appealed to the U.S. Supreme Court when there is a conflict between federal and state laws.

Federal courts interpret national laws

Federal district courts
1. About 100 courts
2. Have original jurisdiction over cases in which someone has broken a federal law

↓

United States Court of Appeals
1. Twelve courts
2. Sometimes called circuit courts because the courts move from city to city within their districts
3. Receive all their cases from people who appeal the decisions of lower federal district courts.

↓

Special United States courts
1. U.S. Court of Patent Appeals
2. U.S. Court of Customs
3. U.S. Court of Claims
4. U.S. Tax Court
These special courts are directly responsible to the U.S. Supreme Court.

↓

United States Supreme Court
1. Chief Justice and eight associate justices
2. Tries cases appealed from state supreme courts and the U.S. courts of appeal.
3. Also has original jurisdiction in all cases involving states, and foreign nations or their ambassadors

Our court system

Constitution are to be settled by the Supreme Court. If the Supreme Court rules that a law passed by Congress disagrees with the Constitution, the executive department must set the law aside and not enforce it.

—to all cases affecting ambassadors, other public ministers and consuls;

Federal courts have power to judge all questions involving people with positions as

ambassadors, public ministers, or consuls.

—to all cases
of admiralty and maritime jurisdiction;

The federal courts deal with questions of ships at sea to avoid difficulties that would involve our whole nation.

—to controversies to which the United States shall be a party;

The United States is a party in cases involving immigration laws, all federal laws, treaties, and in those of the United States government itself.

—to controversies between two
or more states; ~~between a state and~~
~~citizens of another state;~~—between citizens
of different states,—between citizens
of the same state claiming lands under
grants of different states, and between a state,
or the citizens thereof, and foreign states,
~~citizens, or subjects~~.

Citizens of one state can no longer sue another state in the Supreme Court; they must now go directly to that state and sue in the courts of that state under its own laws. This change has been made by Amendment Eleven.

In all cases affecting ambassadors,
other public ministers, and consuls,
and those in which a state shall be party,
the Supreme Court shall have
original jurisdiction.

When a court has **original jurisdiction** it must be the first court to judge a case. Usually cases come to lower courts first and are later appealed to higher ones. But when a case arises that involves a foreign nation, a foreign ambassador, or one of the states, it must be brought directly to the Supreme Court, for in such cases the highest court in our nation holds original jurisdiction.

In all the other cases before mentioned,
the Supreme Court shall have appellate
jurisdiction, both as to law and fact,
with such exceptions and under such
regulations as the Congress shall make.

In all other cases the Supreme Court has **appellate jurisdiction.** That is, the case must first be brought to a lower court for decision. Then, if one of the parties is not satisfied with the judgment, the party can take it to a court of appeals. If the Supreme Court considers an issue of legal principle to be involved, the case can then be taken to the Supreme Court itself. When the Supreme Court *reviews,* or reconsiders, a case, it has the power to change the decision of a lower court.

The same section of the Constitution that gives judging power to the courts also protects the rights of the people who are brought into that court for judgment. The right of trial by jury is guaranteed.

The trial of all crimes, except in cases
of impeachment, shall be by jury;
and such trial shall be held in the state
where the said crimes shall have been
committed; but when not committed
within any state, the trial shall be
at such place or places as the Congress
may by law have directed.

Someone accused of a crime must be tried in the same state in which the crime was said to have been committed. This provides justice because it keeps the accused from being tried in another state, where the laws may be different. Federal laws, however, are the same in all states. If a crime is committed outside of a state (on a ship, or in an area like Puerto Rico or the Virgin Islands), Congress may decide where the trial will be held.

Section 3. Treason
Treason against the United States
shall consist only in levying war against
them, or in adhering to their enemies,
giving them aid and comfort. No person
shall be convicted of treason unless
on the testimony of two witnesses
to the same overt act, or on confession
in open court.

Although the writers of the Constitution provided courts with judges to punish those who break the laws, in Section 3 they made an additional safeguard for the rights of the people.

This section defines treason, one of the worst crimes a person can commit against a country. A person cannot be convicted of treason unless he or she confesses it in open court, or unless at least two persons testify that they saw the wrongdoing.

The Congress shall have power to declare the punishment of treason,

In 1790 Congress said that the punishment for treason was to be death by hanging. In 1862, at the time of the Civil War, Congress said that the punishment was to be death and loss of slaves, or prison and a fine. Today, punishment for treason is either death or not less than five years in prison and a $10,000 fine.

but no attainder of treason shall work corruption of blood, or forfeiture except during the life of the person attainted.

Long ago in England, the children of a *traitor* could be punished, as well as the traitor. In the United States children cannot be punished for a parent's crimes. Our Constitution provides that a traitor may be punished, but the children may keep their rights.

In accordance with their military law, the British executed American Revolutionary officer Nathan Hale for spying.

Reviewing Sections 2 and 3 of Article III

1. What is the difference between original jurisdiction and appellate jurisdiction?
2. Name two kinds of cases in which the Supreme Court has original jurisdiction.
3. How does the right to appeal the decision of a lower court to a higher court help to provide justice in our country?
4. Why is it wise to have a person tried for a crime in the same state in which the crime was committed?
5. Why should the penalty for treason be a heavy punishment?
6. How does the Constitution provide for a fair trial even when a person has become a traitor to our nation?

For further thought

1. Although our three-level court system is structured to provide liberty and justice for all, in actual practice many things delay the average citizen in appealing a court case, or prevent a person from doing so. Discuss the following topics on this subject: The Great Cost of Appeal; How Persuasive Lawyers Have Changed Decisions; The Effect of the Personality of a Judge in a Court Case.
2. Many fear that the Supreme Court is becoming too powerful. How can Congress keep a check on the growing power of the Supreme Court?
3. Although a federal judge can hold office for the remainder of his lifetime if he conducts himself well, a number of judges have been impeached and removed from office. Under what conditions should a judge be impeached?
4. Federal judges are normally appointed to their positions for a lifetime while state and local judges are usually elected by the people for a given term of office. What are the advantages and disadvantages of these two methods?

Memory work
Deuteronomy 1:16-17

Words to study

adhere	maritime
admiralty	overt
appellate	review
controversy	testimony
equity	traitor
forfeiture	

Chapter **11**

The Constitution—federal, changeable, supreme

Important ideas to look for:
- Powers not given to the federal government belong to the states.
- The Constitution can be changed to meet new needs.
- The Constitution is the "supreme law of our land."
- After the states ratified the Constitution, it became effective.

Article IV
The states and the federal government

Section 1. Public records
Full faith and credit shall be given in each state to the public acts, records, and judicial proceedings of every other state. And the Congress may by general laws prescribe the manner in which such acts, records, and proceedings shall be proved, and the effect thereof.

Article IV tells how the states must get along with one another and with the federal government. During the time of the Articles of Confederation, there had been many quarrels between states. The Constitution needed to provide "domestic tranquility." To provide this peace at home, the federal government needed the power to regulate the relations between states.

Although the federal government has many powers, the individual states also have much power over their citizens. In fact, the states had this power first—**the federal government was created by the states.** The delegates to the Constitutional Convention were elected by the states. The Constitution was ratified, or approved, by the states before it went into effect. **All power not delegated to the federal government by the states is still held by the states.**

The men who drew up the Constitution provided in Section I of Article IV that each state must accept the public acts—the laws, the birth and marriage certificates, the court decisions—of all the others. These men realized the need for unity and knew how unity had helped them win the Revolutionary War. This part of the Constitution helps the states work together.

Section 2. Privileges and immunities of citizens
The citizens of each state shall be entitled to all privileges and immunities of citizens in the several states.

When you are in a state of which you are not a resident, you will be treated just like the residents of that state. If the residents of that state pay a sales tax, while you are visiting there, you must pay the same sales tax. You may have most of their privileges, too. A few privileges, such as the right to vote, can be

Our two newest states, Alaska and Hawaii, are the only ones which do not share a common border with any other state. Above is Anchorage, Alaska, and on the right is Diamond Head, Waikiki Beach, Hawaii.

yours only after you have settled there. Some states allow you to vote after you have lived within their boundaries for six months, other states require a residence of one year, and a few require as much as two years.

> A person charged in any state with treason, felony, or other crime, who shall flee from justice and be found in another state, shall on demand of the executive authority of the state from which he fled be delivered up, to be removed to the state having jurisdiction of the crime.

If a person who is accused of a crime in one state flees into another state, the police of the state into which he escaped may arrest him and hold him in jail. For example, if he is accused in Washington and flees to Idaho, the police in Idaho may arrest him, but the governor of Washington may ask the governor of Idaho to return the prisoner. This is called *extradition.* In a few cases a governor has refused because he felt that the person was unjustly accused or would not get a fair trial, but usually the prisoner is returned.

> ~~No person held to service or labor in one state, under the laws thereof, escaping into another, shall, in consequence of any law or regulation therein, be discharged from such service or labor, but shall be delivered up on claim of the party to whom such service or labor may be due~~.

This portion of Section 2 refers to the slaves and provides that slaves who ran away from their masters into another state, regardless of that state's slavery laws, had to be returned to their owners.

Since Amendment Thirteen has freed all

slaves, this part of the Constitution no longer has any effect.

Section 3. New states, territories, and public lands
New states may be admitted by the Congress into this Union;

Land added to the United States is usually first called a *territory*. When a territory has grown in population, it may apply for statehood. Congress must approve the constitution of the new state and pass an act admitting the new state into the Union.

but no new state shall be formed or erected within the jurisdiction of any other state, nor any state be formed by the junction of two or more states, or parts of states, without the consent of the legislatures of the states concerned as well as of the Congress.

A new state cannot be formed within the borders of another state or states unless the states' legislatures and Congress approve.

This happened only once when the western part of Virginia wanted to stay with the North during the Civil War. When Virginia joined the South, Congress passed a law that made it possible for West Virginia to become a separate state.

The Congress shall have power to dispose of and make all needful rules and regulations respecting the territory or other property belonging to the United States; and nothing in this Constitution shall be so construed as to prejudice any claims of the United States, or of any particular state.

The claims of states to Western territory had been one reason the states quarreled during the time of the Articles of Confederation. To avoid such trouble in the future, the

Constitution placed the control of all territories outside the state boundaries under the control of the national government.

"Other property" includes the national forests, parks, forts, and public lands of the United States. Congress may pass laws to "dispose of," that is, sell, public land or national forest timber. Only Congress has power to control national property.

Section 4. Protection for the states

The United States shall guarantee
to every state in this Union a republican form
of government and shall protect each
of them against invasion;

Our national government is a republic; that is, its laws are made and enforced through elected Congress and President. Our states also must be republics; the people must be allowed to make their state laws through their elected representatives. If a dictator should try to take over a state, the national government must step in and restore the rights that God has given to the people.

and on application of the legislature,
or of the executive
(when the legislature cannot be convened)
against domestic violence.

Our national government must also help maintain order in a state when the state itself cannot keep order.

Many times in our nation's history, the President has sent federal troops into a state to maintain order. For example, President Eisenhower sent troops to Little Rock, Arkansas, at the time when black students first enrolled in a local high school. President Kennedy also sent troops to Oxford, Mississippi, when the first black student entered the previously all-white University of Mississippi. By helping to maintain order in times

of tension when riots or other types of crisis occur, our national government can serve as a servant of God for good to the states, as well as to individual citizens.

Reviewing Article IV

1. Why is it a good thing that people have about the same rights in all the states?
2. Who has the most power in our nation, the state governments or the national government?
3. What is the type of government in both our states and our national government?
4. In what way does Article IV help to keep our nation under God?

Research project

Look at the great seal of the United States on a one-dollar bill. How does this seal show the idea of unity among the states?

Words to study

construe   immunity
dispose   jurisdiction
extradition   territory

Article V
Provision for amendments

The Congress, whenever two-thirds
of both Houses shall deem it necessary, shall
propose amendments to this Constitution,
or, on the application of the
legislatures of two-thirds of the
several states, shall call a convention for
proposing amendments, which, in either
case, shall be valid to all intents and
purposes, as part of this Constitution, when
ratified by the legislatures of three-fourths
of the several states, or by conventions
in three-fourths thereof, as the one or the
other mode of ratification may be proposed
by the Congress;

The men who drew up the Constitution realized that the new form of government could not meet all the unknown situations of the future. Only God knows what the future of our country will be. Consequently, the drafters provided that the Constitution could be *amended*, or changed, to meet unforeseen needs. Our Constitution has been amended twenty-seven times.

Amendments can come from two sources. They may be proposed by Congress or by a national convention called by Congress at the request of the legislatures of two-thirds of the states. So far, all the amendments have been proposed by Congress. After both Houses of Congress have approved the proposed amendment, they must send it to the states for *ratification*, or approval.

Proposed amendments can be ratified in two ways—by the state legislatures or by state conventions called for that purpose. All of our amendments have been approved by our state legislatures except Amendment Twenty-one.

The possibility of amending, or changing, our Constitution is one of the basic principles of our government. Even if we do not like a law or part of the Constitution, we may not disobey or disregard it. God tells us that we must be subject to the governing authorities (Rom. 13:1). We have a greater responsibility—that of seeing that our nation in its laws is under God. If a law is against God's law, we must work, and work hard, for the amendment of that law.

If a law has been wrongly interpreted, we ought to do all we can to correct the interpretation of it. Whenever a law is unfair, unjust, or even unnecessary, we must work for its improvement or removal; we should not hastily decide to disobey it because we don't agree with it (see page 6).

Provided ~~that no amendment which may be made prior to the year 1808 shall in any manner affect the first and fourth clauses in the ninth Section of the first Article and~~ that no state,

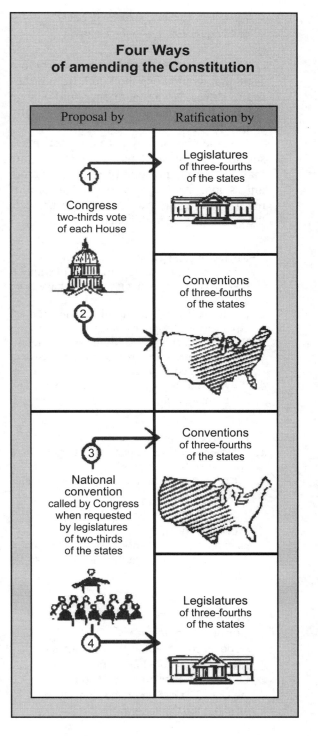

Four Ways of amending the Constitution

Proposal by	Ratification by
① Congress two-thirds vote of each House	Legislatures of three-fourths of the states
②	Conventions of three-fourths of the states
③ National convention called by Congress when requested by legislatures of two-thirds of the states	Conventions of three-fourths of the states
④	Legislatures of three-fourths of the states

without its consent, shall be deprived
of its equal suffrage in the Senate.

No amendment could be passed before 1808 that would keep the South from bringing in slaves. No amendment could change the fact that direct taxes would be equally shared by everyone.

No amendment may give one state more senators than those of another state. No state may be deprived of one of its two senators unless that state agrees to give up one of them. Here again the Constitution protects the rights of the small states.

Reviewing Article V

1. Why didn't the framers of the Constitution make it so flawless that it wouldn't have to be amended?
2. Is it difficult or easy to amend the Constitution? Give reasons for your answer.
3. Why do you suppose all of the amendments have been proposed by Congress rather than by national conventions?
4. Why should we work to change a poor law rather than disobey it?

Research projects

1. What amendments proposed by Congress were not ratified by the states?
2. What amendments are now being considered?

Words to study

amend	prior
deem	ratification
deprive	

Article VI
General provisions

All debts contracted and engagements entered into before the adoption of this Constitution shall be as valid against the United States under the Constitution as under the Confederation.

Our nation had to pay its debts when the Constitution replaced the Articles of Confederation. At that time we had a debt of about $80 million.

Being in debt is no disgrace to any government, business, institution, family or individual, provided the terms of the debt are honored. The United States government has assumed full responsibility for its debts since 1789. It has paid off these early debts, borrowed money to pay for heavy obligations, paid these debts, and borrowed again. To the credit of the United States government, it has never in two hundred years defaulted in any of its financial obligations.

Presently the debts of our national government are owed to individual American citizens, to savings institutions, to life insurance companies and other corporations, and to commercial and federal reserve banks. Anyone may purchase United States saving bonds, upon which interest will be paid.

Other types of government units such as cities, states, counties, and school districts also borrow money at times and are responsible for their debts.

This Constitution, and the laws
of the United States which shall be made
in pursuance thereof; and all treaties made,
or which shall be made, under the authority
of the United States, shall be the supreme
law of the land; and the judges in every state
shall be bound thereby, anything in the
Constitution or laws of any state
to the contrary notwithstanding.

The Constitution states that it is the "supreme law of the land." "Supreme law" means that the Constitution is a higher law than the laws of the states. Judges who work with state laws must promise to uphold the national laws even if the state laws contradict the national laws. The state laws must become secondary because the United States Constitution and the laws made to develop it are supreme. This does not mean that the Constitution is above the law of God; the Constitution is supreme over a state's laws, but God is over all law.

> The senators and representatives
> before mentioned, and the members
> of the several state legislatures,
> and all executive and judicial officers,
> both of the United States,
> and of the several states, shall be bound
> by oath or affirmation to support
> this Constitution; but no religious test
> shall ever be required as a qualification
> to any office or public trust
> under the United States.

The officials of our government are required to take an oath that they will support the Constitution of the United States.

As a citizen you make a solemn promise to be loyal, faithful, and obedient when you pledge allegiance to the flag.

An official has religious freedom just as any other citizen does; therefore no religious test may be given.

Article VII
Ratification

> The ratification of the conventions
> of nine states shall be sufficient
> for the establishment of this Constitution
> between the states so ratifying the same.

When the men who drew up the Constitution had finished their work, the Constitution was not forced upon the people. Instead, the new plan was presented to the Congress of the Confederation, to the thirteen state legislatures, and to the people themselves. It had to be ratified, or approved, by the people through their elected representatives before it could go into effect. So it was put

This final page of the Constitution, which follows the signatures, sets forth the conditions for ratification.

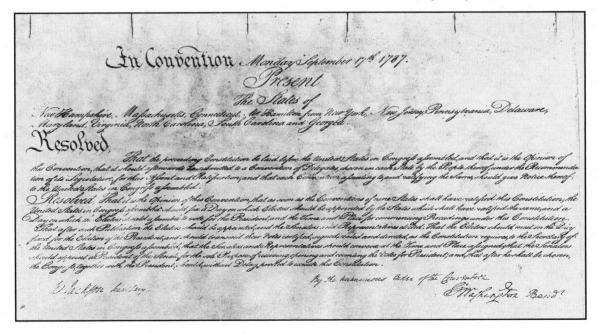

into effect in the same way that it still works today—through representatives elected by the people.

Done in Convention by the unanimous consent of the states present the seventeenth day of September in the year of our Lord one thousand seven hundred and eighty-seven, and of the independence of the United States of America the twelfth. In witness whereof we have hereunto subscribed our names,
George Washington—
President and deputy from Virginia

(These thirty-eight other delegates from twelve states also signed the Constitution.)

New Hampshire
   John Langdon
   Nicholas Gilman
Massachusetts
   Nathaniel Gorham
   Rufus King
Connecticut
   William Samuel Johnson
   Roger Sherman
New York
   Alexander Hamilton
New Jersey
   William Livingston
   David Brearley
   William Paterson
   Jonathan Dayton
Pennsylvania
   Benjamin Franklin
   Thomas Mifflin
   Robert Morris
   George Clymer
   Thomas FitzSimmons
   Jared Ingersoll
   James Wilson
   Gouverneur Morris
Delaware
   George Read
   Gunning Bedford, Jr.
   John Dickinson
   Richard Bassett
   Jacob Broom
Maryland
   James McHenry
   Dan of St. Thomas Jenifer
   Daniel Carroll
Virginia
   John Blair
   James Madison, Jr.
North Carolina
   William Blount
   Richard Dobbs Spaight
   Hugh Williamson
South Carolina
   John Rutledge
   Charles Cotesworth Pinckney
   Charles Pinckney
   Pierce Butler
Georgia
   William Few
   Abraham Baldwin

Reviewing Articles VI and VII

1. Why did our nation have a national debt at the time the Constitution was written?
2. In what way did Article VI help the people to have more trust in the new government than they had in the Articles of Confederation?
3. What does the Constitution mean when it states that it is the "supreme law of the land"?
4. What promise must all government officials make before they take office?
5. Is it a good thing that government officials may not be given a religious test of any kind? Give reasons for your answer.
6. If a religious test could legally be given, why would it be very difficult, if not impossible, to decide what the test should contain?
7. Do you feel that the Constitution was forced upon the people? Give reasons for your answer.
8. Look carefully at the list of the names of the men who signed the Constitution. How many names are familiar to you? What information do you recall about these men?
9. Judging from the representatives who signed the Constitution, what do you think about the distribution from the various states?

Words to study

contract	pursuance
contrary	subscribe

Chapter 12

Amendments to the Constitution

Important ideas to look for:
- The first ten amendments protect the rights we have as image-bearers of God.
- The amendments do not state all the rights that belong to the people.
- Some of the amendments were added to make changes in the Constitution.
- Amendments deal with a variety of problems faced by our nation.

The Bill of Rights

Even before the Constitution was ratified, many people said that it did not protect the rights of the people well enough. They began to talk about a bill of rights. When the first Congress met, the senators and representatives of many states asked that amendments be made to guarantee the rights of the people.

The rights they wanted were written down and organized into ten amendments. Almost as soon as Congress proposed these amendments in 1789, the proposals were sent to the state legislatures and quickly adopted by them. In 1791 these amendments became a part of the Constitution. Shortly after Congress proposed these amendments to protect the rights of the people, North Carolina and Rhode Island, who had been waiting for such a **Bill of Rights**, ratified the Constitution and came under its government.

The first ten amendments protect people's rights against unfair use of power and laws by the national government. Most state constitutions also have a bill of rights to provide similar liberties under the state laws.

Our constitutional Bill of Rights does not give rights to us. Only God who created us can give us the rights of life, liberty, and the pursuit of happiness. **Our Bill of Rights protects the rights we have as image-bearers of God.**

Amendment 1
Freedom of religion, speech, press, and assembly
Congress shall make no law respecting an establishment of religion, or prohibiting the free exercise thereof;

It is easy to see why religious freedom was mentioned first in the Bill of Rights. Many of the first settlers had come to America to find religious freedom; many had come from countries that had a state church. By 1789 there were many different denominations in America. Although a few of the colonies had "established" or official churches, the people wanted to guard their freedom to obey God and their conscience, as they believed was right.

When the New Testament church began, it was separate from the state, or government,

Freedom of the press, guaranteed by the Constitution, is a vital force in preserving our liberty.

and was often persecuted by it. Constantine had become a Christian, and in A.D. 313 he stopped the persecution of Christians. Theodosius, in A.D. 380, made the church a state church. Everyone, believer or not, had to join. Then the troubles began. The church became corrupt, and the state began persecutions of *pagans* in the name of the church.

We may be thankful that the First Amendment prevents our government from establishing a state church and that membership in the Christian church depends upon a love for Christ—not upon a law from Congress. This part of the Constitution as it is now interpreted makes it impossible to teach a religious faith in a government, or public, school. However, it is this very same part of the Constitution that gives parents the right to have Christian schools for their children.

or abridging the freedom of speech,
or of the press;

Congress must allow us freedom to say what we want to say and print or publish what we think. This freedom is limited by the laws of *libel* and *slander* and by the laws of treason. Freedom of speech does not mean that a person may hire a sound truck, drive at midnight into a quiet residential district of a city, turn up the volume, and make a free speech. Nor may one use freedom of speech to turn in a false fire alarm. Freedom of speech and of the press is ours under God. We must use this freedom to glorify Him and praise His name. It surely must not be used to dishonor Him.

or the right of the people
peaceably to assemble,

People may assemble, or meet together, to talk over anything they wish. There may be society meetings in a church to study the Bible; there may be a group of men on a street corner talking about the tax laws. No policeman or other government official may come in and break up a meeting if it is peaceful and is not causing a disturbance to others. We should appreciate this freedom, as well as our other freedoms, for not all of the people in the world enjoy it as we do.

and to petition the government
for a redress of grievances.

We have the right and responsibility to ask our government to correct the things we think are wrong. We do not have to be afraid to ask our government to do this.

Amendment 2
Bearing arms
A well regulated militia, being necessary
to the security of a free state, the right
of the people to keep and bear arms
shall not be infringed.

The states may have militia, or citizens trained to form an army, if needed. This amendment makes our country stronger because it gives citizens the right to defend themselves.

Since the assassinations of President John F. Kennedy, his brother Senator Robert F. Kennedy, and Dr. Martin Luther King, Jr., there has been renewed concern about the misuse of firearms. We still have the right to keep firearms, but most states control this right by saying that pistols and other concealed weapons must be registered, that persons using guns for hunting must have permits, and that shotguns may not have barrels shorter than eighteen inches. The right to keep firearms is often misused by criminals.

Amendment 3
Quartering soldiers
No soldier shall, in time of peace,
be quartered in any house, without the
consent of the owner, nor in time of war,
but in a manner to be prescribed by law.

One of the reasons the colonists had rebelled was that the British soldiers stayed in the homes of the colonists without asking for permission to do so. The Third Amendment keeps our government from placing our soldiers in private homes for food and shelter except during wartime. Even then, soldiers can be *quartered* in the homes of our people only if our elected representatives in Congress pass a law to permit quartering.

Amendment 4
Protection against search
The right of the people to be secure
in their persons, houses, papers, and effects
against unreasonable searches and seizures
shall not be violated, and no warrants shall
issue, but upon probable cause, supported
by oath or affirmation,
and particularly describing the place
to be searched and the persons
or things to be seized.

British officers had often searched the homes of the colonists for smuggled goods. Now the people wanted protection against unreasonable search without a warrant. A *warrant* is a written statement from a judge giving an officer the right to search for a certain thing in a given place. He may neither look anywhere he wishes nor seize anything that has not been listed on the warrant beforehand.

Before the judge issues the warrant, he asks the officer to take an oath giving the "probable cause," or reason why the search is necessary. The freedom from search without warrant applies to one's house, place of business, garage, or vehicle. An open field or lot may be searched without a warrant.

The right to own property was evident in the Old Testament when Abraham bought the cave of Machpelah and the field it was in (Gen. 23:17, 18). The right to own property was protected when God gave the eighth commandment, "You shall not steal" (Exod. 20:15). In the New Testament the right to

Reasons for a search, the specific place to be searched, and the items sought must be spelled out in a warrant issued by a judge. Most warrants are now customized using computers.

own property was evident when Peter asked Ananias, " 'Didn't it belong to you before it was sold? And after it was sold, wasn't the money at your disposal?' " (Acts 5:4). The freedom from search and seizure is based upon God's plan for the earth. Search warrants may be used and are often needed to provide justice.

Amendment 5
Rights of persons

No person shall be held to answer for a capital, or otherwise infamous crime, unless on a presentment or indictment of a grand jury, except in cases arising in the land or naval forces, or in the militia, when in actual service in time of war or public danger;

The right of trial by jury was first given in the Magna Carta. The people in America wanted this same right included in the Constitution.

A person who commits a *capital* crime may be punished with death; a criminal guilty of an infamous crime (now called a felony) may be punished with a prison sentence of more than one year.

A person suspected of a capital crime or felony is brought before a grand jury. A judge appoints citizens for this purpose. They must listen to the evidence. If they decide that there is some worthwhile evidence against the accused person, they pass a *bill of indictment.* The accused is then held in prison or set free on bail until a *petit,* or trial, *jury* meets to try the case. If the grand jury does not indict the person, he or she is granted an *acquittal* and set free immediately.

Members of the armed forces are tried not in a civil court but in a military court called a *court-martial.* Each branch of the service has its own laws, and often the penalties given by military courts are more severe than those of civil courts. A person found guilty in a court-martial has the right to appeal to a higher court called the United States Court of Military Appeals.

> nor shall any person be subject
> for the same offense to be twice
> put in jeopardy of life or limb;

A person can be tried only once for committing a crime but can be placed on trial a second time if the jury did not agree the first time. Also, a person found guilty of a crime can have a second trial if new evidence is found. However, a person who is found innocent cannot be tried a second time for the same offense. Although the framers of the Constitution were probably not aware of it, this plan is similar to God's plan of justice, for since Christ died for our sins, we are not punished for them.

> nor shall be compelled in any criminal case
> to be a witness against himself,

If a defendant is asked a question during a trial and the answer would be harmful to his or her case, the defendant may refuse to answer. An accused person who pleads the Fifth Amendment cannot be forced to answer a self-incriminating question. This clause, as it is interpreted today, also allows a husband and wife to refuse to testify against one another.

> nor be deprived of life, liberty, or property,
> without due process of law;

The "due process of law" clause keeps the law-enforcing (executive) department and law-interpreting (judicial) department from doing as they please with a prisoner. All that is done by a law-enforcement officer or a judge in court must be done according to procedures that have been established or laws that have been made by elected representatives of the people.

> nor shall private property be taken
> for public use, without just compensation.

If the government needs land for a highway or other public use, it must pay the owner a fair price. If the owner refuses to sell, the government can use its right of "eminent domain" and take the land, but must still pay for it.

Reviewing Amendments 1-5

1. Does the Bill of Rights protect us from unjust treatment by the federal government or by the state governments?
2. Why was the Bill of Rights added to the Constitution?
3. Why is religious freedom important?
4. Even though our government must give us freedom of speech, how must our speech be controlled?
5. Why is it sometimes necessary for a judge to issue a search warrant?
6. Complete the following sentences.
   When a grand jury says that a person suspected of a crime must stand trial for it, the result is _____.
   When a grand jury declares that a person suspected of a crime is innocent, the result is

   _____.

   _____ is the process used to force a private citizen to sell property to the government for the good of the country.

For further thought

1. Why are freedom of speech and of the press important in a country with our type of government?
2. Which of God's laws is often broken because of the misuse of the freedom to bear arms? Should this freedom be controlled more carefully today?

Words to study

abridge	jeopardy
acquittal	libel
bill of indictment	pagan
capital	petit jury
court-martial	quarter
grand jury	slander
infamous	warrant
infringe	

Amendment 6
Rights of accused

In all criminal prosecutions,
the accused shall enjoy the right to a
speedy and public trial, by an impartial jury
of the state and district wherein the crime
shall have been committed, which district
shall have been previously ascertained
by law, and to be informed of the nature
and cause of the accusation;

In England during the seventeenth century, trials were often held secretly and sometimes lasted for several years before they were finally settled. The Sixth Amendment guarantees a person the right to a public trial held as soon as possible after charges have been made.

to be confronted with the witnesses
against him; to have compulsory process
for obtaining witnesses in his favor,
and to have the assistance of counsel
for his defense.

A witness in a criminal case must testify in person, not in writing. The person being accused or the lawyer may cross-examine the witness.

The government can force someone to witness in court if the testimony may help the accused person. Such a call to court is referred to as a *summons.*

In 1964 the United States Supreme Court interpreted this part of the Constitution as meaning that the government must hire a lawyer to defend a person if he is unable to hire one.

All of these rights help to provide liberty and justice for all.

Amendment 7
Civil trials

In suits at common law, where the value
in controversy shall exceed twenty dollars,
the right of trial by jury shall be preserved,
and no fact tried by a jury shall be otherwise
reexamined in any court of the United States,
than according to the rules
of the common law.

A **civil court** settles questions or disputes between two citizens. A **criminal court** settles questions between a citizen and the laws of the government. A jury may be used in both types of court.

Right of trial by jury is important. Solomon said, "For lack of guidance, a nation falls; but many advisors make victory sure" (Prov. 11:14). In a jury trial there is less possibility of a mistake because the common sense of many people is brought into our system of justice. Often a jury shows more mercy for the prisoner than a judge does, who spends much time working with those who break the law.

We must, however, be aware that the jury system does have many weaknesses. The jury system is only as strong as the men and women who serve on juries throughout the nation. Trial by jury can make a long, drawn-out case of some act of disobedience against the law and can thus delay justice. Also, highly trained and skillful criminal lawyers can deceive the people who serve as jurors. These lawyers can then cause a jury to declare a criminal innocent even though he may be guilty. People who serve on a jury must have a high sense of justice; they must be able to distinguish between that which is right and that which is wrong. Unless the citizens of our nation realize that they are serving under

God as they carry out their jury duties, the jury system will be of little use in providing the justice it should provide. If the members of a jury have very little honesty and can easily be persuaded by a skilled lawyer, it would be better to have the court case brought before a fair and experienced judge.

The Seventh Amendment helps to draw the line between the duty of a judge and the duty of a jury. The jury must decide on questions of fact, and the judge must interpret the law as it applies to the facts.

Amendment 8
Bail, fines, and other punishment
Excessive bail shall not be required,

A person who is indicted by a grand jury or arrested may pay *bail*, or a sum of money, to the court and then go free until the time of the trial. When the accused returns for the trial, the money is refunded. But if a person does not return to stand trial, the bail is *forfeited* and kept by the court. Bail is often forfeited by a person who is arrested for a minor offense against the law. Even if a person forfeits bail, the court still has the right to try the case.

nor excessive fines imposed,

The amount of bail or fine levied may not be unreasonably high. The more serious a crime is, the higher the bail or fine usually is. But even those for serious crimes must not be *excessively* high.

nor cruel and unusual
punishments inflicted.

No "cruel or unusual punishments" prevents the torture of prisoners but does not prevent execution by hanging, shooting, electrocution, or death in a gas chamber. Everyone has the right to a fair trial and is protected from cruel and unusual punishments, but our government has the authority to punish those who do evil, for it "does not bear the sword for nothing" (Rom.13:4).

Amendment 9
Rights retained by the people
The enumeration in the Constitution
of certain rights shall not be construed
to deny or disparage others retained
by the people.

It was possible to list in the Constitution only a few of the rights of the people. Because a right is not listed in the Constitution does not mean we do not have that right. For example, the right to take part in a political campaign is not listed in the Constitution, but because it is not denied, it still belongs to the people. If all the rights of people were listed, the Constitution would be much too long.

Amendment 10
Reserved powers
The powers not delegated
to the United States by the Constitution,
nor prohibited by it
to the states, are reserved
to the states respectively,
or to the people.

Rights and powers not given to the federal government or state governments still belong to the people. In this plan our government is under God, for God made humans in His own image, and the powers and rights not needed for government must continue to belong to the people themselves.

Reviewing Amendments 6-10
1. How many amendments are there in the Bill of Rights?
2. Why is a public trial better than a secret one?
3. What is the difference between a civil case and a criminal case?
4. If a prisoner puts up bail, when does he get his money back?

Rights and powers under our Constitution

Denied powers. Some things may not be done by either the state or the federal governments:
They may not grant titles of nobility;
They may not place duties on exports;
They may not pass ex post facto laws or bills of attainder.

State powers
Powers of the state government are called "reserved powers." The state governments existed before the federal government. When the states adopted the Constitution, they delegated many powers to the federal government. However, all powers not delegated to the national government were reserved by the states for themselves. A few of these reserved powers are: to establish local governments for counties and cities; to make laws for health and safety of the people; to make laws governing marriage and divorce.

Shared powers
Some things may be done by both the state and federal governments; establishing courts, borrowing, taxing.

Federal powers
Powers of the federal government are called "delegated powers" because they were delegated, or given, to the federal government by the states. Even though the states gave these powers to the federal government, the states are now expected to obey federal laws just as if the power had always belonged to the federal government. We must be careful, however, that the reserved powers of the states are not taken over by the power delegated to the federal government. A few delegated powers are: to declare war; to coin and print money; to regulate commerce; to grant copyrights and patents; to make treaties; to admit new states.

Personal rights. God has given to each individual certain personal rights. Our Declaration of Independence states that "among these rights are life, liberty and the pursuit of happiness." These personal rights are superior to either national or state power.

---

5. Why doesn't the Constitution list all the rights that people possess?
6. Tell the difference between reserved powers and delegated powers. (See chart on this page.)

For further thought

1. Can it be said that Christians have special responsibilities for the way they use the rights granted to them in the Constitution?
2. What should be our attitude toward law enforcement officers? Why is it important to encourage capable people to enter police work? Is there a need for more Christians in this work?

3. In certain large cities there is such a backlog of civil cases that a person may have to wait two to three years to receive a trial. Why is this unfair to the persons involved?
4. The Constitution clearly states that a person cannot be forced to testify against himself. How is this privilege sometimes abused?
5. Some people believe that our country should do away with all capital punishment. Do you agree or disagree? Why?

Research projects

1. Debate: *Resolved:* That the jury system in our courts be abolished.

2 The Ninth Amendment refers to rights retained by the people. Make a list of the rights you have under this amendment. How should these rights be used?

Words to study

ascertain	counsel	impartial
bail	disparage	prosecution
compulsory	excessive	summons
confront	forfeit	

Later amendments

Amendment 11
Lawsuits against states
Adopted 1798

The judicial power of the United States shall not be construed to extend to any suit in law or equity, commenced or prosecuted against one of the United States by citizens of another state or by citizens or subjects of any foreign state.

This amendment changes part of Article 111, Section 2. It says that no individual may *sue* a state in a federal court. If a person has a case against a state, he must present it in the courts of that state under its own laws.

Our national Constitution, under God, protects the rights of states, as well as the rights of individuals. State governments, as well as national governments, have been established by God, and their authority comes from Him.

Amendment 12
Method of Presidential elections
Adopted 1804

The electors shall meet in their respective states, and vote by ballot for President and Vice-President, one of whom, at least, shall not be an inhabitant of the same state with themselves; they shall name in their ballots the person voted for as President, and in distinct ballots the person voted for as Vice-President, and they shall make distinct lists of all persons voted for as President, and of all persons voted for as Vice-President, and of the number of votes for each, which lists they shall sign and certify, and transmit sealed to the seat of the government of the United States, directed to the president of the Senate; —The president of the Senate shall, in the presence of the Senate and House of Representatives, open all certificates, and the votes shall then be counted; —The person having the greatest number of votes for President shall be the President, if such number be a majority of the whole number of electors appointed; and if no person have such majority, then from the persons having the highest numbers not exceeding three on the list of those voted for as President, the House of Representatives shall choose immediately, by ballot, the President. But in choosing the President, the votes shall be taken by states, the representation from each state having one vote; a quorum for this purpose shall consist of a member or members from two-thirds of the states, and a majority of all the states shall be necessary to a choice. And if the House of Representatives shall not choose a President whenever the right of choice shall devolve upon them, before the fourth day of March next following, then the Vice-President shall act as President, as in the case of the death or other constitutional disability of the President.—The person having the greatest number of votes as Vice-President shall be the Vice-President, if such number be a majority of the whole number of electors appointed, and if no person have a majority, then from the two highest numbers on the list, the Senate shall choose the Vice-President; a quorum for the purpose shall consist of two-thirds of the whole number of senators, and a majority of the whole number shall be necessary to a choice. But no person

constitutionally ineligible to the office
of President shall be eligible to that
of Vice-President of the United States.

The Twelfth Amendment is our longest one. It changes Article II, Section 1, dealing with the way a President and Vice-President are to be elected. Today, the electors must still vote for two people. However, they must now tell which one is their choice for President and which is their choice for Vice-President. This helps to provide for the orderly election of our leaders.

Another change deals with the matter of the vote. Before this amendment was ratified, if the vote was a tie, the House of Representatives voted for one of the five candidates with the greatest number of votes. Under Amendment Twelve, they now vote for one of the three persons having the highest number.

Also, the date for the inauguration of the President has been changed by the Twentieth

In Presidential elections, candidates are not elected directly by the people; rather, each state has a certain number of electors who choose the President. Whichever candidate receives the majority of electoral votes becomes President.

Amendment to noon on January 20 instead of March 4.

Amendment 13
Slavery abolished
Adopted 1865

Section 1
Neither slavery nor involuntary servitude, except as a punishment for crime whereof the party shall have been duly convicted, shall exist within the United States, or any place subject to their jurisdiction.

Government is ordained by God, not only for the guidance of the rich and leading citizens but also for the care of the minority—to protect those who cannot protect themselves.

Section 2
Congress shall have power to enforce this article by appropriate legislation.

The Thirteenth Amendment was passed in 1865, shortly after the Civil War, because people weren't sure whether or not President Lincoln had power to free slaves through the Emancipation Proclamation. Although wiping away the traces of slavery as it existed in our country has been a slow process, love for our neighbors requires that we end racial discrimination. Prisoners may still be made to work as punishment for a crime, but one person may not be forced to work for another in payment for a debt.

Amendment 14
Citizenship
Adopted 1868

Section 1
All persons born or naturalized in the United States, and subject

In this nineteenth-century drawing, a Union soldier reads the Emancipation Proclamation to a slave family.

to the jurisdiction thereof, are citizens of the United States and of the state wherein they reside.

When the Constitution was adopted, the slaves were not given citizenship. In fact, the "three-fifths" clause said they were not even worthy to be counted as whole persons. The "three-fifths" compromise (page 48) had served its purpose when it caused the North and South to agree at the Constitutional Convention. After the Civil War, however, the "three-fifths" compromise was useless.

No state shall make or enforce any law which shall abridge the privileges or immunities of citizens of the United States;

The Fourteenth Amendment gave citizenship to the people who had been slaves before the Civil War. It gave them the privileges of citizenship; it also gave them the responsibilities of citizenship. At first, many of them neither appreciated the privileges nor understood the responsibilities.

nor shall any state deprive any person of life, liberty, or property, without due process of law;

The Fifth Amendment says that the federal government may not take away your life, liberty, or property without "due process of law." This amendment protects from unjust treatment by a state government not only the freed slaves but also everyone else.

nor deny to any person within its jurisdiction the equal protection of the laws.

Anybody who is governed by the United States must be treated as fairly as everyone else because we are all image-bearers of God.

Section 2

Representatives shall be apportioned among the several states according to their respective numbers, counting the whole number of persons in each state, excluding Indians not taxed. But when the right to vote at any election for the choice of electors for President and Vice-President of the United States, representatives in Congress, the executive and judicial officers of a state, or the members of the legislature thereof is denied to any of the male inhabitants of such state, being twenty-one years of age, and citizens of the United States, or in any way abridged, except for participation in rebellion, or other crime, the basis of representation therein shall be reduced in the proportion which the number of such male citizens shall bear to the whole number of male citizens twenty-one years of age in such state.

Section 2 of this amendment changes Section 2 of Article I.

The slaves had been set free by the Thirteenth Amendment and had been made full-fledged citizens of our country by the Fourteenth Amendment. Now they could be counted on the same basis as everyone else when a census was taken to decide how many representatives a state would have.

Because all Native Americans must pay federal income tax, they are all counted even though they may live on tax-free *reservation* land. They have all been counted since the 1940 census. This section also says that if a state denies voting rights to those who are eligible, its representation in Congress must be reduced in proportion to the number of citizens who were denied the right to vote.

Section 3

No person shall be a senator or representative in Congress, or elector of President and Vice-President, or hold any office, civil or military, under the United States, or under any state, who, having previously taken an oath, as a member of Congress, or as an officer of the United States, or as a member of any state legislature, or as an executive or judicial officer of any state, to support the Constitution of the United States, shall have engaged in insurrection or rebellion against the same, or given aid or comfort to the enemies thereof. But Congress may by a vote of two-thirds of each House, remove such disability.

Apportionment of Seats in the House of Representatives
2010 Census

State	Seats	State	Seats
Alabama	7	Montana	1
Alaska	1	Nebraska	3
Arizona	9	Nevada	4
Arkansas	4	New Hampshire	2
California	53	New Jersey	12
Colorado	7	New Mexico	3
Connecticut	5	New York	27
Delaware	1	North Carolina	13
Florida	27	North Dakota	1
Georgia	14	Ohio	16
Hawaii	2	Oklahoma	5
Idaho	2	Oregon	5
Illinois	18	Pennsylvania	18
Indiana	9	Rhode Island	2
Iowa	4	South Carolina	7
Kansas	4	South Dakota	1
Kentucky	6	Tennessee	9
Louisiana	6	Texas	36
Maine	2	Utah	4
Maryland	8	Vermont	1
Massachusetts	9	Virginia	11
Michigan	14	Washington	10
Minnesota	8	West Virginia	3
Mississippi	4	Wisconsin	8
Missouri	8	Wyoming	1

Section 3 of the Fourteenth Amendment deals with the serious matter of breaking an oath. Government officials who joined the Confederacy and fought against the Union after promising before God to uphold the Constitution of the United States were not allowed to hold a government office after the war.

Because of this part of the Fourteenth Amendment, the Southern states lost many of their political leaders after the Civil War. In 1872 Congress pardoned many of these men and, in 1898, removed this black mark from the record of the rest. But by that time many of these men had already died; most of those who were left were too old to hold a government job. It was time to take more seriously the words of President Lincoln, "With malice toward none . . . to bind up the nation's wounds . . . ."

Section 4
The validity of the public debt
of the United States, authorized by law,
including debts incurred for payment
of pensions and bounties for services
in suppressing insurrection or rebellion,
shall not be questioned. But neither the
United States nor any state shall assume
or pay any debt or obligation incurred in aid
of insurrection or rebellion against the
United States, or any claim for the loss
or emancipation of any slave;
but all such debts, obligations, and claims
shall be held illegal and void.

The public debt of the United States is the responsibility of every citizen, but the government was not responsible for the debts of the Confederate States of America because that money was used by the South to rebel against the United States. The Southern states could hardly expect to be paid the money they had spent in rebellion.

This amendment also provided that no one needed to pay the slave owners for the slaves who were set free.

Section 5
The Congress shall have power to enforce,
by appropriate legislation,
the provisions of this article.

Congress may make laws to carry out the terms of this amendment. Civil rights laws that deal with *racial integration* have their power today because of this amendment. Although our nation under God seeks to provide equal treatment for all, human sinfulness often keeps complete equality from being put into practice.

Amendment 15
Rights of citizens to vote
Adopted 1870

Section 1
The right of citizens of the United States
to vote shall not be denied or abridged
by the United States or by any state
on account of race, color, or previous
condition of servitude.

The requirements to vote are usually set by the states. In this amendment the federal government tells the states that they may not keep a person from voting because of race or color, or because he was a slave. Recently, Congress has passed laws that seek to avoid racial *discrimination* in the voting requirements of the states.

Section 2
The Congress shall have power to enforce
this article by appropriate legislation.

Reviewing Amendments 11-15
1. Why are electors now asked to vote separately for a President and Vice-President?

2. How many years passed between the adoption of the Twelfth and Thirteenth amendments?
3. Why is it good that slavery is forbidden by the Constitution?
4. Why is it important that an amendment gives Congress the right to enforce it?

For further thought
1. If a state is sued for damages in a court, who actually has to pay the money? Was this a good reason for adopting the Eleventh Amendment?
2. How is civil rights legislation related to the Fourteenth Amendment?
3. In what way has the civil rights problem strengthened federal control of state voting practices?
4. Do the goals of the civil rights movement warrent the support of Christians? Why?
5. What problems in the area of civil rights remain unsolved? What solutions would you suggest for these problems? What responsibilities do Christians have to provide leadership in the solutions to these problems?

Words to study

bounty	reservation
delegated power	reserved power
discrimination	servitude
incur	sue
integration	suit
racial	validity

Amendment 16
Income taxes
Adopted 1913
The Congress shall have power to lay and collect taxes on incomes, from whatever source derived, without apportionment among the several states, and without regard to any census or enumeration.

An income tax law passed in 1894 was declared unconstitutional by the Supreme Court because the tax was not divided equally among the states according to population. Before an income tax law could be passed, this amendment had to be added to the Constitution.

The income tax today is one of the leading sources of revenue for the operation of our federal government. Even though payroll deductions are made by most employers, each individual must personally declare his own earnings and deductions for income tax purposes.

When we pledge allegiance, we promise to be loyal, faithful, and obedient to the tax laws, as well as all other laws of our land. We must be honest in paying our taxes, for the Bible says, "if you owe taxes, pay taxes" (Rom. 13:7).

Amendment 17
Popular election of senators
Adopted 1913
The Senate of the United States shall be composed of two senators from each state, elected by the people thereof, for six years; and each senator shall have one vote. The electors in each state shall have the qualifications requisite for electors of the most numerous branch of the state legislatures.
When vacancies happen in the representation of any state in the Senate, the executive authority of such state shall issue writs of election to fill such vacancies: *Provided*, That the legislature of any state may empower the executive thereof to make temporary appointments until the people fill the vacancies by election as the legislature may direct.
This amendment shall not be so construed as to affect the election or term of any senator chosen before it becomes valid as part of the Constitution.

The framers of the Constitution, you remember, were afraid to give the common people too much power. For this reason senators were elected by the state legislatures rather than by direct vote of the people.

By 1900 the literacy rate in the United

Computers are used in the Automated Collection System to maintain taxpayer account information and update payment information as well as enabling electronic filing of tax forms.

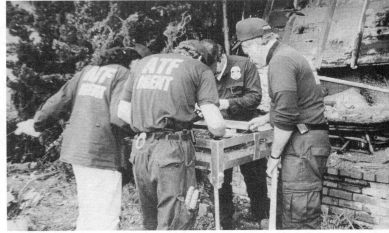

Here, Bureau of Alcohol, Tobacco, and Firearms National Response Team members sift for evidence.

Rescue workers climb around the debris at the Alfred P. Murrah Federal Building, Sunday afternoon, April 23, 1995, searching for victims following a deadly car bomb attack in Oklahoma City.

States was high, and the people wanted the right to elect their senators as they had always elected their representatives.

By means of the Seventeenth Amendment the people received the right to vote directly for their own senators. This amendment increases the voting power of the people, but it also increases their responsibility to select good leaders who can direct our nation wisely under God.

Senators who today are elected by the people should be expected to pay more attention to how the people of their state feel about government than did the senators elected by the state legislature.

Amendment 18
Prohibition of intoxicating liquors
Adopted 1919

Section 1
After one year from the ratification of this article the manufacture, sale, or transportation of intoxicating liquors within, the importation thereof into, or the exportation thereof from the United States and all territory subject to the jurisdiction thereof for beverage purposes is hereby prohibited.

Section 2
The Congress and the several states shall have concurrent power to enforce this article by appropriate legislation.

Section 3
This article shall be inoperative unless it shall have been ratified as an amendment to the Constitution by the legislatures of the several states, as provided in the Constitution, within seven years from the date of the submission hereof to the states by the Congress.

The effects of alcohol on the body have been known for a long time, ever since the days of Noah. Alcohol in itself is not evil; it is part of God's great and good creation. However, its use, even in small amounts and in a careful way, may be habit forming. People soon become slaves to its use. When they are under the influence of alcohol, they lose their sense of judgment, their sense of right and wrong, and the ability to think and act in appropriate ways. Because of this, people who drink alcohol often sin against God by saying and doing things they would never do if they had full control of their minds and bodies.

The people who saw alcohol as evil formed a political party called the *Prohibition* party. Antisaloon leagues were formed. Churches gave their support. Many states passed laws against alcohol; such states were called *dry* states. Even in *wet* states many cities had *local options* that prevented the sale of liquor.

When the Eighteenth Amendment was passed, it made the entire liquor industry illegal. Enforcing this part of the Constitution was a difficult task—if not an impossible one. People who were addicted to alcohol were willing to pay very high prices for it. Some people even began to drink wood alcohol and other impure substances containing alcohol because the purified type could not be obtained. These impure products often caused paralysis, blindness, and even death. *Smuggling* and *bootlegging* were common; hidden stills for the manufacture of liquor were everywhere.

The federal courts were filled with lawbreakers. In two years there were about 3,500 civil cases and 65,000 criminal cases in the courts. Disobedience was everywhere. Gangs grew in many cities, and gangsters fought to decide who would control the profitable, illegal liquor trade. Some thoughtful people began to see that the Eighteenth Amendment did not solve the problem of liquor evils; it only added the problem of bootlegging gangs. Our government sought to enforce this part

On July 14, 1917, suffragists picketed in front of the White House.

of the Constitution, but it was impossible to deal with all the offenses that took place.

Amendment 19
Equal suffrage
Adopted 1920
The right of citizens of the United States to vote shall not be denied or abridged by the United States or by any state on account of sex.
Congress shall have power to enforce this article by appropriate legislation.

The Nineteenth Amendment is often called the "Equal Suffrage" or "Women Suffrage" amendment.

Before 1920 several states had given women the right to vote, but not until the Nineteenth Amendment was passed did the vote become a national right.

The political and social rights of women have grown under the democratic influence of Western culture. Equal voting rights for women are based upon the value of the individual—the fact that everyone, whether man or woman, is an image-bearer of God.

Amendment 20
Beginning of terms of office
Adopted 1933
Section 1
The terms of the President and Vice-President shall end at noon on the 20th day of January, and the terms of senators and representatives at noon on the third day of January, of the years in which such terms would have

ended if this article had not been ratified; and the terms of their successors shall then begin.

When the Constitution was drawn up in 1787, communication was poor, mail was slow, and roads were bad. After an election had taken place, several months were needed for counting the votes, for notifying the winner of his election, and for his moving to the capital to take up his work.

However, several things happened to improve communication and transportation. The invention of voting machines improved ballot counting; the invention of the telephone and telegraph speeded communication; and the improvement of roads and highways made transportation to and from the capital faster and easier.

Under Articles I and II of the Constitution, a President assumes office on March 4. This amendment makes it possible for him to take office on January 20—about forty-four days sooner than before.

Section 2
The Congress shall assemble at least once in every year, and such meeting shall begin at noon on the third day of January, unless they shall by law appoint a different day.

The Twentieth Amendment also changes the opening date of a new Congress. Under the old plan members of Congress elected in the November election would not take office until December 4 of the following year, almost thirteen months later. During the time between these two dates, those who were not reelected did very little. They were often called *lame ducks* because the power given to them by the people had been transferred to someone else who had been elected in their place.

Under the Twentieth Amendment a member of Congress elected in November now takes office on the following January 3, only about two months later. This is good because it allows the "lame ducks" to go home and gives the newly elected delegates the opportunity to put their ideas to work almost immediately.

Section 3
If, at the time fixed for the beginning of the term of the President, the President elect shall have died, the Vice-President elect shall become President. If a President shall not have been chosen before the time fixed for the beginning of his term, or if the President elect shall have failed to qualify, then the Vice-President elect shall act as President until a President shall have qualified; and the Congress may by law provide for the case wherein neither a President elect nor a Vice-President elect shall have qualified, declaring who shall then act a President, or the manner in which one who is to act shall be selected, and such person shall act accordingly until a President or Vice-President shall have qualified.

Section 4
The Congress may by law provide for the case of the death of any of the persons from whom the House of Representatives may choose a President whenever the right of choice shall have devolved upon them, and for the case of the death of any of the persons from whom the Senate may choose a Vice-President whenever the right of choice shall have devolved upon them.

The Twentieth Amendment also gives Congress the right to say who will be President or Vice-President if either or both of them should die between the November election and the time they should take office on January 20. Although this has never happened, the Constitution does provide for such an emergency.

Section 5

Sections 1 and 2 shall take effect on the 15th day of October following the ratification of this article.

This amendment was ratified in 1933. It made the first term of Franklin D. Roosevelt a little shorter than a regular presidential term.

Section 6

This article shall be inoperative unless it shall have been ratified as an amendment to the Constitution by the legislatures of three-fourths of the several states within seven years from the date of its submission.

A limit of seven years was given by Congress to the states for ratification of this amendment. A time limit like this one is wise because otherwise the process of adding an amendment could stretch over a very long period. This kind of rule forces the states either to accept or to reject an amendment quite soon after it is proposed by Congress.

Amendment 21
Repeal of the Eighteenth Amendment
Adopted 1933

Section 1

The eighteenth article of amendment to the Constitution of the United States is hereby repealed.

Section 2

The transportation or importation into any state, territory, or possession of the United States for delivery or use therein of intoxicating liquors, in violation of the laws thereof, is hereby prohibited.

The Eighteenth Amendment, which prohibited the sale, manufacture, or transportation of liquor, was *repealed* in 1933. The federal government would no longer try to control the use of liquor. Does that mean that you are free to use as much alcohol as you wish, whenever and wherever you wish? Not at all!

First, our state and local laws still control the use of liquor through such laws as drunken driving laws and laws that forbid the sale of liquor to minors.

Second, when the Eighteenth Amendment was passed, the churches felt that the evils produced by alcohol would end. Today, many churches seek to persuade people not to drink alcoholic beverages because of the sin and sorrow that often follow.

Third and above all, each individual is under God. All people are responsible directly to God. We may not become addicted to alcohol. In writing to the Corinthian Christians Paul asks, "Do you not know that your body is a temple of the Holy Spirit . . . ?" (I Cor. 6:19). People may not lay aside responsibility for their words and deeds by turning the controls over to liquor.

When this amendment was passed in 1933, our nation was in a business *depression*. Our government needed all the tax money it could get. People knew that liquor taxes would bring much money into the treasury. But the millions of dollars received in liquor taxes do not cover the cost of caring for the people whose minds and bodies are impaired because of liquor. Alcoholism has become one of our society's worst problems.

The Eighteenth Amendment has been repealed, but the need for Christian citizenship has not changed. We are still under God.

Section 3

This article shall be inoperative unless it shall have been ratified as an amendment to the Constitution by conventions in the several states, as provided in the Constitution, within seven years from the date of submission hereof to the states by the Congress.

Because the subject of repealing prohibition was so important, Congress felt that the people should decide the matter directly. This is the only amendment that has been added to our Constitution after being ratified by special conventions held in each state. All our other amendments have been ratified by our state legislatures.

This amendment also points out the flexibility of the Constitution, for it proves that amendments can be not only added but also repealed.

Amendment 22
Presidential tenure
Adopted 1951

Section 1
No person shall be elected to the office of the President more than twice, and no person who has held the office of President, or acted as President, for more than two years of a term to which some other person was elected President shall be elected to the office of the President more than once. But this article shall not apply to any person holding the office of President when this article was proposed by the Congress, and shall not prevent any person who may be holding the office of President, or acting as President, during the term within which this article becomes operative from holding the office of President or acting as President during the remainder of such term.

Section 2
This article shall be inoperative unless it shall have been ratified as an amendment to the Constitution by the legislatures of three-fourths of the several states within seven years from the date of its submission to the states by the Congress.

This amendment shows how a tradition or custom that people like can be made into a law. Both President Washington and President Jefferson decided not to run for a third term. They felt that eight years were enough for any one person to direct the affairs of our nation.

Other presidents followed this tradition from the days of Washington until 1940, when Franklin D. Roosevelt ran for a third term as President and was elected. Four years later he was reelected to a fourth term of office. These elections took place just before and during World War II. However, when the war was over the people of our country decided that the two term custom started by Washington should be made into a law.

Amendment 23
Presidential elections
in the District of Columbia
Adopted 1961

Section 1
The District constituting the seat of government of the United States shall appoint in such manner as the Congress may direct:
A number of electors of President and Vice-President equal to the whole number of senators and representatives in Congress to which the District would be entitled if it were a state, but in no event more than the least populous state; they shall be in addition to those appointed by the states, but they shall be considered, for the purposes of the election of President and Vice-President, to be electors appointed by a state; and they shall meet in the District and perform such duties as provided by the twelfth article of amendment.

Section 2
The Congress shall have power to enforce this article by appropriate legislation.

This amendment gives the people living in Washington, D.C., the right to vote in presidential elections. They did not have this right until March 29, 1961, when Kansas became the thirty-eighth state to ratify, or approve, the amendment, making it a part of our national Constitution.

The District of Columbia may have as many electoral votes as it would have if it were a state. However, the District may not have more electors than the smallest state may have.

Amendment 24
Removal of the poll tax
Adopted 1964

Section 1
The right of citizens of the United States to vote in any primary or other election for President or Vice-President, for electors for President or Vice-President, or for senators or representatives in Congress, shall not be denied or abridged by the United States or any state by reason of failure to pay any poll tax or other tax.

Section 2
The Congress shall have power to enforce this article by appropriate legislation.

The *poll tax* was a tax that a person had to pay before voting. It was used in several Southern states to keep black citizens from voting since most of them were too poor to pay the tax. This amendment eliminated the poll tax as a requirement to vote for federal officials such as President, Vice-President, senators and representatives, and electors.

Just as the Twenty-third Amendment extended the voting rights to the people living in the District of Columbia, so the Twenty-fourth Amendment removed voting restrictions of those people who were limited by the poll tax. Both the Twenty-third and the

Twenty-fourth amendments help our nation as, under God, it seeks to provide liberty and justice for all.

Amendment 25
Presidential and Vice-Presidential disability and succession
Adopted 1967

Section 1
In case of the removal of the President from office or his death or resignation, the Vice-President shall become President.

Section 2
Whenever there is a vacancy in the office of the Vice-President, the President shall nominate a Vice-President who shall take office upon confirmation by a majority of both houses of Congress.

Section 3
Whenever the President transmits to the President pro tempore of the Senate and the Speaker of the House of Representatives his written declaration that he is unable to discharge the powers and duties of his office, and until he transmits to them a written declaration to the contrary, such powers and duties shall be discharged by the Vice- President as Acting President.

Section 4
Whenever the Vice-President and a majority of either the principal officers of the executive departments, or of such other body as Congress may by law provide, transmit to the President pro tempore of the Senate and the Speaker of the House of Representatives their written declaration that the President is unable to discharge the powers and duties of his office, the Vice-President shall immediately assume the powers and duties of the office as Acting President.

Thereafter, when the President transmits to the President pro tempore of the Senate and the Speaker of the House of Representatives his written declaration that no inability exists, he shall resume the powers and duties of his office unless the Vice-President and a majority of either the principal officers of the executive department, or of such other body as Congress may by law provide, transmit within four days to the President pro tempore of the Senate and the Speaker of the House of Representatives their written declaration that the President is unable to discharge the powers and duties of his office. Thereupon Congress shall decide the issue, assembling within 48 hours for that purpose if not in session. If the Congress, within 21 days after receipt of the latter written declaration, or, if Congress is not in session, within 21 days after Congress is required to assemble, determines by two-thirds vote of both houses that the President is unable to discharge the powers and duties of his office, the Vice-President shall continue to discharge the same as Acting President; otherwise, the President shall resume the powers and duties of his office.

This amendment tries to provide a better answer to the question of who is to govern the nation when the President is unable to do so because of illness or some other reason. President Eisenhower suffered a severe heart attack while in office and this caused the nation to think about the problem of who takes over until the President is well again. Then, immediately following the assassination of President John F. Kennedy, Lyndon Johnson became President and for a while the nation was without a Vice-President. This amendment, like fire insurance, is something we hope will never be needed. In a responsible way our nation's leaders have tried to anticipate emergencies and provide for them.

Amendment 26
Lowering the voting age to eighteen
Adopted 1971

Section 1
The right of citizens of the United States, who are eighteen years of age or older, to vote shall not be denied or abridged by the United States or by any State on account of age.

Section 2
The Congress shall have power to enforce this article by appropriate legislation.

In brief language this amendment extends the privilege of voting in federal elections to young people between the ages of eighteen and twenty-one, assuming other eligibility requirements have been met. Following the adoption of this amendment many states changed their voting age requirements to coincide with those of the federal government.

Amendment 27
Congressional Pay
Adopted 1992

No law, varying the compensation for the services of the Senators and Representatives, shall take effect, until an election of Representatives shall have intervened.

The 27th Amendment keeps members of Congress from giving themselves pay raises shortly after they are elected. It was originally proposed by James Madison and approved by Congress in 1798. To become a part of the Constitution, 3/4ths of the states needed to ratify it. On May 7, 1992, Michigan became the 38th state to do so and Amendment 27 became a part of our Federal Constitution.

Our Constitution has been amended twenty-seven times. More amendments may be added whenever the need arises.

This is our Constitution. It is the basic set of rules that tells us how our republic must be governed. When we pledge our allegiance "to the flag of the United States of America and to the republic for which it stands," we promise to obey these laws. We pledge our loyalty and faithfulness to our nation under God.

Reviewing Amendments 16-27

1. Why is it impossible to divide an income tax equally between the states?
2. What advantages are there to having senators elected directly by the people rather than by the state legislatures?
3. Why was the Eighteenth Amendment difficult for our government to enforce?
4. Why do you suppose the Eighteenth Amendment did not go into effect until one year after it was ratified and added to the Constitution?
5. Should women have the right to vote? Give reasons for your answer.
6. Why is it wise to let the newly elected members of Congress begin their work as soon as possible after they are elected?
7. Should the Eighteenth Amendment have been repealed? Give reasons for your answer.

For further thought

1. The Constitution contains a Bill of Rights but no "bill of obligations." If it did contain a "bill of obligations," what would you like it to include?
2. What should be the attitude of Christians toward the payment of income tax? Any tax?
3. Many states operate liquor stores. What do you think of this system?
4. Amendment 25, Section 4, states that under certain conditions a president may be declared unable to carry out his duties. Under what conditions should this be done?
5. If you were allowed to make one more amendment to the Constitution, what would you suggest?

Our Constitution at a glance

Articles

I Legislative branch— the making of laws
II Executive branch— the enforcement of laws
III Judicial branch— the interpretation of laws
IV Relationship of states to one another and to the nation
V Methods of amending the Constitution
VI General provisions—national debts, supremacy of the Constitution

Amendments

1-10 Bill of Rights
11 Jurisdiction of state courts in lawsuits against the states by foreigners and citizens of other states
12 Separation of election of President and Vice-President
13 Abolishment of slavery
14 Grant of citizenship to freed slaves; equal treatment for all
15 Grant of the right to vote to freed slaves
16 Authorization of income tax
17 Election of senators by popular vote
18 Prohibition of intoxicating liquors
19 Grant of the right to vote to women
20 Beginning dates for terms of office (the "lame duck" amendment)
21 Repeat of prohibition
22 Limitation to two terms of office for any President
23 Right of citizens of District of Columbia to vote in Presidential elections
24 Removal of poll tax
25 Presidential and Vice-Presidential Succession
26 Lowering voting age to eighteen
27 Congressional pay

Research projects

1. Appoint a committee to study the activities and program of Alcoholics Anonymous or a temperance society in your community.
2. Have a committee of your class arrange a bulletin board display illustrating ways in which the misuse of alcohol causes problems for our citizens and law-enforcement officers.

Words to study

bootlegging
concurrent
depression
devolve
"dry"
"lame duck"
local option

poll tax
populous
prohibition
repeal
smuggling
"wet"

UNIT RESEARCH PROJECTS

1. Compile a scrapbook. Divide it into three sections: legislative, executive, and judicial. Collect articles dealing with activities of these three branches.
2. Make an original booklet with illustrations tracing the steps by which a bill becomes a law.
3. Draw a map showing the congressional districts of your state. Give the number of each district, the name of the representative, and the political party he represents.
4. Stage a class debate or forum on the question: **Resolved:** That the President should be elected by a direct vote of the people.
5. Write a report giving the reasons for limiting the President to two full terms (Twenty-second Amendment).
6. Make a booklet illustrating the many powers of the President. Divide the booklet into five sections: executive powers, diplomatic powers, military powers, legislative powers, and judicial powers. List the presidential powers that belong under each section and illustrate with pictures and articles.
7. Report on the Census Bureau. Describe how the census is taken every ten years and how the government uses the results.
8. Hold a debate on the following topic: **Resolved:** That the income tax is unfair and should be abolished.
9. Make a report on recent efforts by women to achieve equal rights. Include the history of the women's suffrage movement.
10. Draw a chart comparing the rights found in your state constitution with those found in the U.S. Constitution.
11. Using various reference materials, have a committee draw a large map of the District of Columbia for your bulletin board. Locate the main public buildings, monuments, and other points of interest.
12. Section 111 of Article IV on pages 107-108 refers to "other property" including the national parks, forests, and public lands of our country. Obtain information about this land by contacting the Department of the Interior. Make a report to the class about the use of this land and discuss ways its use could be improved.

Unit four
One nation under God, indivisible

I pledge allegiance
to the flag of the United States of America
and to the republic for which it stands,
one nation under God, indivisible . . .

Under the Articles of Confederation,
each state was allowed to keep its
"sovereignty, freedom, and
independence." Each state was free to
go its own way, to make its own decisions
no matter what the national government
asked it to do. At that time,
our nation was very much divided
on nearly all questions.
But when we pledge allegiance today,
we do not promise to be loyal,
faithful, and obedient to a divided nation.
We say instead that our nation is
"indivisible." This means that we have
unity, a close relationship among the different parts of our country.

The unity of our country is not based
on the fact that we all do the same
type of work, for people from different
areas do work of many different kinds.
Nor is our nation indivisible
because we all have the same religion,
for our people belong to many different
churches. Neither are we united in
having the same interests, for the
interests of the people in one state
or community are very different
from the interests of people in other states
or communities.

Why then is our nation indivisible?
Our nation is indivisible because our
civil governments—national, state, city,
county, and township—are similar to
one another in many ways.
Naturally there are many differences
among these levels of government,
but the ways in which they are the same
are most important. In this unit
we shall study many of the similarities
that keep our nation from becoming
divided, those which make our
nation indivisible.

Chapter 13

State government

Important ideas to look for:
- The authority of state government, as well as that of national government, comes from God.
- Every state must submit to the authority of the federal Constitution.
- There must be complete cooperation among the fifty states to ensure good government in our land.
- All the states have three branches of government: legislative, executive, and judicial.

Ways in which our nation is indivisible

First, our national, state, and local governments must be indivisible because **they have the same source of authority.** Romans 13:1 says, "Let every person be subject to the governing authorities. For there is no authority except from God, and those that exist have been instituted by God." It is not speaking of national government alone. It says that the authority of our state and local government also comes from God. We must obey our state and local laws for the same reason that we must obey our national laws—because God has commanded that we do so.

Second, the different levels of government must be indivisible because **they have the same general functions.** They all provide good services for the people because they must all be servants of God for good. They also have power to punish evildoers as they bear the sword.

Third, **all levels of government work together** to provide these good services and to control evil. An example of the way our levels of government work together to provide good services for the people would be the support given by the national government to the state programs to help the physically challenged and aged. The state helps local authorities in such projects as building roads, bridges, hospitals, and schools. These levels of government work together to control evil when the F.B.I. helps local police and state patrols to capture lawbreakers. Our federal Supreme Court accepts some cases from state supreme courts.

Fourth, **the form of our government on all levels is very similar.** Our national government is a republic. The people make laws and enforce them through their elected representatives. Our nation can be united because all our states also use the republican form of government. It would be impossible to have one indivisible nation if some of our states had kings instead of governors, or if some cities had dictators instead of mayors. Because we have **the same form of government on all levels,** we can be indivisible.

The Union and the states

We live in the **United** States of America. **Our states are united under one supreme law of our land—the Constitution.** All of our states must submit to the authority of the national government. During the days of the Articles of Confederation, each state was allowed to keep its "sovereignty, freedom, and independence." It was a "firm league of friendship" with all real power remaining with the state governments. Under the Articles of Confederation our government was not indivisible, but was instead very divided. When the states had this independent power, trade did not prosper; quarrels and troubles of many kinds arose. After the Constitution was written, the states had to ratify it before it could go into effect. **By doing so, they delegated the needed power to the national government.**

We see, then, that when the states ratified the Constitution as the "supreme law of the land," they promised to obey the national government. Therefore, when a state violates the federal Constitution, the Constitution must always win. For this reason state officials must take an oath to uphold the national government. No state may go its own way or even decide to leave the Union. At the time of the Civil War some of the states tried to break the union among the states, but those who left were forced to return.

Our national government does more than just ask for the allegiance of the citizens of all of the states. It also seeks the welfare of each and every state in the Union. In time of danger, in time of floods, or in time of famine—whenever there is an emergency or a disaster—the federal government is always ready to help any state.

The relationship between the federal government and the states can be compared in many ways to a family. The national government would be the parents, controlling, guiding, and providing for her children, the states. The children, or states, accept the benefits given by the parents, but they are expected to obey parental authority and to work together to provide for the needs of the group. You can see that this is not a perfect comparison, for the states existed before the national government, and yet this comparison can help us to understand the present-day relationship between our states and the national government.

Relationships among the states

There are fifty children in the federal family. How do these brother-and-sister states get along with one another?

Children in a family must recognize the rights of one another. So our states must recognize that each one has its own laws, court decisions, and other public acts. Before you use your brother's bicycle for an outing or wear your sister's sweater to school, you need his or her permission and the approval of your parents. So one state may not move its borders without the agreement of the other state or states involved and the consent of Congress. You must treat the property of your brothers and sisters as carefully as if it were your own. So also a state must treat the citizens of every other state as fairly as they treat their own, using exactly the same laws.

Just as the members of a family must work together for peace and harmony, so our states must work together to enforce justice and to maintain order. The law enforcement agencies of the nation, as well as of our states, work together to enforce the laws of all.

But children quarrel occasionally in a home. The parents must settle these quarrels in a fair way before they become serious disagreements. Our national government has, in its federal courts, the authority to settle disputes among the states.

Children within a family sometimes quarrel with one another, yet when an outsider starts a fight with one of them, they all get together to help overcome the outsider. So our states must stand together when any one of them is attacked by a foreign power.

Territorial governments

The area between the Appalachian Mountains and the Mississippi River belonged to the United States at the end of the Revolutionary War, but it was mostly unsettled forest. This area outside of the state boundaries was called a territory. Under God's providing care, our nation grew; the unsettled territory gradually became settled. When the population of a certain area increased, the people there could ask Congress to place a territorial boundary around them and appoint a territorial governor over them. The federal government was able to make wise laws to care for this territory, and the people were given the right to make a few of their own laws.

Later, when the population of the territory became large enough to entitle the people to have one member in the House of Representatives, they could apply for statehood. This same process was repeated over and over as new land was added to the United States and as people moved into the new territory.

Throughout our nation's history we have

had two classes of territorial government. The first was for **unorganized territory.** This type had very few people. All officials were appointed by the President and all laws were made directly by Congress. Most of the western half of our country was once unorganized territory. We have no unorganized territory today.

A second type was for governing **organized territory.** Here people had a legislature to make their own laws. Congress still exercised a strong control over this territorial legislature because it could veto their laws if the laws were unwise. The governor and judges of the high courts in an organized territory were appointed by the President and approved by the Senate. Besides having the right to make most of their own laws, the people of an organized territory could also elect the judges in their lower courts and other public officials. Such a territory could send a delegate to Congress. He could serve on a committee that was considering a law for his territory; he could take part in debate, but he could not vote.

Nearly all of our fifty states except the original thirteen were once territories. Before these territories could become states, Congress had to pass statehood bills to admit them into the Union. The Alaska and Hawaii statehood bills are the most recent bills of this kind passed by Congress. Before each bill could be passed, the territorial legislature had to create a constitution which would regulate the new state in harmony with the national Constitution.

Today, the United States has several territorial possessions, including Guam, Wake Island, the Midway Islands, American Samoa, the Virgin Islands, and Puerto Rico. Most of these are called *dependencies* because they have no self-government. In 1977 we signed a new treaty with Panama which provided for an increase in their responsibility for the canal until December 31, 1999, when full control was transferred to them. Puerto Rico

---

How a territory becomes a state

1. Territory must have enough population for one representative.
2. Territory applies for statehood.
3. Congress passes an enabling act.
4. Territorial legislature draws up a state constitution.
5. Congress approves the state constitution.
6. Congress passes a statehood bill.
7. President signs bill.
8. Territory holds a referendum on the bill and elects federal and state officials.
9. Admission is officially proclaimed by the Secretary of State or, in special instances, by the President.

Pago Page Harbor, American Samoa. One of the major American territories in the Pacific along with Guam, Midway Islands, and Wake Island. Two other major territories are Puerto Rico and the Virgin Islands in the Caribbean.

has a special relationship to the United States and is called a *commonwealth*. It has its own constitution and is completely self-governing, but has no voting membership in the United States Congress.

The United Nations gave the United States *trusteeship* over the Marshalls, the Marianas, and the Carolinas. These Pacific island groups have since gained independence and have signed a Compact of Free Association with the United States.

State governments

Our state governments are very important to us. The laws of our state affect our daily lives in many more ways than the laws of our national government do. This is because our national laws are more general, while state laws are made to fit the area closer to our homes. As a servant of God for good our state laws provide many services:

Provide for a healthy environment through laws that reduce pollution.

Make laws that provide for and govern public schools.

Help to preserve parks, historic sites and wildlife sanctuaries.

Regulating traffic on highways outside cities.

Issuing birth and death certificates.

Making laws to govern marriage and divorce.

Protecting the rights of children and providing care for orphans.

Assisting the unemployed, the aged, and the mentally ill.

State governments must also maintain law

Preamble
Statement of purpose
for organizing
state government

Bill of rights
Fundamental rights of
the state's citizens

Provisions for three branches of government:

Executive   Legislative   Judicial

Their qualifications, duties,
and powers

Special provisions
Regulations
for voting, taxation,
expenditures, etc.

Provision for amendments
Procedures for changing
the constitution

Provisions for local government
Broad outline
of organization
and authority

**A TYPICAL
STATE CONSTITUTION**

and order and punish those who disobey the law. For that reason each state government must provide a police force, a system of courts, and prisons to punish and rehabilitate criminals.

State constitutions

The legal basis for the operation of each of our state governments is in the constitution of that state. The constitutions of the original thirteen states were made shortly after the Declaration of Independence. Each new state that entered the Union had to draw up a constitution before it could be admitted. Most of these later constitutions were modeled after those of the original states and also after our national Constitution. Whatever changes or additions were needed to meet the needs of the new state were made. Today, our state constitutions are quite different from one another. They are all the same in at least one way, however, in that they all provide for three branches of government: the legislative, the executive, and the judicial.

State constitutions can usually be amended more easily than our national Constitution. As the years have gone by, many states have amended their constitutions to meet changing conditions. Amendments have also been added to regulate the many new departments and agencies of the state governments. Pressure groups, such as the liquor industry, labor organizations, and the agricultural interests, or *farm bloc,* often work for amendments, rather than laws, that will help them. They know that an amendment cannot be changed as easily as an ordinary law passed by the legislature.

Because of the many amendments made, the constitutions of our states have become longer and longer. California's constitution has over 70,000 words and more then 450 amendments. Compare this with our national Constitution which has about 7,500 words including all of the amendments. Louisiana's constitution had been amended more than 525 times, contained over 250,000 words, and filled over 200 pages before it was rewritten in 1974 and reduced to about 35,000 words. Many states have recently improved their constitutions by eliminating the parts that are no longer useful.

State legislatures

The lawmaking body of a state government is generally called the state legislature. A few states use the name general assembly, legislative assembly, or general court. Whatever the name may be, the duty remains the same—to make laws needed for the good government of that state.

All the state legislatures are bicameral (two chambers) except Nebraska's, which is unicameral (one chamber). All of the other states call their upper house the Senate. Nebraska also calls its one house the Senate. Like the lower house in Congress, the lower house of the state legislature is usually called the House of Representatives. A few states still call their lower house the Assembly or the House of Delegates.

The state senate The number in a state senate is determined by the state constitution. Alaska and Nevada have the smallest senates, with twenty each, while Minnesota with sixty-seven senators has the largest senate. The problem of establishing the boundaries of *senatorial districts* is a very real one.

Many states began by allowing each county to have one state senator. Others divided the state into areas of about equal size and then permitted the people of each of these senatorial districts to elect one senator. Recently, however,

State legislatures use committees to study issues and monitor government functions. Here, the Idaho legislature is in session.

court decisions and shifting population patterns have made it necessary to redistrict so that each senatorial district has approximately the same number of voters.

State senators are elected directly by the people. In most states their term of office is four years, although in several it is two years. A state senator is required to be a citizen and a qualified voter of the district which he or she represents. Most states require that a senator be at least twenty-five years of age, but several say that if you are old enough to vote you are old enough to hold an office in state government.

Just as the Vice-President of the United States serves as the president of the United States Senate, so the lieutenant governor of a state usually presides over the state senate. In states that do not have a lieutenant governor, the members of the senate elect their own chairman.

The Oregon State Capitol is an imposing building where the functions of state government are carried out.

The state house of representatives In our Congress the House of Representatives, or lower house, has many more members than the Senate, and the term of office of each representative is shorter than the term of a senator. Similar facts apply to the houses of representatives of our state legislatures. Alaska with forty members has the smallest house of representatives, while New Hampshire has the largest at 400.

Although some states elect their representatives to the state legislature by county or township, most of the states now divide the state into districts of nearly equal population for this purpose, just as they do for the election of state senators. A representative's district is smaller than the district of a senator.

In most states a representative's term of office is two years. To hold this office a person must generally be at least twenty-one years of age and a citizen and qualified voter of the district he serves.

The state house of representatives elects its own speaker or chairman, just as the national House of Representatives does.

Lawmaking in state government The lawmaking process in the state legislatures is very much like that used in Congress. The committee system is used for the study of bills. Joint committees made up of members of both the senate and house of representatives often work together to speed up the lawmaking process. A simple majority in each house is usually needed to pass a law, but a two-thirds majority is needed to override a governor's veto.

Legislative meetings About two-fifths of the state legislatures meet *biennially*. Their meetings are usually held during the first part of the year following the November elections. Because state business often makes it necessary to hold a special session during the next year, many states have been changing their constitutions so that the legislatures are required to meet *annually* like the Congress.

About one-third of the states have no time limit on a legislative session. The other states have time limits—from thirty days in Alabama to a traditional six months in Missouri. If the legislature must meet longer than the specified days to do its business, the lawmakers are not paid for the extra days. This can be both good and bad. It can be good to have a time limit because it forces the senators and representatives to keep at their work. It can be bad if they do not take enough time to study a law thoroughly before passing it or if they adjourn before finishing what should be done.

Direct legislation

Most of the laws in our states are made by state legislatures. But laws can also be made by the people themselves through the use of the *initiative* and the *referendum*.

An initiative is a law or an amendment that

State representatives use legal assistants to review potential legislation and committee minutes.

is drawn up by a citizen or group of citizens. These people must then get a large number of voters to sign a *petition* that the initiative be placed on the ballot. In some states 10,000 signatures are required; in others 10 percent of registered voters must sign the petition. If they succeed in getting enough signatures, the initiative is placed on the ballot at the next general election. If it is passed by a majority of the voters, it may become a law without going through the state legislature.

If the lawmakers are not sure that the people would like a new law, they may "refer" it to the voters at the next election. By voting on this referendum, the people decide whether the law should be enacted. If the legislature passes a law that the people do not like, the people may petition, with many signatures, that it be placed before the voters for approval. If the voters of the state do not sustain the law, it is repealed.

In a republic the elected representatives usually make the laws. But by the use of the initiative and referendum, the people can make state laws directly.

When we pledge our allegiance to our nation under God, we make a solemn promise to do our part in the lawmaking process regardless of the method that is used.

Lawmaking powers

Under the old Articles of Confederation the states had all the powers of government. When the Constitution was ratified, some of these powers were delegated, or given over, to the federal government. Most of the powers, however, were *reserved* by the states. Of course, there are some things that neither the state nor the national government can do because they would take away the rights of the people to life, liberty, and the pursuit of happiness. The reserved powers of the states govern that large area between the delegated powers of the national government and the inalienable rights of the individual citizens.

State executive department

The executive department of a state government is headed by the governor. Most of the states also elect a lieutenant governor who would fill the executive office if the governor should die or be unable to fill his office. States not having a lieutenant governor usually make the secretary of state the alternate to the chief executive.

The governor The requirements for the office of governor are different in the various states. All states, however, say the person must be a citizen of the United States. Many say he or she must be at least thirty years old, and must have lived in the state for five years.

In most states the governor's term of office is four years; in others, it is two years. The salary a governor receives varies a great deal from state to state. In 2009, California had the highest listed salary of $206,500 while the lowest was in Maine at $70,000. The average salary for governors was $124,398 per year. Most state governors are provided with a home and expense account while in office. Two governors have opted to forego their salary.

The duties of governor are very much like the duties of our President except that the governor performs executive duties within the state he or she serves. Another reason our nation is indivisible is that the chief executives of our nation, our states, our cities, our townships, and our counties carry out their work in a similar way. Study the chart on page 148 to see how our executive departments are similar.

The beautiful New York State Capitol, Albany, N.Y.

Inspector from the Food and Dairy Division of the Michigan Department of Agriculture checks the temperature in a refrigerated unit at a grocery store.

Other state officials Besides the governor and lieutenant governor, each state has many other officials. The secretary of state is responsible for the records of the legislature; his department regulates state elections, keeps the state seal, often issues automobile and driver's licenses, and does much other work.

Each state has a treasurer to care for its funds, a superintendent of public instruction to regulate the school system, an *attorney general* to provide advice about the law and represent the state in trials, and an *auditor* or *comptroller* to audit or check the records of all the other departments of state government.

Other officials, many of whom are appointed rather than elected, run departments which provide various state services. The state highway commission tends to the road systems of the state; the board of state institutions regulates mental hospitals and state prisons; the fish and game commission helps to preserve our natural resources; many other boards and commissions also help to carry on the work of state government.

State judicial department

Our system of state courts is an important part of our state government because these courts try all cases in which a state law has been broken.

Our state court system, like our national court system, has three levels. We have local or district courts, we have courts of appeals, and we have a state supreme court. Most of the judges for the lower courts are elected by the people. Judges for the higher courts are usually appointed by the governor and then approved by the legislature. The judges of our state courts as well as the judges of our national courts are under God. They must try to provide justice for all.

Federal influence

Our Constitution provides for the division of authority between the federal and state governments. The intent is to keep the decision-making process as close to the people as possible. President Lincoln, in his Gettysburg Address, summarized this abiding principle of our nation's heritage: "government of the people, by the people, and for the people." The founders of our nation grappled with the division of authority, recognizing that many issues affected all of the colonies, yet each desired to deal with the

Similarities of executive departments

Office	Federal	State	City	County
Chief executive	President	Governor	Mayor or city manager	Sheriff (and county commissioners)
Duties	Commands the armed forces	Commands the state militia	Appoints police officers	Personally engages in law enforcement in the county, outside of incorporated cities and towns
	Welcomes ambassadors and foreign officials	Welcomes official visitors to the state	Welcomes conventions and official visitors to the city	
	Signs or vetoes laws made by Congress	Vetoes or signs laws made by the state legislature	Usually presides at council meetings, can veto council ordinances	Has no legislative authority
	Sends "State of the Union" message to Congress	Suggests laws to the legislature, works with committees	May ask the city council to consider ordinances	May ask the board of county commissioners to consider laws
	May pardon crimes against United States laws	May pardon crimes against state laws	Has no pardoning power	Has no pardoning power
Alternate executive	Vice-President	Lieutenant govenor	Mayor pro tem	Deputy sheriff
Law-enforcement agencies	FBI Secret Service Border Patrol	State patrol or police	City police	Sheriff's posse

Convicted criminals are often sent to state prisons for punishment, where they serve out a sentence behind bars.

issues differently. Throughout our history, the debate continued between the role of the national government, known as federalism, and the protection of states' rights included in the Constitution.

As issues became more complicated, the federal government's role expanded. This opened the door to campaign platforms running against the idea of "big government," including Ronald Reagan's successful presidential bids. One factor muddying the waters in this debate is the role of federal monies offered to the states and local governments. It is said that whoever holds the purse strings, influences policies. There are two major forms of government dollars available: aid grants and revenue sharing. Grants are funds allotted for specific purposes, such as upgrading roads and other infrastructures or for urban renewal.

In the vast majority of cases, grants must be matched by other funds, whether from the state or outside private sources. Revenue sharing is where the national government passes along some of the federal tax revenues to the states. Revenue sharing became popular during the last part of the twentieth century when there was a federal budget surplus. The goal was to return some of the policy control back to the states and reduce federal involvement and overhead.

What happens when the federal government's revenues fall? Or worse, when the federal government takes in less monies than it spends? This shortfall is called a *budget deficit*. State and local governments that depend on federal monies to finance projects or make up short-falls in their budgets are particularly vulnerable to the changes in federal funding. In recent decades, the federal government offered enticing incentives to encourage new programs and expand existing ones, particularly those affecting families (such as unemployment benefits, welfare eligibility, and federal subsidies and educational loans). When the federal funds were cut, the states had to scramble to find the funds to sustain the programs that the people had come to expect. More recent federal funding proposals, such as the Race to the Top education initiative, have pitted state against state to compete for the federal dollars. A few of the states that initiated the required federal policies received the funds; many who made the changes received nothing. A handful of states refused to enter the competition, preferring to maintain their independence. In this indirect way, the federal government could impose its wishes without mandating policies directly by making them the law of the land. This gave the appearance of divided authority, but not the reality of it.

Deficit impact The U.S. government has run a multi-billion-dollar deficit almost every year in modern history, with notable exceptions from 1998 to 2001. Since the government must pay its bills, it is forced to borrow the necessary funds from independent, private sources. This mushrooming debt load is known as the *national debt*. As with any loan, the debtor must not only repay the funds that were borrowed in the first place (the principal) by a set time, it must also pay interest, which adds significantly to the total amount to be paid back. In 1901, the federal government had a surplus of 63 million dollars. In 1991 it had a deficit of just over 269 billion dollars. The projected deficit for 2011 was $1.5 trillion dollars.

Such a large number is hard to imagine, even when adding all the zeros (1,500,000,000,000). But the effects of it

	Recent Budget History - Congressional Budget Office (dollar amount unadjusted for inflation)	
Fiscal Year	**Deficit/ Surplus**	**Fiscal Year Amount ($)**
1969	surplus	3.2 billion
1970	deficit	2.8 billion
1975	deficit	53.2 billion
1980	deficit	73.8 billion
1985	deficit	212.3 billion
1990	deficit	221 billion
1995	deficit	164 billion
2000	surplus	236.2 billion
2004	deficit	412.7 billion
2008	deficit	455 billion
2012	projected deficit	1 trillion

are easier to understand because they impact every household. A higher national debt raises interest rates, making it harder for families to get home mortgages and car loans. Higher interest rates also make it harder for businesses to get the capital they need to purchase expensive machinery or expand the business. Less expansion means fewer jobs. Fewer jobs fuel unemployment, which causes less economic growth. Less growth leads to lower tax revenues. Lower tax revenues force tax increases on the dwindling number of workers. Consumer confidence falls. A dismal economic outlook further reduces the job and loan markets, leading to families defaulting on loans and possibly losing their homes.

Unlike the federal government, individuals and families do not have the option of borrowing more and more money every year. If they do go into debt, at some point they will reach their credit limit. Their budgets must be balanced. Likewise, almost every state in the union has some form of a balanced budget provision, whereby the state government cannot spend more than it takes in.

Currently, there is no balanced budget provision in our Constitution. Several amendments have been proposed, but none have passed. Most of these proposed amendments allowed for the provision to be waived in times of war or national emergency, but only by a very large majority of Congress. The Balanced Budget Act of 1997 was an all-encompassing legislative package that instituted a budget reconciliation process. The goal was to balance the federal budget by 2002. Subsequent legislation undermined much of that effort, as well as the economic fallout of the 9/11 attacks and the war on terrorism. The goal fell short.

During recent decades, the inability of the federal government to agree on an operational budget, let alone a balanced one, has undermined the constitutional checks and balances in an unusual way: by forcing the shutdown of the federal government. While the threat of a shutdown has occurred often, actual shutdowns are rare. A few select government agencies were closed for a long weekend in 1990, while a much larger shutdown occurred in 1995. Some 800,000 government employees who were considered "nonessential" were sent home. More recently, the impasse has forced the government to extend the budget deadline through "emergency funding," leaving the government limping along without a formal budget. The budget problem persists no matter which political party is in office, in part because it is rare for one party to control the Executive Branch and both parts of the Legislative Branch, and in part due to the conflicting demands of interest groups and lobbies.

It didn't take long for the thirteen original colonies to realize how dependent they were upon one another. The Articles of Confederation, and later the Civil War, showed that our nation could not ignore the necessity of being indivisible. We must always be on guard to identify and deal with forces that work to divide us and undermine the Constitutional principles on which our nation is founded.

Do you remember what you have read?

1. In what three ways are our local governments like our national government?
2. How is the relationship of a state to our national government similar to the relationship of a child to parents? In what ways is it different?
3. Does a state have more rights of self-government than a territory? In what way?
4. Name three things that were necessary before a territory could become a state.
5. Why are state constitutions amended so often?
6. In what ways are the state legislatures like the national Congress?
7. Explain the difference between an initiative and a referendum.
8. What are the advantages and disadvantages of a time limit on the meetings of state legislatures?

For further thought

1. Do you think your state legislature meets often and long enough?
2. Why do most states have a bicameral legislature?
3. Have recent court decisions about redistricting lessened the need for bicameral legislatures?
4. The governor of Texas from 1925-1927, Mrs. James A. ("Ma") Ferguson, pardoned 3737 prisoners during her two-year term of office. Was this a wise use of the governor's pardoning power?
5. Do you think it is wise or necessary to have our country divided into states? Wouldn't it make more sense to have a number of our smaller states combine into a few large ones? Is the present state structure performing well? Why or why not?

Research projects

1. Obtain a copy of your state constitution and read its articles and amendments. How many amendments does it have? When was the last amendment added?

2. Research the voting regulations in your state. When were they last changed and why?
3. Research the salaries of officials in your state. See if you can obtain a financial report from your state treasurer and evaluate it.
4. Invite your state representative to speak to your class to discuss his job.
5. Make a study of the penal system in your state. Research the prison policies of your state as well as the conditions for prisoners. Write to your state director of prisons for information about prison policies and conditions. Present the information you gather as a bulletin board display for the class.
6. Since many prisons are overcrowded a number of state and local governments have started to utilize private prison systems. What are the advantages and disadvantages of such a system?
7. Make a study of the Panama Canal. Include information about the building and operation of the canal as well as the 1977 treaty which provided for the transfer of our interest in the Canal to Panama by the year 2000.
8. Research your state's budget process, identifying specific requirements, if any, for a balanced budget. Determine if your state has functioned without a budget or if state offices and services have been suspended due to the legislature not meeting the budget deadline.

Words to study

annually	"farm bloc"
attorney general	initiative
auditor	national debt
biennially	petition
budget deficit	referendum
commonwealth	reserved
comptroller	senatorial district
dependency	trusteeship

Chapter 14

Local government

Important ideas to look for:
- Local and state governments have a relationship that is different from that between state and national governments.
- Most counties throughout the country perform similar duties.
- There are several types of municipal governments.
- All levels of government are under God and thus must receive our respect and obedience.

County government

Every state in the Union is divided into counties except Alaska, which is divided into boroughs. (In Louisiana a county is commonly called a *parish.*) There are over 3000 counties in our nation. The largest is San Bernardino County in California with 20,064 square miles; the smallest is New York County with twenty-eight square miles—about one-fifth of New York City. Delaware has only three counties while Texas has 254. Loving County, Texas, has a population of less than 100 while Los Angeles county, California, has close to 10 million people.

County government has jurisdiction over the people of our nation who live in the rural areas—outside of the incorporated cities and towns. This type of government is not new. The Anglo-Saxons in early England called such small divisions of land "shires." Here the "shire reeve" (*sheriff*) was the chief law-enforcement officer. When the Normans came to England they called the shires "counties" because they resembled the areas ruled by counts in Normandy.

Under God's Providence, the states of our country grew from unsettled territory to organized territory and then became states. To provide for the needs of the citizens of these states, the state constitutions provided for county government. The relationship between these local governments and the state government is different from the relationship between the states and the national government.

We have seen how the states have delegated certain powers to the national government while other powers have been reserved by the states. These reserved powers have their legal basis in the state constitutions. These state constitutions provide for townships and counties. The state assigns some of its powers to the local governments. A state has the power to strengthen, weaken, or even remove certain powers from a county or township. The national government cannot do this to the states. A state therefore has more authority over its counties and townships than the national government has over the state. The power that the state holds over the counties and townships also helps to make local governments work together; it helps to make the state indivisible.

Services provided by county governments

Law enforcement

Keeping the peace
Maintaining courts
to settle
differences between
citizens and punish
those who break
the law
Providing jails and
workhouses

Record keeping

Recording births,
deaths, and
marriages that
take place in
the county
Recording deeds,
mortgages, wills,
court decisions,
and other
important papers

Public works

Building roads
and bridges
Providing ditches
and drainage for
flood control
Helping to
maintain schools
and other
public buildings

Public welfare

Caring for the poor
and orphans,
and often
building hospitals
for the sick
Protecting
the health
of the people

Revenue

Assessing property
(setting its fair
value for taxation
purposes)
Collecting
real-estate taxes
Spending
county funds

Another reason our nation is indivisible is that most of our county governments follow the same general pattern. They have similar officers, even though they may be called by different titles in different areas. The main officers of county government are a board of commissioners or supervisors, sheriff, treasurer, county clerk, coroner, district attorney, county judge, and county superintendent of schools. Some counties also have a road commissioner, surveyor, and county recorder, as well as others that may be needed for the work in a particular county with special needs.

The **board of county commissioners** may be made up of from three to eighty persons. It forms the legislative branch of county government, making decisions about government programs in the county. In many cases it also does some of the executive work by helping the sheriff carry out some of its decisions. The board of county commissioners also checks to see that all departments of county government are working smoothly. It is responsible for setting the tax rate. It also decides on and supervises the construction of public improvements in the county.

The **county treasurer** is responsible for the money of the county government. This money is used to pay the bills for improvements that are made and to pay wages of county employees. The treasurer receives the taxes, court fines, and other fees paid by the citizens to the county. Special *levies* are often collected for the state, for school districts, and for special purposes like roads and drainage districts. The county treasurer is required to send this money to its proper place.

All government employees who handle public money must be placed under *bond* when they take office. The bond of the county treasurer protects the citizens from losses because of dishonesty or carelessness. If money is misplaced or taken, the bonding company, not the citizens, must make up the loss. Any officials who handle public money must also be aware of the fact that they are under God. Their work must be done honestly.

The **county clerk** (often called the county recorder) prepares ballots for elections and counts votes. This person also issues marriage licenses and other permits, serves as secretary to the court, and keeps a record of court decisions and the records of those who break the law. The county clerk also acts as clerk for the board of county commissioners. Much of the clerk's work is the filing of important papers. Sometimes we joke about the red tape and duplicate copies of government papers, but the business of record keeping is very important for the orderly operation of government.

The **county sheriff** investigates crimes, makes arrests, and is responsible for the operation of the county jail. In addition, the organization of search and rescue work is often called for, patients from mental hospitals may need to be transported, or stray animals recaptured. The sheriff's duties may also include directing traffic, storing abandoned cars, selling real estate when people fail to pay their taxes or even reclaiming personal property when people do not pay their monthly installments. If the need arises, the sheriff may appoint deputies or a *posse* to help perform these and many other tasks.

The **district attorney** is called the prosecuting attorney in some states and the county attorney in others. One of the requirements for this office is that the person be a qualified lawyer. Television programs sometimes give the impression that the "DA" lives entirely in a world of screaming sirens, midnight arrests, and narrow escapes. Although many district attorneys have had tense moments in their fight against crime, most of their work is careful routine. This includes directing investigations, collecting evidence against a person suspected of a crime

and presenting the case against the accused person in a trial.

A district attorney must also defend the county in lawsuits against it. For example, if someone should have an accident with a county road-grader or fall from a county bridge and sue the county for damages, the district attorney would defend the county in court. Whether prosecuting or defending, this person must work closely with law enforcement officers to secure any evidence.

Whenever county departments need advice or information about the law, or when school districts and townships need legal advice,

The Bureau of Alcohol, Tobacco and Firearm's Integrated Ballistics Identification System is used to match bullets and shell casings recovered at crime scenes.

they call on the district attorney.

The **county coroner** has the responsibility of investigating all deaths that take place where no doctor is present. If the circumstances under which a person died look unnatural and indicate suicide, manslaughter, or murder, the coroner may call for an *inquest*. When an inquest is held, a small jury is called and witnesses may be summoned to clear up the details of how the death happened.

Sometimes an *autopsy* is performed. In an autopsy a doctor performs an operation on the dead person's body to try to determine the cause of death. The doctor might look for poison in the victim's stomach or perhaps take a blood test to see if the person died of a heart attack or of drowning. An autopsy might be authorized by one of the relatives of the dead person or by a court order. If the inquest or the autopsy shows that the person did not die of natural or accidental causes, the facts of the case are turned over to the court and law enforcement officers.

Because the duties of the coroner involve medical knowledge, many counties elect medical doctors to this office. Some call the coroner the Medical Examiner. Large counties have a morgue; it is supervised by the coroner. If a person who died cannot be identified immediately, the coroner must try to identify the body and keep the possessions for surviving relatives.

". . . Man is destined to die once . . ." (Heb. 9:27). When our government provides for a coroner, it recognizes that death is a very real thing, a thing that concerns each citizen. Our coroners are also under God's law as they perform their duties for our government.

The services that a government provides for its citizens cost money. Taxes paid by the people provide this money. Romans 13 tells us that we must pay our taxes, but who can tell how much of the tax money must be paid by each person?

This is the job of the **county assessor**. Farmers are asked how many head of cattle they own and their worth. The assessor also wants to know the size of the farm and what type of soil it has, so the value of the land can be determined. The owner of a house will be asked about its foundation, its roof, the date of its construction, and the value of the furniture. Businesses are asked to take an inventory of their goods. The value of what a person owns determines how much property tax needs to be paid.

Here, too, all citizens are responsible to God as they place an honest value on the goods they own. This is a part of their Christian *stewardship*. On the other hand, if they feel that the assessor has placed an unfair value on their property, they may appeal to the county tax *equalization* board. Cases not settled here may be appealed further to the state tax commission.

The **county superintendent of schools** is elected to exercise careful supervision over the common schools in the county and help teachers and school districts in their choice of textbooks and equipment. Advice is given to help schools develop and to be sure that they follow a balanced program of study. The county superintendent also sees to the budgets and financial reports of the common schools, checks the private schools to see that their programs of study meet the requirements of state law, and requires schools to provide attendance records of their pupils. The county superintendent also gives advice to school boards about school problems.

The county officials we have discussed are the most important ones. There are many others.

Township government

In colonial days each town in the New England area governed itself. Town meetings were held and most of the citizens helped to make the laws and settle the problems of the town. This would have been a pure democracy if everyone had been allowed to vote.

As more settlers arrived, other towns grew up. Boundaries were then needed to tell where the government of one town ended and another began. Lines were drawn. The town's shape was often irregular. These "townshapes" came to be called townships. **The township is still the most important unit of local government in the New England states.**

Because of the increase in population, not everyone can attend the town meeting today. Instead, elected representatives meet to make the laws. *Selectmen*, a smaller group of trustees, make up a board of supervisors to carry on the business of the township. Each township has its own officers: treasurer, clerk, *constable*, assessor, overseer of the poor, overseer of the roads, and others. The duties of these township officers are very much like the duties of the county officers we have already discussed.

The irregular shape of many of these early townships made it hard to record property deeds and to survey unsettled land. To solve this land problem, Congress, under the Articles of Confederation, in 1785 passed an *ordinance* saying that unsettled land must be mapped out on a grid system. Township boundaries for survey purposes would now be straight lines running north and south, crossed by lines running east and west. After this was done each piece of land six miles square (thirty-six square miles) was called a township.

Township government is another "governing authority." It is another building block that fits smoothly into the structure with county, state, and national government to act as a servant of God for good and to bear a sword. As these levels of government work together, they help to make our nation, under God, indivisible.

Under the Land Ordinance of 1785, the Northwest Territory was surveyed and laid out in townships. Each township was six miles square and contained thirty-six sections. Each section was one mile square and contained 640 acres. Section sixteen in each township was set aside for the use of schools.

Do you remember what you have read?
1. Who makes up the legislative branch of a county government?
2. Why is a county or township treasurer bonded?
3. Why should a district attorney be a lawyer?
4. What is the difference between an inquest and an autopsy?

For further thought
1. Why is it wise that an autopsy be performed only after permission is given by a relative of the dead person or by the court?
2. How does the work of the county assessor affect property taxes?
3. In what way is a township in New England different from a township in the western part of the United States?
4. What are the advantages of the town meeting?

The conduct of affairs at town meetings was not always handled peaceably, as is evident from this old drawing.

Research projects

Local government in one part of the United States may be quite different from local government in other parts. To become better acquainted with the local government in your own area, work in teams to find the answers to the following questions. Your class may wish to add other questions to the list. Report the information you find to the class.

1. Is county or township government the more important in your area?

2. What is the lawmaking board called? Who are its members?
3. What are the borders of your township? Make a map of the townships in your area.
4. Learn the names of those who hold office in your local government. Try to find out how long they have held office. See if the duties they perform for your community are similar to the ones listed for their office in the material you have just read.

Things to do

1. Make a bulletin board display about your county or township government. You may be able to find pictures of your local officials on old election campaign posters or in your local newspaper.
2. Invite a deputy from the sheriff's department to speak to the class about his duties and experiences.
3. Try to determine which section of land in your township was originally set aside for school use.

Evaluation

Our state and local government officials are under God, as are those who serve in federal office. Our state and local laws and ordinances must also meet the high standard of God's Word. Because of sin and evil in the world, our laws, government leaders, and citizens fall far short of being perfect. Sometimes laws permit citizens to do sinful things, and occasionally laws themselves are evil.

Do you know of a state or local law that is unfair, or that permits citizens to do things that are wrong? Discuss this law with others. Try to determine how it was originally passed and what could and should be done to improve or remove it.

Words to study

assessor	morgue
autopsy	ordinance
bond	parish
constable	posse
coroner	prosecuting attorney
equalization	selectman
inquest	sheriff
levy	stewardship

Municipal government

A *municipality* is a town, borough, village, or city that has certain rights of local self-government.

Unincorporated communities When early pioneers settled near one another to form a small community, they could name their settlement. Outside the edge of such a village or small town, you would usually find a sign giving the name of that community. Under the name you would probably find the word *unincorporated*. An unincorporated village or town is governed by the laws of the county in which it is located, in exactly the same way as the more thinly populated area around it is governed.

Incorporated towns When more people begin to live in a small area, the need for government increases. The people who live in a village know that those living in an *incorporated* town have better streets and better police and fire protection. The people living in an unincorporated village cannot expect all of the citizens of the county to pay taxes for the sidewalks and streetlights they would like to have in their community.

In order to get these services for themselves, the people of an unincorporated community may hold a meeting and decide to become an incorporated town or village. They must then ask the state legislature for a *charter* that will allow them to make certain local laws for themselves.

Such a charter sets the borders or limits of the town and also provides the way by which the borders or limits may be enlarged as the city grows. It permits the citizens there to tax themselves for the services that they want, such as sidewalks, sewers, streetlights, and libraries. It gives them the right to elect certain town officers.

An incorporated town or village usually has a city council to make the laws, or ordinances. The mayor, the chief executive, appoints a chief of police to help carry out the laws. A *justice of the peace* usually serves as the local court system. Other officers, such as city clerk, treasurer, health officer, and attorney, are appointed or elected according to the needs of the town and the type of charter granted by the state.

In many of our eastern states, an incorporated village or small town is called a *borough*.

The laws made by the towns and villages must not conflict with the laws of our state or nation. As we "pledge allegiance to the flag of the United States of America and to the republic for which it stands, one nation under God, indivisible . . . ," we are promising to be loyal, faithful, and obedient to our local government as well as to our national laws.

Larger municipalities: cities

We have seen that a municipality is any village, town, or city that has received a charter from the state legislature allowing local

Christmas in April unites volunteers of all faiths and all walks of life who donate materials or their time to help those in need. Each year, all across the United States, these volunteers set aside one day to do the much needed home repairs for elderly, handicapped, or low income families. Below, a young man from Oakland County, Michigan helps a group of volunteers restore the beauty and safety of this old house.

Many cities are rebuilding while trying to retain important or interesting landmarks from their past. Above you see the Gem Theater coming to rest at its new home at Madison and Brush Streets in downtown Detroit. The movement of this building from its former location was, according to the Guiness Book of Records, the largest building ever moved, 5,500,000 pounds.

self-government. Villages and towns are small municipalities. Their charters do not allow as much self-government as the charters of larger cities will permit. Some state legislatures will give a community a "city" charter if it has a population of only two hundred people, other states require 10,000 people in a small area before a city charter will be given, but the average is about 2500.

Importance of city government When the Constitution was adopted in 1789, only about five percent of the people of our country lived in cities. Since that time, factories have been built, and industry and business have brought people together in large cities. This movement of the population from the country to the cities is still going on. Because the use of farm machinery makes it easier for

one man to cultivate more land, many young people who were born and raised on farms are moving to the cities in search of jobs. Today about two-thirds to three-fourths of the people of the nation live in cities. City government, therefore, is more important than ever before.

Types of city government Although the first kind of city government was the town meeting, today there are three leading types: the mayor-council type, the city commission type, and the council-manager type. Some states divide their cities into classes according to population; they may then ask cities of the same class to have the same type of government. The charter of a small city often states the type of government it must have. Larger cities usually have the right to choose

Boston's famous Faneuil Hall Marketplace
emerged from what had become a rundown
waterfront neighborhood. Above 1.5 million
people gather on January 1, 1996 to enjoy
performances, concerts, and art exhibits
throughout the city during Boston's 20th
First Night celebration.

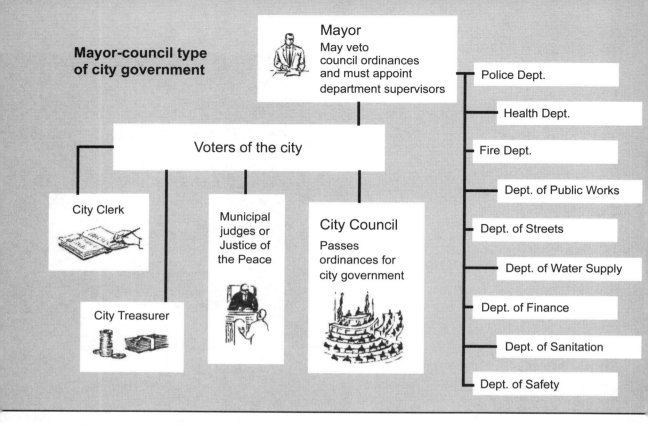

Mayor-council type of city government

Mayor — May veto council ordinances and must appoint department supervisors

Voters of the city

City Clerk

City Treasurer

Municipal judges or Justice of the Peace

City Council — Passes ordinances for city government

Police Dept.

Health Dept.

Fire Dept.

Dept. of Public Works

Dept. of Streets

Dept. of Water Supply

Dept. of Finance

Dept. of Sanitation

Dept. of Safety

the type they consider best for them.

The **mayor-council** type is the most widely used form of city government. The council is usually made up of from five to eleven members; Chicago has the largest city council with fifty members. The council is the law-making department of city government. City laws are usually called ordinances. Although a few cities have bicameral councils, most city councils meet as one group. Council members, sometimes called *aldermen*, are elected by the people in the different *wards*, or districts of the city.

Mayors are also elected by the people. They chair council meetings and in some cities they have power to veto ordinances passed by the council. They appoint most of the city officials, such as the heads of the different departments, and must see that laws are enforced for the good of the people.

Far fewer cities use the **commissioner** type of government. Under it, the people do not elect a mayor and council. Instead they elect the head of each department of city government. Department chairpersons are called commissioners. There are usually five departments under this plan: Public Works, Public Safety, Streets and Public Improvements, Parks and Public Property, and Finances.

The commissioners of these departments meet to make the ordinances for the city. Then each commissioner serves as the chief executive to carry out the ordinances that apply to that department. The commissioners appoint their own assistants and hire their own workers. The commission type of city government is able to act quickly because the small group of commissioners has both legislative and executive power. If things do not go well in a department, it is possible to recall (remove from office) the commissioner who is responsible.

One disadvantage of this type of city government is that each commissioner tries to get as much of the tax money as possible for his department. The departments often act as if they were entirely separate, instead of remembering that government should be indivisible.

The **council-manager** type is the newest form of city government. The people elect a city council or commission to make the ordinances and policies for city government. This council hires a city manager, who is usually trained for this position, to carry out these policies. The city manager must appoint the heads of all the city departments and check to see that all departments are run for the welfare of the people. With a city manager the city government operates in much the same way that the president of any large company conducts business.

City managers hold their offices as long as their work is satisfactory. If the work is not done well, the city council may dismiss the person and hire someone else. A good city manager can do much to make city government operate as efficiently as any modern business.

Services of city government One of the most important services that a city performs for its citizens is to provide a plentiful supply of pure water. Pipelines from distant rivers, filtering plants, and pumping stations are often necessary before the water can be piped into the homes and industries of a city.

The city also checks the food that is sold

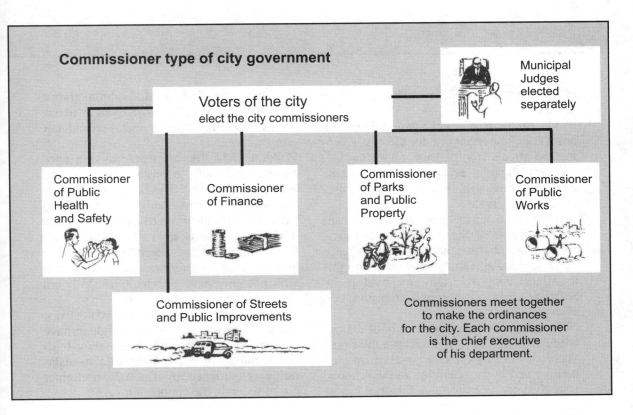

Commissioner type of city government

Voters of the city
elect the city commissioners

Municipal Judges elected separately

Commissioner of Public Health and Safety

Commissioner of Finance

Commissioner of Parks and Public Property

Commissioner of Public Works

Commissioner of Streets and Public Improvements

Commissioners meet together to make the ordinances for the city. Each commissioner is the chief executive of his department.

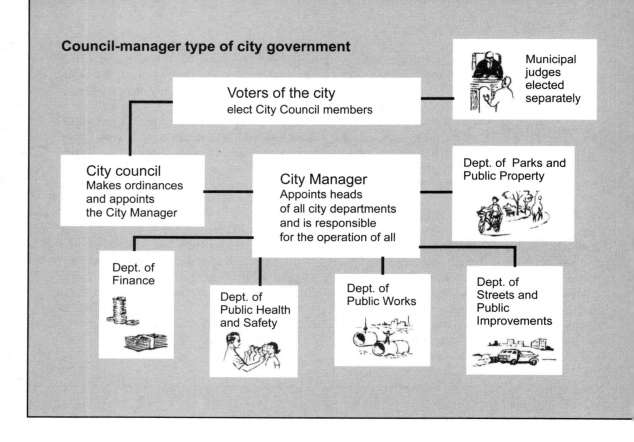

Council-manager type of city government

Voters of the city
elect City Council members

Municipal judges elected separately

City council
Makes ordinances
and appoints
the City Manager

City Manager
Appoints heads
of all city departments
and is responsible
for the operation of all

Dept. of Parks and
Public Property

Dept. of
Finance

Dept. of
Public Health
and Safety

Dept. of
Public Works

Dept. of
Streets and
Public
Improvements

in stores and in restaurants to be sure that it is pure.

The problem of sewage and garbage disposal is an important one for the city. Keeping the streets free of trash and providing a means whereby every home can dispose of its waste material is a task that requires continuous service.

The people of a city need adequate means of transportation. Street building and care, naming, numbering, and mapping streets, building sidewalks and putting up streetlights are all services provided by city government. Some cities also operate public transportation systems.

In some cities the public school district boundaries and the city limits are the same. When this occurs the city government may be involved in the operation of the schools. Usually, however, the school district has its own board of directors and administrative officers. It also has its own system of tax levies to raise revenue for operation and new construction.

Police and fire departments provide needed services that help to protect the lives and property of the citizens. These services are seldom appreciated enough by those who benefit from them around the clock every day of the year. To answer a call of alarm at any time of night or day, regardless of weather and circumstances, requires men and women who not only have occupational skills but also a dedication to their work.

Risk and danger are part of their daily lives. Since 1970 over one hundred firefighters have been killed each year in the line of duty. Injuries, including those caused by smoke inhalation, are experienced by at least one firefighter out of seven in the course of a year.

The number of police officers who are killed in the performance of their duties each year is even greater than that of firefighters. Because of sinful tendencies, crime becomes more prevalent when police and firefighters are unavailable. Looting and arson become more frequent. These public servants are worthy of prayer, respect, and adequate pay.

The amount of tax money spent for these important services is quite large when compared to the amount spent by other city departments.

As the population of a city grows, the city council must plan for city expansion. *Zoning* laws are made to keep businesses and factories from overrunning the growing residential areas. Such city planning and zoning makes living more pleasant.

Parks, playgrounds, libraries, museums, parking facilities, sports facilities, and many other services may be provided by city government for its residents.

Summary

It is in one's own community that the average citizen is made most aware of the need for and the functions of government. The closer the level of government is to a person, the more opportunities there are for citizen involvement in Christian political action.

Each of us is affected by many different levels of government at the same time; we are citizens of a city, a township, a county, a state, and a nation. To each of these governments we must be obedient, loyal, and faithful. We cannot be loyal to these governments if their laws conflict; the laws of one level must agree with and strengthen the laws of the others. When we pledge allegiance to one of these levels of government, we pledge allegiance to all of them. We must be subject to each because each is under God.

Do you remember what you have read?

1. Does an unincorporated or an incorporated town provide the most services for its citizens?
2. How would taxes differ between the two types?
3. Where does a village or town that wishes to incorporate get its charter?
4. Why has city government been increasing in importance?
5. Name the three types of city government.
6. What do we call a municipal law?
7. How does the mayor-council type of government differ from the council-manager type?

For further thought

1. With the concentration of so many people in urban areas today, is it wise to continue to have three separate units of local government (county, township, city) within a county? Would it be better to have one unit of government to serve the whole county?
2. What is a citizen to do when different levels of government, each "under God," disagree?
3. Most city commissioners or councilmen are paid a very meager salary. Would it be wise to increase the salary so that these officials could give full time to their offices?

Research projects

1. Have committees from your class do the following assignments and report their findings to class:
   a. Learn about your city's water supply, its source, pumping system, and purification processes.
   b. Find out how your city disposes of its sewage and garbage.
   c. Get information on the operation of your police system: the number of officers employed, the type of equipment used, and the salaries paid.
   d. Visit a council meeting, if it is open to the public.
   e. Investigate the fire protection provided by your city or county government.
   f. Try to find and read a copy of your city charter. When did your city receive it? Where is it kept?
   g. Find out the zoning regulations of your city.

Urban living can be crowded, fast-paced, and impersonal. Large cities provide services people in smaller communities often provide for themselves, either individually or cooperatively.

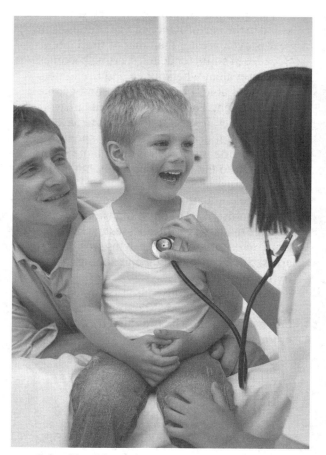

Emergency aid

School health service

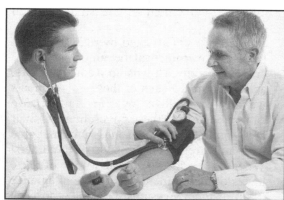

Library facilities

Health care

Specialized police service

Recreational facilities (New interactive water playground at Piotrowski Park, Chicago, IL)

Road repair (Milford, MI)

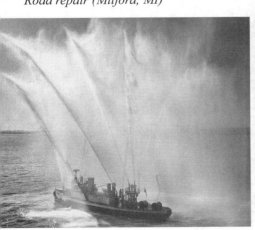

Specialized fire protection

Fire protection

h. Name an incorporated and an unincorporated city in your area. Tell how their governments differ.
2. Make a chart showing the names of your city officials and the offices that they hold.
3. Make a study of city and county election campaigns. Note that candidates for city offices are generally non-partisan, while candidates for county offices generally run on a political party ticket. Try to determine how this difference affects campaign issues.

Words to study

alderman	municipal
borough	municipality
charter	unincorporated
incorporated	ward
justice of the peace	zoning

UNIT RESEARCH PROJECTS

1. How did your state come into the Union? Was it one of the original thirteen? If not, try to trace its movement in history from unorganized to organized territory and on to statehood.
2. Organize the class into a city or village council and conduct the business likely to be important for your community.
3. Draw a map of your state showing all the counties and important cities.
4. Prepare a speech describing the qualities one needs to be a good mayor.
5. Make a map of your county showing the township and city boundaries or a map of your local community showing main roads, public buildings, parks, and other important features.
6. Nebraska is the only state with a unicameral legislature. Make a report on how this body conducts its business and why Nebraska prefers this type of organization to the usual bicameral legislature.
7. Make a scrapbook about your state. Include information about the following: government, history, capital, motto, resources, industries, state flower, bird, song, and nickname. Include maps of your state and newsclips.

Unit five
Liberty and justice

I pledge allegiance
to the flag of the United States of America
and to the republic for which it stands,
one nation under God, indivisible,
with liberty and justice . . .

The pledge that you have made
so often states that our nation under God
provides liberty and justice for all.
Our nation must provide liberty for
our people because we have received
this inalienable right from the Creator.
Our government must provide justice
because government was ordained by God
to rule in His place. Because God is just,
our government, which rules for Him,
must also be just.

In this unit we shall look carefully
at what liberty is and how it is
related to justice. You will be asked
to think about how the two are kept
in balance. We will study the types
of courts and the process of trial by jury.
The many executive departments
and agencies of our national government
will be considered, for they seek
to provide liberty and justice in the
faithful execution of our laws. A study
of political parties and the process
of electing national leaders will
show liberty in action.

Chapter 15

Liberty and justice compared

Important ideas to look for:
- Liberty is the freedom to act under the law.
- The freedom of the Christian is guided by the law of God.
- Justice requires a court system operating to provide equal treatment before law.
- Justice prevents liberty from being misused.

What is liberty?

"Where the spirit of the Lord is," we read in II Corinthians 3:17, "there is freedom." This is why the Apostle Paul could speak of the freedom and liberty he had in Christ even while he was in prison. Paul experienced true spiritual liberty because he wanted to do what the Lord wanted him to do.

Political liberty is a reflection of spiritual liberty. **Liberty means freedom to do what we please as long as we choose to do that which is according to the law.** Such liberty includes negative freedom, that is freedom *from* control and oppression. It also includes positive freedom, or freedom *to* plan our activities and speak our thoughts. We experience liberty when we choose to live within the limits set by the laws of our country.

Romans 13:5 reminds us that we must submit "not only because of possible punishment but also because of conscience." We should not obey the law simply to avoid punishment. Rather, we should do what is right for the sake of our conscience. Then we will enjoy liberty under law.

If we misuse our liberty, we will soon find it taken from us. Political liberty can be enjoyed when there is a right balance between citizens who exercise their personal freedom in a responsible way and a government that must enforce laws for the well-being of all. Liberty is a precious thing. To acquire it and to maintain it requires a high sense of personal responsibility on the part of all citizens. The government must avoid tyrannical laws that are neither necessary nor good. Citizens have an obligation to oppose laws which hinder their liberties. They must also live in such a way that many government restrictions would not be necessary.

What is justice?

When our government provides justice for all, it guarantees all our people fair, honest, and **equal treatment before our laws**. We may not have titles of nobility, nor should our government have especially favored groups or classes of citizens that receive privileges not given to others. Our nation must seek to provide justice for all—rich or poor, famous or unknown, young or old—because God has commanded, ". . . Maintain justice, and do what is right . . ." (Is. 56:1).

For whom must liberty and justice be provided?

Our civil government must provide liberty and justice for the **church**. The Bible tells us ". . . Fear God and keep his commandments, for this is the whole duty of man" (Eccles. 12:13). The church must be free to lead its members in the worship of God. It must be free to do mission work so others may hear the Gospel.

The **home** must be granted the rights of liberty and justice because God has commanded parents to bring up their children in the fear of the Lord. The civil government must give parents the freedom to carry out this command.

Our nation must also provide liberty and justice for **individual citizens** so they can exercise their God-given, inalienable rights to life, liberty, and the pursuit of happiness.

What courts do we have to provide justice?

Our court system provides local courts where every citizen who has a complaint involving the law may have a hearing. Here also lawbreakers may be brought to justice. Courts of appeal are willing to hear the cases of those who feel that the judgment of the lower court was unfair. Our state and national supreme courts try cases that come under their special jurisdiction. Our state court systems hear all cases dealing with state laws, and our national court system tries offenses against our federal laws. By means of our three-level system in both state and national courts, our nation seeks to provide justice for all of our people.

Types of lower courts

Justice courts The local courts in some small villages or communities are headed by justices of the peace. The justice of the peace in such a justice court has jurisdiction over civil cases that involve small amounts of money, injuries to property, traffic violations, breaches of the peace, disobedience of health department regulations, or similar local offenses. A justice of the peace generally does not rule in cases that deal with *tort* (wrongs done to a person), or titles to land, or such more serious cases. However, he or she may *bind over*, or transfer, the accused person to a higher court for trial, issue warrants for the arrest of persons suspected of serious crimes, and perform civil marriages.

Police or magistrate courts Police or magistrate courts are often found in middle-sized towns or small cities. The judges are usually elected in much the same way and have the same type of jurisdiction as a justice of the peace in a justice court. Although a local lawyer is often elected to serve as a justice of the peace or as a judge in a police or magistrate court, many people not trained in law, such as farmers, truck drivers, ministers,

---

Justice of the Peace

During the past fifty years modern technology has caused many changes in American society and the way that the government carries out its responsibility.

At one time the office of the justice of the peace was a very important one for the administration of local justice. The justice of the peace, in spite of limited training in law, tried to do a good job and often showed much wisdom.

Today, with improved transportation and communication, plaintiffs and defendants usually travel to the county court house or some other district court where the matter is handled by judges who have special training.

The office of justice of the peace has become less important in most areas and in some cities has been discontinued altogether.

Qualified people must be elected or appointed as judges if justice is to be served.

teachers, store clerks, real estate agents, and druggists, have held these positions. Justice in such courts may be well intended, but decisions are sometimes biased and inconsistent.

Municipal courts Many larger cities have municipal courts that have both local and state jurisdiction over criminal and civil cases that arise within their city limits. These municipal courts are often divided into branches, such as civil, criminal, traffic, juvenile, misdemeanor, small claims, and *probate*. This type of organization helps the courts to function more efficiently. For example, the juvenile court division would handle only cases involving persons under 18 years of age. Judges in such courts may be specially trained in the laws governing juvenile cases and be particularly concerned about the problems of minors. Special advis-

ers trained in psychology or counseling may assist the judge. When a case is heard, the judge may simply give a warning or advice. In other cases, a minor may be placed on *probation*, fined, or even sent to a school of correction, often called a reform school. In this same way the probate court division is able to have judges who are skilled in dealing with the wills and estates of people who have died. The small claims court is another example of a special type of municipal court. Cases handled in a small claims court usually involve amounts of money less than $1000. For example, a newspaper carrier wishes to collect money owed by a customer for a few months' subscription; a man wishes payment for repair of his car fender which was dented in a shopping center parking lot; a landlady wishes a boarder to replace a mattress that was burned with a cigarette. These people can hardly afford to pay attorney fees and court costs for an expensive trial. In the small claims court the judge settles the trouble between the *plaintiff* (the person making the complaint) and the *defendant* (the accused) without the presence of lawyers.

General trial courts The general trial court is an important link in the chain of justice in our nation. It handles cases, both civil and criminal, that are too difficult for the justice and magistrate courts. Officials of the general court include the *judge*, who is usually trained in law; the *clerk* of the court, who, with the help of stenographers, records the actions of the court; and a *bailiff*, who is in charge of the prisoners while they are in the courtroom. This person maintains order in the court, and usually swears in the *jury* and the witnesses.

Court procedure in a criminal trial

Before the trial Suppose that a crime has been committed in a small community. The law enforcement officers arrest the person suspected of the offense. The defendant is then brought before the magistrate or justice of the peace. When the magistrate has heard the evidence presented by the police officers, he may decide to have the accused "bound over to the grand jury." The *prosecutor* or district attorney then assumes responsibility for bringing the evidence gathered by the police to the attention of the grand jury. If the grand jury finds that the evidence is sufficient to charge the defendant with the crime, the person is *indicted* and held for trial. In some cases the defendant may be freed on bail; in others the accused is held in prison until the date of the trial.

The trial Although the courtrooms throughout our nation may vary a great deal in size, in style of furnishings, and in age, most of them have basic arrangements that are quite similar. The United States flag is displayed. A Bible is usually provided for swearing in witnesses and jury members. In the front of the room on a raised platform is the judge's *bench*, or desk. A desk for the clerk of the court is provided on one side; a chair for the witness, or a *witness stand*, is usually found on the other. A *jury box* seating twelve people and enclosed by a bannister or railing is along the wall next to the witness stand. In front of and below the judge's bench are tables and chairs for the lawyers, the defendant, and others involved in the case. The rest of the courtroom is filled with benches or chairs for people who may wish to watch the proceedings. The public may observe trials because a "public" trial is one of the rights guaranteed in the Sixth Amendment to the Constitution.

On the date of the trial, the court opens when the judge leaves the *chambers*, usually an adjoining room, and enters the courtroom. The bailiff calls everyone present to rise as the judge enters. After calling the court to order, the judge begins by conferring with the lawyers for the prosecution (state's side) and for the *defense* (accused's side) about the rules for the conduct of the trial. Next, the accused is called before the judge's bench, and the clerk reads the charges in the statement of indictment that has been prepared by the prosecutor. The judge then asks whether the accused will plead "guilty" or "not guilty." If the defendant pleads "guilty," no further trial is held; instead the judge, after considering the case, prepares the sentence according to the law.

If the accused pleads "not guilty" he must next choose whether the case will be heard by the judge alone or by a jury. When the accused wants a jury trial, the bailiff of the court summons a group of citizens for jury duty. From this panel or group, the lawyers agree upon twelve persons who they feel are able to give a fair judgment. After being sworn in, the jury listens to the case.

The prosecuting attorney generally begins with an *opening statement* to acquaint the jury with the case. To introduce various pieces of evidence, the prosecutor may call several *witnesses*.

These witnesses will be questioned in a way that will bring out facts against the accused. After the prosecutor has completed the questioning of each witness, the *defense attorney* may *cross-examine* a witness in an effort to find weak or inconsistent points in the testimony. Next, the defense has a turn at producing witnesses and evidence to prove the innocence of the accused.

Summing up After the testimony by witnesses has been completed, the prosecuting attorney reviews the facts of the case to the jury and attempts to convince them that the accused is guilty. The defense attorney next addresses the jury in an effort to prove that the defendant is innocent.

When the lawyers have finished, the judge *charges* the jury, drawing their attention to the points of law involved in the case and to their responsibility to find the accused innocent if they think that the facts do not prove

Before the trial, the attorney for each side will go over the evidence, check the laws which may apply to the case, and research previous cases of a similar nature which may serve as "precedent."

otherwise beyond a "reasonable doubt."

The jury decides After the jury has been charged by the judge, the bailiff escorts them into a private room where they remain until they have reached a *verdict*. To reach such a decision, all twelve persons on the jury must agree. If they cannot reach complete agreement because even one member consistently disagrees, the jury is said to be *hung.* When this happens, either the case is dismissed or a new jury is selected and the case must be tried again. In most cases, however, the jury reaches an agreement. They then call in the bailiff, who is outside the door. The bailiff in turn tells the judge, and the court is called back into session. When the jury returns to the courtroom, the *foreman,* whom the jury members have selected to serve as spokesperson, announces the verdict to the court. If the accused is found "not guilty," the person is released. If, however, the foreman of the jury states, "We, the jury, find the defendant guilty as charged," the judge is responsible for sentencing or fining the accused according to law.

Civil cases

In court cases between citizens much the same procedures are followed as in criminal cases. One important difference is that in a civil case, the district attorney does not prosecute the defendant. Rather the complaint of a private citizen is involved. Suppose that one man is suing another for $5000 because of damages and injury received in an automobile accident. Because the person who is trying to collect the damages has a complaint, he or she is called the plaintiff. The lawyer for the plaintiff has the case placed on the court's *docket*, or list of cases to be tried. Before the date set for the hearing, the lawyer for the defendant and the lawyer for the plaintiff may decide to settle out of court to avoid court costs. If no *settlement* can be reached, both sides of the *lawsuit* may be presented to the judge, or, if the defendant chooses, to a jury. The case is usually closed in one of two ways. One way is for the court to issue an order for the defendant to pay the amount of the *judgment* to the plaintiff. However, the court may decide to change the amount of damages to be paid, even though the defendant is found to be at fault. The second way is for the court to declare the defendant innocent of the charges.

Appeal to a higher court

Even when a lower court does all that is possible to provide a fair trial and the jury reaches a verdict with great care, there is

Before testifying, a witness must take a solemn oath that his or her testimony will be the truth.

always the possibility of error. Our court system, therefore, provides that the decision of a lower court may be appealed to a higher one. If a person *convicted* of a crime (or a person against whom a judgment was made) feels that the decision was unjust, or if an attorney thinks that the trial was improperly conducted, the case may be appealed. The judges of the appellate court then review, or reexamine, it. They do not hold a second trial. Instead, they read carefully all of the lower court's proceedings, including the testimony and verdict of the trial in the lower court. The judges of the court of appeal may change the decision of the lower court, or they may uphold it. They may even order a new trial if they feel that this is in the best interest of justice. Sometimes a decision is appealed several times, all the way up to the Supreme Court.

The necessity of courts

The courts are open to the people of our land as they seek justice. Courts are necessary because we are sinful: we break the laws of government and quarrel with our neighbors. Sometimes court cases are brought because of differences of opinion. The causes of these differences—the lack of harmony and of love for one another—are due to our sinful nature.

The courts are a blessing from God, for

they prevent war by peaceably settling many of these quarrels. Their judges help fulfill the second function of government because they do not bear the sword in vain as they levy fines and impose sentences on those who are found guilty of breaking the law.

When should we take a disagreement to court? I Corinthians 6 tells us that rather than going to court, Christians should either settle a disputed matter among themselves or be willing to suffer wrong. This is the way things should be, but today a court case may be necessary before an insurance company is willing to pay a claim or can legally do so. If Christians are on opposite sides in such a lawsuit, there should be no bitterness or hatred on the part of those involved. While going to court with such an attitude keeps the intent of the Bible passage, we recognize that it would be better if no lawsuit were necessary.

Liberty and justice; how they balance

Liberty and justice may seem to be quite opposite. Liberty gives us the right to do as we please as long as what we choose to do is in accordance with the law; and justice is equal treatment before our laws. Justice controls and balances liberty because it keeps liberty from being misused. It also places a criminal in prison where his liberty is taken away. Our nation under God has the responsibility of keeping a balance between the liberty of the people and the justice enforced upon lawbreakers.

Liberty and justice; how the balance is kept

Our government seeks to keep the balance between liberty and justice by providing for a division of power among the three branches of our government.

The **legislative branch**, or Congress, helps to preserve liberty and provide justice for all by making the laws necessary to guard the rights of the people and to punish those who do wrong. When our lawmakers raise an army to protect our country, when they pass tariff laws to guard the welfare of our industries, when they establish courts or prisons, when they pass any law that provides a good service or punishes those who do evil, they are helping to provide liberty and justice for all.

The **judicial branch** does much to balance liberty and justice. Juries, basing their decisions on the testimony of witnesses and on the law, decide whether accused persons are innocent or guilty. Judges in our courts interpret the laws for the juries and use the laws passed by the legislative branch as they make judgments. Judges cause a law to be removed if they find that it does not agree with the principles of liberty and justice as they are written in the Constitution.

The **executive branch** does more, perhaps, to serve as a servant of God for good and to "bear the sword" than do either of the other two branches. In Article II of our Constitution, our President is given this task: "He shall take care that the laws be faithfully executed." Seeing that the laws are faithfully carried out is the President's biggest task. As the President and other members of the executive department carry out the laws of our nation, they seek to provide liberty and justice for all. In the next chapter we will consider the many departments and agencies that assist the President.

Do you remember what you have read?
1. What is liberty?
2. Why may our government not allow all people to do as they please?
3. Why do the home and church need liberty?
4. What is justice?
5. How does justice control the use of liberty?
6. How do the laws of liberty balance the laws of justice?
7. What qualities should a good juror have? Why is serving on a jury often difficult?

8. What responsibility does each of the following have in court procedure?

bailiff	judge
clerk	jury
defendant	plaintiff
(accused)	prosecutor
defense attorney	(or district attorney)
foreman	witness

For further thought

1. Why should it not be necessary for a Christian to go to court to settle a dispute with another Christian? (Refer to I Corinthians 6.)
2. Why are courts necessary?
3. Why do people who have been ordained by God to positions of authority (parents, teachers, judges, officers of the law) have difficulty using their authority with perfect justice? What should our attitude be when we learn of misuse?
4. Most judges are elected to office on a nonpartisan ballot. Why is this wise?
5. How do individuals and groups misuse their liberty? Give examples from history and the present to illustrate this.
6. How have individuals and groups been denied justice (equal treatment before the laws)? Give examples from history and the present.

Things to do

1. Draw an original sketch, cartoon, or chart to illustrate the balance between liberty and justice.
2. Have a panel discussion dealing with the following subject: "The Difficulty of Maintaining a Balance Between Liberty and Justice in the Home, School, and Community."
3. Ask a local judge or attorney to speak to the class on the nature of the law, the legal profession, and the court system.
4. Visit a local court while in session. To understand the complete court procedure, attempt to be present when the case begins.
5. Draw a chart showing the court system of your own state. Include the exact names of the various courts, the number of judges, and the types of cases heard in each.

Words to study

bench	jury box
bind over	justice of peace
chamber	lawsuit
charge	opening statement
convict	probate
cross-examine	probation
defense	settlement
docket	summing up
hung	tort
indict	verdict
judgment	witness stand

Chapter 16

Executive departments maintain balance

Important ideas to look for:
- Many departments and agencies assist the President as he "takes care that the laws be faithfully executed."
- Faithful execution of our laws helps to provide liberty and justice for all.
- Government employees, like all other citizens, need to take seriously their pledge of allegiance.
- Civil Service examinations help to provide qualified persons for government positions.

The executive branch enforces laws

If liberty and justice are to be maintained for all of our citizens, it is important that Congress make laws that are adequate for our needs and honest in their purposes. Our courts must interpret these laws fairly. The responsibility of the executive branch, however, is perhaps even more complex than that of the legislative or judicial, for the executive branch must execute these laws; that is, it must enforce them, must put them into action. Of course, our President, who is our chief executive, could not administer or carry out all of our laws by himself. Our country is far too large, and our population is far too great for that.

The Cabinet— assistants to the President

Soon after George Washington was inaugurated as our first President, he appointed four department heads who later came to be called his *Cabinet*. He chose the most able men of our country to be his helpers.

Although our Constitution does not say anything about a Cabinet, each President has followed Washington's example and has appointed a Cabinet of his own. As our country grew in size, many new departments had to be formed. Today, our President has fifteen Cabinet members—each in charge of a department—to help him carry out our laws.

These departments aid the President as he "takes care that the laws be faithfully executed" and seeks to provide liberty and justice for our nation. Each Cabinet member must manage his department efficiently and well; each must make reports to the President and advise him of improvements that could be made.

Cabinet meetings are held once or twice a week at the White House. Besides his Cabinet members, the President may ask other high government officials to attend, such as, the Vice-President, our ambassador to the United Nations, the head of the Office of Management and Budget, and the heads of various other agencies when matters related to their work are considered.

These were the men Abraham Lincoln chose to assist him. Secretary of State Seward (foreground) negotiated the purchase of Alaska.

The Constitution does not give a set of qualifications for Cabinet members; in fact, it says nothing at all about the President's Cabinet. It is up to the President to appoint persons he feels are best suited to do the work. The members appointed must be approved by the Senate. Although the President may ask a Cabinet member to resign at any time that the member's work is unsatisfactory, the Cabinet member's term of office normally ends at the conclusion of the term of the President who appointed him. However, the President may prefer to retain some of the Cabinet members of his *predecessor.*

The Department of State

Our Department of State is in charge of the foreign affairs of our nation. It seeks to provide liberty and justice for our own people

as it regulates the complex relationships that we have with other nations of the world. Our Secretary of State works for world peace by making treaties with other countries and by reaching trade agreements with them. Our ambassadors and their staff members in foreign nations and our representative to the United Nations are employees of the State Department. This department of our government also gives *passports* and *visas* to citizens who want to visit or travel in other countries.

As the members of the State Department deal with the nations of the world, they must realize that not only is our nation under God's rule and providential care but so also are all the others. They must apply the teachings of

This design is from the flag of the Secretary of State. The olive branch symbolizes our desire for peace; the thunderbolts, our might.

finances. The Secretary of the Treasury is responsible for collecting the customs, duties, and taxes for our government according to the laws made by Congress. Officials of the Treasury Department pay the wages of all government employees and other bills of our nation. They also borrow money on the credit of the United States. Much of this money is borrowed from citizens, banks, and insurance companies through the sale of United States Bonds. The Treasury Department provides for the engraving, printing, and coining of money. Once each year the Treasury Department must make a financial report to Congress. The Federal Reserve System of our banks helps to control interest rates and also insures the money placed in our banks.

Another very important part of the nation's financial work is the preparation of the national *budget*. The Office of Management and Budget draws up a list of expected government expenses for the coming year. This office must also estimate the amount of taxes our Treasury will receive. The President, through the Office of Management and Budget, does all he can to see that our national budget *balances*—that is, as much money as is spent should be collected by taxation. If this is not done, our national debt will increase even further.

How money is spent is decided by Congress but the President, as chief executive, must see to it that the budget is met even if the treasury has a *deficit*.

The Office of Management and Budget was once part of the Treasury Department, but since it has such a large responsibility, is has now been made a separate agency of the Executive Branch. The Office of Management and Budget is responsible directly to the President rather than to the Secretary of the Treasury.

Law enforcement agencies that are controlled by the Treasury Department are the United States Secret Service, which guards the President and tracks down counterfeiters, the Narcotics Squad, and the Department of

Christ on a worldwide basis when dealing with other nations. The Bible teaches that "from one man he made every nation of men . . ." (Acts 17:26). When we deal with people of other lands, we must do so according to the law of God, for they too are image bearers of Him.

Although the chief duty of the State Department is to help our President decide on our foreign policy and world problems, it also has several duties within our country. It keeps all the original copies of treaties and agreements made with other nations, and it publishes information about the international relations of the United States. It must keep the great seal of our nation. Also, it supervises the work of over 200,000 persons, many of whom work in foreign countries.

The Treasury Department

The more than 115,000 people of the Treasury Department are in charge of our nation's

Treasury Department agencies fulfill many functions. Above, secret service agents guard the President as he greets people; below are counterfeit twenty dollar bills and printing equipment seized by the U.S. Secret Service in 1995/1997.

Cadets at the Air Force Academy in Colorado Springs, Colorado are trained in both military and academic subjects. They will graduate as second lieutenants.

Internal Revenue which checks on the accuracy of income tax payments. Taxpayers who cheat run the risk of being imprisoned under federal law.

Just as the State Department works for freedom from fear of other nations, so the Treasury Department serves as a servant of God for good by caring for the economic well-being of the people.

The Department of Defense

The Department of Defense is responsible for the protection and security of our nation. When this department defends our nation, it spends much of its time bearing the sword. When our armed forces protect us from our country's enemies, the Department of Defense is helping to provide liberty and justice for us.

The President is involved in the business of this department because he is the commander-in-chief of the armed forces. He asks the Secretary of Defense to contract for military supplies and equipment, to arrange for enlisting or drafting and the training of needed personnel, and to provide needed air bases, navy yards, and army posts.

The Department of Defense is composed of three smaller departments: the Department of the Army, the Department of the Navy, and the Department of the Air Force. Each of these military departments has its own regulations, organization, plans for research, and officer-training programs. The United States Military Academy at West Point, the Naval Academy at Annapolis, and the United States Air Force

Four soldiers from the 82nd Airborne Division walk around camp wearing rain suits, gloves and M-17A1 protective masks to acclimate their bodies to the Saudi heat during Operation Desert Shield.

Academy near Colorado Springs are under the control of the Defense Department.

The Secretary of Defense who, by tradition, has always been a civilian, must see that each of these departments is ready to fulfill its purpose. The President often meets with the Secretary of Defense and the Joint Chiefs of Staff so that all military departments work well together to defend our nation from its enemies.

In spite of all our military power, the defense of our nation is first of all under God's care, for ". . . Unless the Lord watches over the city, the watchmen stand guard in vain" (Ps. 127:1). Our citizens must continue to ask God's blessing so that ". . . we may live peaceful and quiet lives . . ." (I Tim. 2:2).

Since waterways were once very important in war, the improvement of harbors and rivers was assigned to the Defense Department. Although their connection with defense is rather remote today, the Department of Defense continues to be responsible for our waterways, primarily through the US Army Corps of Engineers. The USACE is responsible for investigating, developing, and maintaining the nation's water and related environmental resources.

More than a million civilian workers together with all the men and women in uniform, carry on the work of the Defense Department.

The Department of Justice

The Attorney General of the United States is the head of the Department of Justice. Just as the district attorney prosecutes a prisoner in a lower federal court, so the Attorney General is responsible for prosecuting persons brought before the United States Supreme Court. The Attorney General very seldom tries a case personally. Instead, deputies and lawyers try the cases. The Attorney General must see that our lower courts are in operation and that our United States district attorneys are doing their work as they should. The Attorney General must provide legal advice for the President and other officials of the executive branch. In addition, he or she is the defense lawyer of the United States whenever any case is brought against our country in court. More than 100,000 people carry out the work of this department.

The Department of Justice helps to provide liberty and justice for many new citizens by carrying out our immigration and naturalization laws. Under the supervision of this department of our President's Cabinet, people from many foreign lands come to live in our nation to enjoy our freedom with us and become citizens. The Border Patrol of the Immigration Service is under the supervision of the Department of Justice. The patrol guards our borders against persons who attempt to enter our country illegally.

One of the major law enforcement agencies of our nation is the **Federal Bureau of Investigation**, under the supervision of the Justice Department. The law enforcement officers in the FBI are the most highly trained of those in our nation. Whenever someone breaks a federal law, the FBI officers go into action. They do not stop at state borders but can go anywhere to arrest a lawbreaker. They may have to trail a criminal both day and night, from state to state, and from one hideout to another until they bring him to justice. In unusual cases the FBI may be called upon to coordinate the work of state and local law enforcement agencies.

Would you like to become an FBI officer? Becoming one is not easy. You must have a good education, be able to pass a physical examination that proves you are in excellent health, and be between twenty-five and forty years old. After you have applied and are accepted for this work, you will be trained in all the latest methods of criminal investigation. You must become an expert in the use of firearms.

The crime laboratory maintained for the FBI by the Department of Justice is one of the best in the world. The FBI has in its files in Washington, D.C., copies of millions of fingerprints. By fingerprints the FBI can help to promote liberty by identifying the innocent who are thought to be involved in a crime; they can also help to provide justice by bringing evidence against those who are guilty.

The crime problem

Through the use of its police power, the Department of Justice does much to arrest criminals and bring them to trial for their crimes. But the Department of Justice cannot solve the crime problem of our country by itself. It needs our help. Many people say, "I'm a law-abiding citizen. Why should I worry about the crime problem in our country?" This is not the correct attitude. Crime prevention must be the concern of every citizen.

Crime is sin, and sin dishonors God. Disobedience to law is disobedience to God, who says in His Word, "Everyone must submit himself to the governing authorities . . ." (Rom. 13:1). The only exception to this rule is when, in obeying earthly authorities, we would be forced to break the law of God (see page 6).

The crime problem should also concern us because it may affect us personally. Your parents' automobile might be stolen, your home might be burglarized, your life or the life of a family member might be taken by a criminal. We should all be aware of the high cost of crime—millions of dollars are spent each year for prevention and punishment of crimes. Everyone who pays taxes must help pay the cost.

Other citizens ask, "How can I keep all

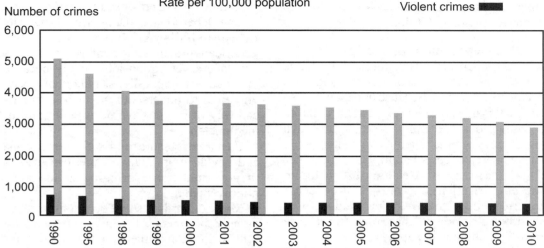

Crime Rate in the United States
Rate per 100,000 population

Crimes against property ▨
Violent crimes ▬

Number of crimes

of the laws when I don't know them all?" Most people are quite familiar with the more serious crimes: murder, treason, robbery, and kidnapping. But these crimes are not the only ones that break the law. Traffic violations, such as speeding and failing to stop at stop signs, are also crimes. Destroying or damaging another person's property is breaking the law. Tearing down signs, disfiguring public parks, and fishing out of season are all violations of law.

We should ask ourselves how sincerely we try to keep the laws of our land. We can be sure that if we have an earnest desire to obey God's laws, we will be serious about obeying our nation's laws at the same time.

The prison program

In spite of efforts to improve prisons, conditions are often very bad. Certainly our government must punish crime, but because there are so many criminals nearly every state and federal prison is overcrowded. But the state and federal governments do not always wish to budget funds to build new prisons or expand existing ones.

Almost half of released prisoners find themselves back in prison after only a year or two. It's hard to understand why an ex-

convict, after being locked up for so long, would continue to commit crimes and risk being put back in prison. It would seem that a person would avoid doing anything that might cause him to lose his new-found freedom. Unfortunately, many released convicts are unable to adjust to the "outside." In addition, ex-convicts often have a hard time finding an honest job, so many of them turn back to a life of crime.

Although some prisons have classrooms where inmates may complete their education and learn a trade, many prisons don't have such programs. Prisoners who show continued evidence that they are reliable and worthy of trust are often released with minimum sentences under the *parole* system.

Christians need to pray for people who are serving time in our country's prisons. But a greater challenge is to become personally involved in prison ministry. Charles Colson spent time in jail for covering up crimes committed by government officials. The experience made him realize just how much work is needed in our prison system. He started "Prison Fellowship," a program designed to bring the Christian message to inmates across the United States. Although much has been accomplished in this area, there is much that still needs to be done to improve prison conditions.

The Department of the Interior

The Department of the Interior is in charge of the vast natural resources that God has given to our nation. Because our country is so large, this department is divided into smaller commissions and bureaus, each of which must carry out the federal laws that apply to its own area of responsibility.

The **Bureau of Reclamation** helps to develop irrigation projects to permit better use of arid land and to develop the production of hydroelectric power. These projects increase our food and power supply.

The **Bureau of Land Management** is in charge of about 245 million acres of nationally owned land. Laws for tidelands and grazing areas are enforced by officials of this division. The **Geological Survey** conducts studies of land and resources, publishing maps available to all. The **Bureau of Mines** promotes safe mining operations by a mine inspection program. It also makes surveys of mineral resources and encourages opening of new mines.

Game wardens of the **U.S. Fish and Wildlife Service** enforce the laws that protect our fish, birds, and wild animals. The **National Park Service** cares for more than 84 million acres of land containing 58 national parks. Their purpose is:

to conserve the scenery and the natural and historic objects, and the wildlife therein, and to provide for the enjoyment of the same in such manner and by such means as will leave them unimpaired for the enjoyment of future generations.

The National Park Service helps us to appreciate God's handiwork in nature.

The Department of the Interior, through its **Bureau of Indian Affairs** works with Native Americans in achieving their just goals. It has not done a very good job, mainly because many government officials either have been unwilling to understand the Native American way of life or have been indifferent or incompetent.

Increased pressure from Native Americans, and having more Native American leaders in government are bringing about some improvement.

Many other duties that do not fit into any other department of our government are sent to the Department of the Interior for enforcement. Among these other duties are the carrying out of laws for the territories and dependencies and also the enforcement of regulations dealing with the flag. Whether the officials are supervising the work of the smaller units, or whether they are dealing

Information gained through the banding of birds helps the Fish and Wildlife Service take measures which will protect the flocks.

with the great problems of the proper use of our natural resources, the officials of the Department of the Interior can do much as servants of God for good.

The Department of Agriculture

Agriculture is one of the basic industries of our nation. Everyone from the richest to the poorest must depend upon the soil for the food needed to live. The raw materials for most of our clothing and houses come directly or indirectly from the soil. Because the growing of food is so important, and because the farmer has many problems in his work, this department is a very busy place.

The effects of sin in the world are very real to the farmer in his daily work. Weeds, plant and animal diseases, insect pests, drought, and crop failures are common enemies that need to be overcome. Our Department of Agriculture seeks to help the farmers of our nation by searching for new ways to improve crops. Specialists of this department try to find better ways of controlling plant and animal diseases and other enemies of the farmer. The department supplies relief to farmers in areas of crop failure.

Improving the production of food is only one part of the work of the Department of Agriculture. Providing a good way of marketing and distributing the food to people who need it is even harder. World needs and world markets—surpluses in one area and hunger in another—are difficult and complicated problems. The officials of the Department of Agriculture are often severely criticized for their work. In our prayers we must also ask God to give wisdom to them so that they may be able to govern well—that through their efforts people everywhere may enjoy the blessings of enough food.

The Department of Agriculture is in charge of our national forests. By means of the **Forest Service** it seeks to regulate the cutting of timber and to protect our forests from fire. Soil conservation is an important responsibility of this department because if the soil of our country would lose its fertility or would be lost through serious erosion, farmers would soon be unable to produce enough food.

The 4-H program helps boys and girls in our country by encouraging them to take up worthwhile projects. The Department of Agriculture provides books and records for the 4-H club members, and it gives assistance and advice for the club leaders. As boys and girls take an active part in their 4-H work, they learn how to work together. They need to learn more about dealing honestly and fairly with one another.

The Department of Commerce

Some of the most serious disagreements between states under the Articles of Confederation were about the problems of trade. At that time the federal government could not control the commerce between states and with foreign countries. But under our Constitution, Congress may make laws to control trade and to promote commerce. These laws have helped to prevent quarrels between states. They have helped to make our nation more orderly and therefore closer to the way God would have it be.

Just as the Department of Agriculture helps the farmers of our nation, so the Department of Commerce seeks to assist business people—manufacturers, merchants, truckers, owners of railroads and airlines, and even fishermen. Our government helps these business people with a variety of services through the Department of Commerce.

One of these services is provided by the **Weather Bureau**. This department seeks to help commerce by giving weather reports that can be used by airlines, fishing fleets, and trading vessels. At hundreds of weather stations information on air currents and storm movements is collected. Storm warnings and weather forecasts are provided for the public by means of radio, television, newspapers and the Internet.

The National Weather Service uses computers and advanced technology to track the weather.

Before trade can be carried on successfully, a country must have a standard set of weights and measures. This is important as it guarantees a fair trade to both the buyer and the seller. The **National Bureau of Standards** must set up the specifications for sizes in clothing and shoes, as well as all other items for sale to the people of our country. A rod of fencing, a yard of lace, a pound of hamburger, a gallon of gas, a dozen oranges, or an ounce of gold—the measures of all of these items and many others have been approved for our nation by the National Bureau of Standards.

The Bureau of Standards also establishes measures for testing the quality of items that are offered for sale. For example, a blanket that is labeled "all wool," a billfold stamped "genuine leather," or coffee that is marked "98 percent caffeine free" must fulfill all advertising claims. If goods are not what the manufacturer claims, the manufacturer may be prosecuted.

The scales in grocery stores, the meters in the gasoline pumps of filling stations, and all other types of measuring or weighing devices operate on standards that have been set by the Department of Commerce. These standards are generally enforced according to state or local laws. Government officials carry on a continuous system of testing to make sure that standards are being met. Such testing is necessary because of man's sinful and selfish nature. As our government sets a standard for weights and measures, and as it enforces them in the daily business transactions of the people of our nation, it helps to provide justice for all.

Since most *patents* apply to products that are manufactured and sold by businesses, the Department of Commerce has been placed in charge of the Patent Office. Here more than 8 million patents have been recorded. A patent encourages inventions by giving the inventor the right to control the making and selling of an invention without competition for seventeen years after it has been registered. The patent can be renewed.

Among the thousands of new inventions that have recently been patented are a long-range projector to place advertisements on clouds, a fine, stainless steel thread that can be used to make stockings as sheer as silk or nylon, and a plastic insulation that can be sprayed on cows to keep them cool in summer and warm in winter.

The thousands of patents in the Patent Office show that humans are image bearers of God. God is the great Creator; because we are made in His likeness, we can be creative and invent new things. Our government provides liberty so we are free to work on new ideas; after people make a new product, our patent laws provide justice so that they will benefit from their work. God has given us the ability to invent, and therefore we have the responsibility to use our inventions for good and not for evil.

Other duties of the Department of Commerce include maintaining a Copyright Office to protect the rights of authors in much the same way the Patent Office protects inventors, supervising our national highway and road-building program for the improvement of interstate commerce, and building lighthouses. The department is in charge of licensing merchant ships, enforcing laws for safe shipbuilding, and regulating docks used by ocean trading vessels. *Seismologists* of this department make a record of all earthquakes. The **Bureau of the Census**, another division of the Department of Commerce, has many employees to carry out its work of counting our population.

The Department of Labor

The Secretary of Labor is also a member of the President's Cabinet and is therefore in the executive branch of our government. The chief purpose of the Department of Labor is to see that all labor laws are properly carried out. This department seeks to improve the working conditions and promote the welfare of the wage earners in our country. Since 1913, when this department was added to the President's Cabinet, many labor laws have been passed by Congress. A law limiting the regular working time to forty hours per week, with one and one-half times the regular pay for overtime, the minimum-wage law, and laws that provide pension and medical care are among the many laws that are now in effect to promote the general welfare of American workers. Child-labor laws state that boys and girls under sixteen years old may not be hired to work in factories. The age limit is eighteen in more dangerous industries like mining and lumbering. The child-labor laws do not affect newspaper carriers.

The **Bureau of Labor Statistics** provides information for the President about the number of workers employed and unemployed. The **National Labor Relations Board**, an independent government agency, works with the Department of Labor to help the labor unions and employers to obtain fairer working contracts. When strikes and picketing result from disagreements between labor unions and employers, the National Labor Relations Board tries to help settle the troubles.

The Department of Labor helps to provide liberty and justice for all. It seeks to give to all the opportunity to work at the tasks they choose for themselves.

Some people think that work is a curse, that it is the result of Adam and Eve's fall into sin. They forget that Adam worked before he sinned. He had to keep the garden and watch over the rest of God's creation. After sin entered the world, however, the work that people had to do was different and much harder. Before the fall, Adam could do his work with ease; but after sin came, work often became unpleasant and burdensome. Yet God in His mercy has given us the ability to make many labor-saving inventions. Work is not only a

A dispute between a company and its workers can affect the whole nation. The National Labor Relations Board helps settle such disputes.

means of earning a living; it is also a task that God has given us to do. If a person knows that work is a God-given task, it is easier to obey the boss and to work hard.

A person should receive fair wages; " . . . for the worker deserves his wages . . . " (Luke 10:7). If the employers of our nation realize that they are under God's watchful care and that they own their factories and businesses because of God's blessings upon them, then they will not try to take unfair advantage of their workers. They will never hold back their wages or oppress their workers. Instead, they will deal with their employees in the spirit of brotherly love, as Boaz did with his servants (Ruth 2:4).

But a worker is also responsible to the Lord for the proper use of time. In the Old Testament we have the command, "Six days you shall labor . . ." (Exod. 20:9), and the New Testament says "If a man will not work, he shall not eat" (2 Thess. 3:10). An employee should respect the employer and attempt to do what the employer requires. Doing this is not always easy, especially if the employer is hard to get along with. But even if an employer is unreasonable, a worker still should recognize that serving God is important in every part of life—at work, school, home, or church.

When you grow up and join the ranks of American workers, remember, "Whatever your hand finds to do, do it with all your might . . ." (Eccles. 9:10). The work habits you will have when you are an adult are being formed every day as you mature. If you develop work habits based upon Christian principles, you will be helping to keep our nation under God.

The Department of Health and Human Services

The Preamble to our Constitution states that the general welfare of our people is one of the goals of our national government. Our President has always had the responsibility of enforcing federal laws dealing with health, education and welfare. As the population of our country increased and our federal government became more concerned about these matters, more such laws were passed. In 1953, the agencies that had been formed to carry out these laws were drawn together into the Department of Health, Education, and Welfare. In 1979, this department was divided and a separate Department of Education was formed. The remaining agencies were regrouped and named the Department of Health and Human Services.

The Public Health Service The Surgeon General is in charge of the public health service. Together with many other medical officers, he is in charge of our national hospitals, medical care in federal prisons, and the medical examination of new immigrants. The National Leprosarium in Louisiana cares for leprosy patients in our country and carries on research for control and prevention of leprosy. The National Institutes of Health include the National Heart Institute, the National Cancer Institute, the National Institute of Mental Health, the National Institute of Dental Research, and others. These research programs work on problems that are too complex for local city and county health officers. The officers of the National Public Health Service inspect serums and vaccines, they destroy rats on ships that come to American ports, and they provide a variety of health services for our people. The discoveries made through these research programs and the enforcement of our health laws have done a great deal to cure or to control the spread of disease.

The Food and Drug Administration The Food and Drug Administration works to protect the health of the people of our country by testing many samples from the foods that are sold in our markets. Long ago when our nation was thinly settled, most people grew their own food or at least knew the person who had grown it for them. Today, more people buy canned or frozen goods and food that has been grown in distant places. People can no longer check on the purity of food themselves; the government must now do it for them. Because of humanity's sinful and selfish nature, the Food and Drug Administration must constantly check to see that persons making or selling goods do not substitute poor quality or harmful material for the genuine article in the hope of making a quick profit. Tests made by this department have uncovered such impurities as clay mixed in candy, white sand in table sugar, and poisonous spray on cranberries. Narcotic drugs must be marked, "warning—may be habit-forming." Poisons must be clearly marked, and *antidotes* must be listed on the label. The content of patent medicine is closely regulated. Inspectors from the Food and Drug Administration constantly check on the purity of meat and the sanitary conditions at slaughter houses and meat-packing plants. This department also serves as a servant of God for good as it protects our health.

The Social Security Administration The Old Age and Survivors Insurance Program, or Social Security, as it is commonly called, is a plan to have the government provide for the needs of people who have reached retirement age and for the families in which the wage earners have died. Money for these payments is collected through payroll taxes. Under the Old Age Assistance Program, the national government helps the states care for the old people who are not covered by Social Security. Through the Department of Health and Human Services, the national government also helps the states carry out their plans to help the blind, to meet the needs of dependent

Social Security provides those who are retired or unable to work with income collected through payroll taxes.

children, and to teach a good trade or business to those who are handicapped.

The Department of Housing and Urban Development

In 1965 the Department of Housing and Urban Development was formed. One of its areas of concern is the improvement of housing conditions for our people. Many families of unskilled laborers, of the unemployed, or of minority groups live in crowded slum areas, in very poor housing. Slum conditions are related to both the increase in our nation's population and a wide range of complex economic and social conditions. New shopping centers and large districts of new homes have been built in the suburbs of cities, while the original downtown area has been allowed to deteriorate. Vacant and improperly maintained buildings invite vandalism. Thousands of automobiles choke public thoroughfares. Since no one individual or business is able to deal with these urban problems, the national government, in cooperation with the local authorities, works to bring about improvement.

The Department of Transportation

The Department of Transportation came into existence in 1967 after Congress had passed legislation spelling out its purpose and organization. With over 58,000 employees it regulates or operates a wide range of transportation activities in the air through the Federal Aviation Administration, on land through the Federal Highway Administration, and on the sea through the United States Coast Guard. The major duties of this department, however, are not only to keep present transportation systems working efficiently, but also to plan and encourage new transportation systems which are fast, safe, and convenient as well as economical. This does not mean that all transportation will be operated by the government but that the federal government wishes to stimulate advances in transportation. People who do much traveling agree that better ways of transportation are needed. Unsafe transportation or the kinds which waste time or resources must be replaced by something better.

The Department of Energy

In 1977 Congress enacted a bill that formed the Department of Energy to coordinate the nation's energy policies and programs. It encourages the conservation of fuel and electricity and conducts research to develop new energy sources as well as to discover more efficient ways to use our present supplies. Agencies within the department regulate electric power projects and coal research programs. A five-member commission of the department has authority to set prices for natural gas and electricity as well as to approve proposed pipelines for the transportation of oil.

The Department of Education

Since the Constitution says nothing about education, the matter of making laws for schools, setting regulations for school attendance, and providing buildings and books for public schools has generally been left to the states. The states in turn assign much of the responsibility for schools to the counties and local school districts.

With the increase in mobility and expansion into the global economy, the states, and particularly the federal government, have expanded their roles by setting curriculum standards, mandating standardized testing, and influencing local policies through the control of funding.

The Department of Veterans Affairs

Over the years, our nation has shown special concern for the needs of veterans who were injured while serving their country. The supervision of Veterans Hospitals, pensions, and other veterans affairs were formerly handled by an independent agency of the government known as the Veterans Adminis-

tration. In 1989, however, a bill was signed by President Reagan that changed the Veterans Administration to the Department of Veterans Affairs and gave it a Cabinet post.

The Department of Homeland Security

Eleven days after the September 11, 2001 terrorist attacks, the Office of Homeland Security was established in the White House to oversee and coordinate a comprehensive national strategy to protect the nation against this type of threat and respond to any future attacks. In November of 2002, Congress established it as a Cabinet-level department. Five years after the 9/11 attacks, a review of the department led to it being restructured in order to streamline operations and facilitate better coordination with federal, state, and local partners. Further changes were instituted in 2007 as a result of the Post-Katrina Emergency Management Reform Act, which also clarified issues related to defense of our ports and preparedness for radiological and chemical emergencies.

Throughout these organizational changes, the basic mission of the department remained unchanged: to secure the nation and keep Americans safe. As you can imagine, this is no small task. Over 240,000 persons are employed by the department in vital areas that range from: transportation, agriculture, justice, energy, defense, and health. The Federal Emergency Management Agency (FEMA) is best known for responding to natural disasters within our borders.

The department now includes the Customs and Border Protection, Immigration and Customs Enforcement, National Communications System, and the National Infrastructure Protection Center. Yet the component that students are most likely to encounter is the Transportation Security Administration. These are the people who screen luggage and passengers boarding commercial airlines.

The U.S. mail

A Things that may not be sent through the mail:

1 Poison of any kind, including poisonous animals and reptiles
2 Chemicals or other inflammable materials
3 Indecent pictures or reading material
4 Materials used in a game of lottery or chance
5 Libelous matter (material that defames someone)
6 Intoxicating beverages
7 Threats to a public official
8 Narcotics of any kind
9 Concealable weapons

B Sealed mail is to be opened only by the person to whom the mail is addressed or by an official in the dead-letter office.

C Stealing from the mail is a federal offense. Cases of this kind are handled by the officials of the postal department itself.

D Mailmen may read postcards; it is hard for them to avoid doing so.
D Local damage to mailboxes is con-

Independent Agencies

In addition to the fifteen departments of the President's Cabinet, in the executive branch of our federal government there are nearly 200 independent agencies. Each of these special commissions or agencies has its own work to do. A few of these special agencies are the **Nuclear Regulatory Commission**, the **Consumer Products Safety Commission**, the **Federal Communications Commission**, and the **Federal Reserve System**.

The U.S. Postal Service

Benjamin Franklin became the first Postmaster General in 1775. Since then mail has been carried on foot, by pony express, stagecoach, train, ship, and plane under the authority of Section 8 of the Constitution: "To establish post offices and post roads." The Zone Improvement Plan (ZIP) was established in 1963 to help speed delivery of the billions of pieces of mail handled each year. In October 1983, a new voluntary nine-digit zip code system went into effect to help process the mail more efficiently.

The United States Post Office was a regular department represented in the President's Cabinet until 1971, when it was reorganized as an independent agency of the executive branch. Although the head of the Postal Service is no longer a member of the President's Cabinet, he is still called the Postmaster General. One of the reasons for the change was to provide for even greater efficiency in handling the mail.

There was a time in American history when government officials could provide post office jobs for people who had helped them win election to office. Happily this era has passed; postal employees now obtain their jobs by scoring well on Civil Service examinations. Handling the mail is a public trust; those who do so must be honest, efficient, and considerate. We must in turn be appreciative of their efforts, cooperative, and grateful to God for this useful means of communicating with others.

The Civil Service Employment

Several million citizens are employed by the United States government. These people must not only be qualified to do their work well but they, as other citizens, must also take their pledge of allegiance seriously as they perform their tasks. Their loyalty, faithfulness, and obedience are extremely important.

How are the persons who fill these positions selected? When George Washington began to make appointments to governmental positions, he thought that fitness for office was the leading qualification. Soon, however, appointments began to be given only to members of a president's political party who were fit for office. President Jackson misused his power to appoint government workers under the "spoils system" when he dismissed many faithful government workers and gave their jobs to those who had helped him to become President. Only after President Garfield was shot by a disappointed office-seeker did Congress pass the Pendleton Act in 1883. This act provided that the Civil Service Commission be appointed.

Part of the Commission's task was to find the necessary qualified people to keep the government running smoothly, primarily through a series of standardized tests that ensured a level of proven competency. In

The Fermi 2 power plant, located 35 miles south of Detroit, safely produces more than 1,100 megawatts of electricity, enough power to serve a city of about one million people. In operation since 1988, the plant is one of over 100 commercial nuclear plants in the country, which supply about 19 percent of the nation's electricity. Nuclear plants do not burn fuel for energy, so they emit no greenhouse gases or other pollutants. They are part of the nation's fuel mix, including coal, oil, natural gas, solar and wind, that ensures we are not reliant on one type of fuel source to generate electricity.

1972 and 1981, lawsuits were filed that claimed the tests were biased because African-Americans and Hispanics who didn't score as well on average. Temporary makeshift hiring procedures were put in place, which are still in effect over twenty years later. Federal hiring is now a decentralized hodge-podge of forms and interviews across the departments. About 80% of government jobs are filled through questionnaires and background checks of work and educational experience, and not though a written test, despite the fact that most businesses, universities, and now federally-mandated standardized testing for public schools, employ the testing method for evaluating competency.

Do you remember what you have read?

1. Make a list of the departments of the President's Cabinet. Beside the name of each, write the name of the present department head.
2. Which department of the President's Cabinet would be responsible for each of the following items?
   a. granting a patent
   b. helping to settle a strike
   c. assisting in providing housing for people with low incomes
   d. prosecuting a person who entered our nation illegally
   e. making a trade treaty with Japan
   f. studying air safety
   g. closing a mine that is unsafe
   h. operating the Denver mint
   i. carrying on a research program on heart disease
   j. helping a farmer plan for contour plowing
   k. signing a contract for the building of an aircraft carrier
   l. approving proposed oil pipelines
   m. supporting educational research projects
3. What are the qualifications for a Cabinet member?
4. How does a person become a Cabinet member?
5. How do Cabinet members help the President?

For further thought

1. Suppose you were the only one who witnessed an accident caused by someone who broke the law. What would be your responsibility as a Christian citizen?
2. Some say that inmates in prison are treated so well that a term in prison is not a real punishment. What do you think?
3. Does the United States have a duty to provide food for people outside of its own borders?
4. The Treasury Department collects income taxes. What are some of the difficulties that face the Internal Revenue Service each year?
5. Which cabinet member do you feel is most important? Why?
6. Why is it wise to invite the Vice-President and the delegate to the United Nations to the meetings of the President's Cabinet?
7. Why is it good that a person does not have to write race or religion on the application for a Civil Service job?
8. Why is the merit system better than the spoils system?
9. Why is it a good thing that a member of a subversive organization cannot be hired to work for our government?
10. How do present-day child labor laws affect you?

Research projects

1. Labor problems demand a large amount of attention from government agencies. To learn more about the labor union movement and labor laws, select one of the following for careful study:
   Union Development
       Knights of Labor, Railroad Brotherhood, AFL (American Federation of Labor), CIO (Congress of Industrial Organizations), Christian Labor Association
   Labor Laws
       Norris-LaGuardia (Anti-injunction) Act, Taft-Hartley (Labor-Management Relations) Act, Wagner (National Labor Relations) Act.
2. Select a problem that our nation is facing as it deals with other nations. Write a brief report

on it, giving some reasons or causes for the problem and some possible ways to solve it.

3. The Federal Bureau of Investigation has gathered information about many persons and organizations in our nation and throughout the world. Should their power to do so be limited or expanded? Why?

4. Give an oral report on the United States Secret Service (called the "T-men").

Things to do

1. Construct a bulletin board using the caption, "The State Department in Action." Mount news items about its activities.

2. Make a study of solar, wind, and atomic energy and try to determine which would be the best solution for our nation's energy needs.

3. Draw a map of the United States. Put on it ten of the major national parks and give important features of each.

4. Research the budget and financial reports of the expenditures of one of the Cabinet departments. Discuss the ways in which federal funds have been used.

5. Give a written or an oral report to your classmates on "The Cabinet—the President's Helpers." Aspects that could be the basis for your report are: origin, number of members, method of appointment, term of office, basis of selection, and duties.

6. Hold a class discussion on ways the Department of Transportation should deal with the nation's transportation problems.

7. Select a topic of importance to your community from the following list and make a study of possible solutions: Pollution of some aspect of the environment; Availability of good health care; How is the government helping to resolve these concerns?; What else should the government be doing to resolve them?

Words to study

antidote	passport
balance	patent
budget	predecessor
Cabinet	seismologist
deficit	slum
immigration	subversive
parole	visa

Chapter 17

Selection of leaders— liberty in action

Important ideas to look for:
- Throughout most of our history a two-party system has existed.
- The two-party system helps to bring stability to our government.
- Political parties have important responsibilities in the affairs of government.
- Voting is one of our most precious liberties.

Liberty demands responsible citizenship

The tyranny of a prince in an oligarchy is not so dangerous to the public welfare as the apathy of a citizen in a democracy.

—Montesquieu

In a republic laws are made by leaders elected by the people. One of the chief ways of using our liberty in America is to select these leaders to make our laws. Intelligent voting is one aspect of liberty in action.

Voting demands a choice

When voting, a person must make a choice among candidates. When an initiative, a referendum, or some other issue comes up at an election, the voter must choose to be for or against it.

To select the most qualified candidate for a government office, or to support the best provisions before the people, the voter must study the issues and know the candidate's stand on political questions. The voter has the liberty to choose, but a choice must be made.

Not only must the voter prepare for the day of election by studying candidates and issues, but many other preparations also need to be made. Candidates must be selected and issues presented. Campaigns must bring the political questions of the day to the attention of the voters. Office seekers must take a stand on political questions that face the nation or community. Much of this preparatory work is done by the leaders of our political parties.

A two-party system

Political parties are not new. They had existed in other nations for many years before our nation began. They developed in the United States when it was time to ratify the Constitution. Then the Federalists favored the strong national government that the Constitution would provide. The Anti-Federalists were not in favor of such strong federal government. Since that time there have been two major political parties in our nation. During some periods of history, the party differences have been small but at other times there have been sharp differences on many issues. Party names have changed, and questions about government have shifted through the years, but the two-party system has remained.

Occasionally a third party gathers around

an issue. For example, the Greenback Party grew out of an issue about printing more paper money. When the problem was settled, the political party concerned about it was dissolved. In the 1992 election, an Independent Party candidate, Ross Perot, received over 19 million votes (over 18.6% of the popular vote) because people were dissatisfied with the candidates of the two major parties. The ideas of minor parties are often taken over by a major party. Thus the minor party may influence political life even though no minority party candidate has won a presidential election.

Advantages of the two-party system If there were fifteen political parties, a candidate could get more votes than any of the other candidates and still not have the support of very many people. In a two-party system the winning candidate can enter office with the assurance that a majority of the voters preferred him. Thus a two-party system helps to stabilize our government. Under this system, a candidate who is unsuccessful in one election is free to run for office again in the next election. We have the freedom to disagree with the party that holds the power of governmental office. We may use our freedom of speech and the freedom of the press to work for removal of that party from office at the next election. This is not revolution. It is simply the use of our liberty. This liberty could not be used under a one-party system, for to work against a government with a one-party system would be trying to overthrow the government. The two-party system has served quite well as a means of keeping the party in office sensitive to the concerns of the voters.

Disadvantages of the two-party system Although the two-party system has provided elected officials as often as the Constitution demands, some have questioned whether there might possibly be a better way. The Constitution says nothing about political parties, whether there should be one, two, many, or none.

Presidential elections since 1900
by percentage of popular vote
Note: the percentages of popular vote for the Democrats plus the Republicans
do not equal 100% because of the Independent voters.

		Democrat	Republican			Democrat	Republican
1900	McKinley (R)	46.5	52.8	1956	Eisenhower (R)	42.2	57.8
1904	Roosevelt (R)	38.8	58.2	1960	Kennedy (D)	50.1	49.9
1908	Taft (R)	44.2	53.0	1964	Johnson (D)	61.3	38.7
1912	Wilson (D)	42.5	23.6	1968	Nixon (R)	42.9	43.6
1916	Wilson (D)	38.8	36.3	1972	Nixon (R)	37.7	60.9
1920	Harding (R)	34.9	61.6	1976	Carter (D)	50.6	48.5
1924	Coolidge (R)	29.0	54.3	1980	Reagan (R)	42.4	51.0
1928	Hoover (R)	40.9	58.3	1984	Reagan(R)	36.8	63.2
1932	Roosevelt (D)	57.8	39.9	1988	Bush (R)	46.1	53.9
1936	Roosevelt (D)	62.2	37.4	1992	Clinton (D)	43.3	37.7
1940	Roosevelt (D)	54.9	44.9	1996	Clinton (D)	50.1	41.4
1944	Roosevelt (D)	53.7	46.1	2000	W. Bush (R)	52.1	47.9
1948	Truman (D)	49.7	45.2	2004	W. Bush (R)	49.3	50.7
1952	Eisenhower (R)	44.6	55.4	2008	Obama (D)	52.9	47.1

One disadvantage of having only two main political parties is that this system leaves little choice to voters who may think that both parties have weak programs or poorly qualified candidates. These voters now have their choice of: (1) not voting at all, (2) voting for representatives of a very small party who will probably not win or even be generally noticed, or (3) voting for candidates of the party that has the better of the two programs offered by the two major parties. Christians especially have been uneasy about having to vote between two candidates who have little or no concern for the principles of the Bible. Perhaps a multiple-party system of electing officials would give each group of voters a better opportunity to vote in keeping with its principles.

One way in which some democratic nations have tried to become more fair to each group of voters is to have proportional representation. By this arrangement each political party is allowed to elect a percentage of representatives roughly equal to the percentage of votes the party received in the last election. Whether or not such a multiple-party system would be a good arrangement in our nation is difficult to determine, for it has never been tried. Many changes in our political procedures would be necessary before this could happen. In any case, Christians should always be on the lookout for new and better ways to be an influence for good in the political life of our country as well as in every other area of life.

To succeed, a candidate also needs campaign funds. Many citizens send small contributions to support the campaign of their favorite candidates. In the last few decades many corporations, unions, and professional groups have formed Political Action Committees (PACs). These PACs exercise their influence in both the choice of candidates and in collecting larger sums of money to support the candidate's campaign.

Duties of political parties One of the main functions handled by political parties is the **selection of candidates for public office**. After a candidate has been chosen, the political party also helps his campaign by giving him publicity and by urging party members to vote for him.

The **adoption of a party platform** is important because the platform tells the voters what stand that political party has taken on public issues. Also it contains goals which the party will attempt to achieve if elected.

Political party campaigns help to **arouse the interest of citizens in their government**. They force government leaders to give information to the voters. By criticizing the opposition party and by answering the people who criticize them, the political party leaders give the voters a look at both sides of a question. Newspapers, radio, television, billboards, signs, buttons, the Internet and personal appearances are all used to arouse interest and gain the votes of the people.

But the political party has services to perform between elections as well as during the campaign. In fact, its real function is most evident in the lawmaking process. The legislation proposed by the President or a governor, and the laws passed by the Congress or a state legislature, will generally reflect the political thinking or position of the party members.

After a candidate has been elected, the political party tries to **make the officeholder do his work well**. To accomplish this, the members of the party in each legislative body (national, state, or local) usually appoint one of their members to be *party whip*. The party whip tries to convince each member to vote the way the party promised in its platform. Party members realize that unless officeholders do their work well, they will not be reelected when their terms expire.

Under our two-party system, members of the party which is out of power **carefully watch everything done by those in office**.

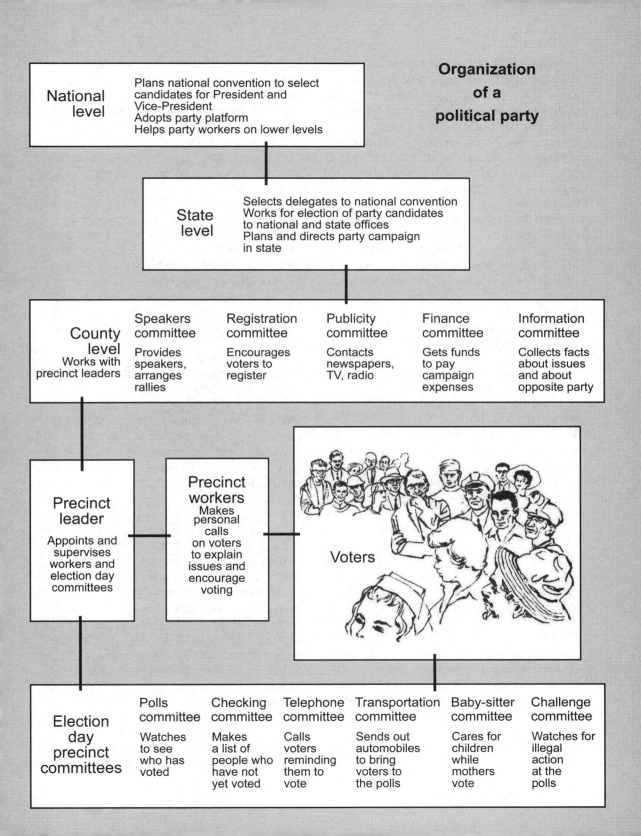

Organization of a political party

National level
Plans national convention to select candidates for President and Vice-President
Adopts party platform
Helps party workers on lower levels

State level
Selects delegates to national convention
Works for election of party candidates to national and state offices
Plans and directs party campaign in state

County level
Works with precinct leaders

Speakers committee	Registration committee	Publicity committee	Finance committee	Information committee
Provides speakers, arranges rallies	Encourages voters to register	Contacts newspapers, TV, radio	Gets funds to pay campaign expenses	Collects facts about issues and about opposite party

Precinct leader
Appoints and supervises workers and election day committees

Precinct workers
Makes personal calls on voters to explain issues and encourage voting

Voters

Election day precinct committees

Polls committee	Checking committee	Telephone committee	Transportation committee	Baby-sitter committee	Challenge committee
Watches to see who has voted	Makes a list of people who have not yet voted	Calls voters reminding them to vote	Sends out automobiles to bring voters to the polls	Cares for children while mothers vote	Watches for illegal action at the polls

Organization of political parties A political party is an organization of citizens who agree in a general way on what government policies should be. Often members of the same political party differ from one another on many details, but they think the same way about most of the main problems. These political parties try to control the government in a legal way by having their candidates elected to public office.

Both the Republican and Democratic parties are made up of citizens from every part of American society—farmers and business people, factory owners and their workers, servicemen and civilians, citizens of every race, and members of all religious faiths. **Membership in our American political parties depends merely on a matter of agreement with the party platform and willingness to vote for the party candidates.** The freedom to choose a political party is part of the liberty that our nation provides.

To succeed, an organization needs active leadership. This leadership is provided in the political parties by those members who are most earnest and eager for the success of the organization.

Not enough Christians take the challenge for political leadership seriously. Nevertheless, Christian leadership in political parties is very necessary if our nation is to be a Christian nation.

Just as we have local, state, and national governments, so the political parties are organized on these same three levels. The local level, or "*grass roots*," of the party is made up of the *precinct* and county leaders. The precinct organization is closest to the people. On this level party workers call on the voters, explain and discuss the issues, and do all they can to get people to vote for their candidates. The county committee helps the leaders of all the precincts in a county.

The state committees are in charge of campaigns for the election of state candidates. They also regulate the election or appointment of delegates to the national convention. The national committee directs preparations for the national convention, plans campaigns for the Presidency and Vice-Presidency, and helps all state and local committees in their efforts to win elections.

Although many people belong to a party and vote a *straight ticket* for that party's candidates, many other citizens are *independent voters*. Independents do not belong to any party; they feel free to vote for one party in one election and the other party in the next. Often they vote a *split ticket*, voting for some of the Democratic candidates and some of the Republican candidates. Independent voters sometimes form organizations to work for candidates they consider well qualified, regardless of the candidates' political affiliation.

Presidential primaries Political leaders who desire to be nominated as the presidential candidate for their party often enter primary elections and campaign for votes in many states before the time of the national convention. The voters of these states show by their ballots in the primary elections whom they would like to have as the presidential candidate for their party. The convention delegates from such states are thus guided in their choice. In this way a candidate may be assured of a large number of votes before the balloting officially begins at the national convention, and demonstrates to party members that he is a good vote-getter.

National conventions National political conventions are usually held in July, several months before the November presidential election. The political party assigns each state a definite number of votes according to a formula drawn up by the national committee. At one recent convention the Democrats allowed each state to have twice as many votes as it had members in Congress. In addition, each state that voted Democratic in the last presidential election was allowed a bonus of four votes. The Republican plan for

THE CRADLE OF THE G.O.P.

ROLL OF HONOR
A. LINCOLN
U.S. GRANT
R.B. HAYES
J. A. GARFIELD
B. HARRISON
W. McKINLEY

FIRST REPUBLICAN CONVENTION HELD AT LAFAYETTE HALL, PITTSBURG, PA, FEB. 22ᴰ 1856.

The aim of the Republican Party, formed in 1854, was to prevent the extension of slavery.

assigning votes to states was a bit different, but it also gave bonus votes to states that had voted Republican. Both parties also assign delegates to the District of Columbia and to possessions and territories of the United States. According to these formulas, there were more than 2000 delegates in attendance at each convention.

Often states send more delegates than they have votes, so each delegate has only part of one vote. Each delegate usually has an alternate.

From the moment delegates begin to arrive, the feeling of tense excitement begins. Newspaper reporters, radio announcers, and television crews prepare to bring the convention proceedings to the people of the nation. The hall is gaily decorated with flags and banners. Red, white, and blue ribbons are everywhere. The delegations of the states gather around their state banners. Many delegations bring their own bands. Sounds of shouting, clapping, and singing fill the air. When all the state delegations have arrived and have been officially seated by the Credentials Committee, the party officials enter the hall. Wave after wave of applause is accompanied by many hats thrown into the air. Much handshaking and backslapping is done.

Soon the temporary chairman calls the convention to order, and the huge hall becomes silent. Everyone rises while "The Star-Spangled Banner" is played and a chaplain may lead an opening prayer asking for God's blessing upon our nation and His guidance in the selection of a presidential candidate.

During the opening days of the convention, many party officers are elected. The party platform, which tells what the party has accomplished in the past and what it plans to do if elected, is presented by the committee that was asked to prepare it. The policies of the party are debated and changed so that they will please the greatest number of party members and independent voters. When the party platform has been approved by the delegates, the important business of nominating and electing a presidential candidate begins.

The chairman of the convention calls the roll of the states in alphabetical order. The chairman of any state delegation that wishes to do so then makes a speech nominating a candidate for President. After much applause, another speech supporting the nomination takes place. Sometimes a state delegation honors a favorite person called a *favorite son* from its own state by nominating him for the office of President.

After all the nominations have been made, the roll call for voting begins. On the first ballot the states sometimes vote for their own candidate. When the name of a state is called, the chairman of the delegation rises to announce the state's votes. As the voting continues, the states' "favorite sons" change their votes to the candidate that they feel is best qualified to serve as the President of our nation. When one candidate receives a majority, the excitement of the convention reaches its peak. The delegates wave banners and parade around the hall as they sing and shout. Another vote is generally taken to give unanimous support to the candidate of the party. Occasionally a candidate who is the choice of all the delegates may be nominated by *acclamation* rather than by the usual voting process.

The procedure for selecting a vice-presidential candidate is similar, but the delegates generally follow the wishes of the presidential candidate. This is done to make sure that the candidates will work well together during the campaign and throughout their term of office. After the candidate for Vice-President has been selected, the candidates generally make their acceptance speeches amid the overwhelming applause of the delegates.

Although it would seem that a national political convention is disorderly and run more by emotion and political pressure than by good judgment, it is serious business. Here the party platform is adopted. Through the convention processes the candidates who will run for the highest offices in our land are officially chosen, although the party members may have already indicated their choice through the primary elections. The delegates realize that their party must have candidates who are capable of providing good leadership. They choose the best they have, because otherwise the citizens would not vote for their candidates and their party would lose the election. A political party must pick its best candidates, not only to win the election, but primarily to lead our nation, under God, in the years ahead.

Selecting our candidates through the national convention is one good illustration of liberty in action. You are free to become a member of any political party; you have the liberty to work and to become a leader in that party. If you become a leader, you may be able to represent your area as a delegate to a national convention and help in the selection of presidential candidates.

Freedom to help in the selection of candidates is only one part of liberty in action. We also have the freedom to run for office ourselves. Whether we are seeking to become a senator representing our state in Congress or a city council member representing our neighborhood in our own town, we have the liberty to *campaign* for votes in order to be elected to office. We may even choose to run for office as a *nonpartisan* candidate;

Political conventions are attended by elected delegates, candidates, and other party leaders.

that is, without belonging to any particular political party.

The freedom to hold office in our government is not taken seriously enough by most Christians. It is a task they usually leave for someone else. Although we may be thankful for the Christians who are willing to use their time, talents, and freedom to run for public office, we need many more who are willing to do so. This is an opportunity of service to God that has been overlooked too long.

Do you remember what you have read?

1. What advantages does the two-party system have over a system with many political parties? Over a one-party system?
2. Why does voting demand a choice?
3. Name five things that political parties do for our country.

4. What is required of a person who wants to join a political party?
5. What do we mean when we say a person is an independent voter?
6. How does a person become a leader in a political party?
7. In what order do states vote at a national political convention?
8. Why do the leaders of a political party generally ask the presidential candidate whom he would like to have as a vice-presidential candidate?

For further thought

1. Discuss Christians who you know are in politics or government on the local, state, and national levels. What positions do they hold and what parties do they represent?
2. Do Christians generally realize they should

Selection of leaders—liberty in action 205

take a more active role in politics? In what ways can an elected Christian official exert a good influence in government?

3. Recent presidential candidates have successfully received the support of a majority of the delegates prior to the convention itself. Is there a danger that this method of choosing a candidate fails to reflect the wishes of the people who support the party?

Research projects

1. Write an essay on or discuss the topic "Why I Choose to Belong to the . . . (Democratic or Republican) . . . Party."
2. Arrange for an interview with some local office-holder. Try to find the answers to the following questions and obtain any other information you can about his work:

    Why did he decide to run for office?

    What things did he do to win the election?

    What are some of the main problems connected with serving in his office?

Words to study

acclamation	party whip
favorite son	precinct
"grass roots"	split ticket
independent voter	stabilize
nonpartisan	straight ticket
party platform	

Campaign Process

James Garfield, the twentieth president of the United States declared, "Next in importance to freedom and justice is popular education, without which neither freedom nor justice can be permanently maintained." The process of educating the voting public about the choices to be made in each election is called the campaign process. Much of the work of the political parties centers on the campaigns. Their primary role is to nominate a candidate for office and work to get that person elected. But there is much that goes on long before that step.

A person who wants to be considered as a candidate must first meet the specific qualifications for that office, such as age and residency. But beyond these concrete requirements, there are general expectations that should be considered, such as experience, character, and leadership abilities. This, of course, assumes that the general public knows enough about the potential candidate to evaluate these qualities. So the first step in the campaign process is to examine the viability of a run for office. This is known as testing the waters. This can be done informally by talking with people involved in the government, party politics, and potential donors. But much of it is done formally through public opinion polls, *focus groups*, and research, in an effort to measure how many people have heard of the potential candidate and know his or her stance on the issues. Name recognition is a key factor in raising the necessary funds and volunteers to run a successful campaign. As you can guess, the person who currently holds the office has a big advantage in these areas already. The current office-holder is called the *incumbent*.

If the campaign seems viable, the potential candidate will assemble a campaign staff. The staff will consist of a few paid individuals, a host of volunteers, and often a political consultant who specializes in running campaigns. The team will then set a campaign strategy. This strategy will include defining the candidate's position on key issues, the theme of the campaign, how to raise and spend the funds available, and how to schedule the candidate's time. Part of the theme of a campaign is whether it will be a positive or negative campaign. A positive campaign focuses more on what the candidate can do if elected to office. A negative campaign focuses more on the job the incumbent did or did not do while in office. When the negative reports deal more with the candidate's character or lifestyle rather than the voting record, and purposely cast suspicion, this is called *mudslinging*.

The goal of the campaign strategy is to reach as many *constituents* as possible. The constituents are those people who reside in the district being represented by that office. Ideally, the purpose of the campaign strategy should be to find the best way to inform the voters. In practice, it often has more to do with swaying than providing information. In our diverse and splintered society, too many specifics can alienate potential voters. Much effort goes into saying just enough to gain votes, and saying it in a general way without offering details, so that a wide array of special-interest groups can support the candidate.

Given the size of the constituency in a presidential campaign, it can take a lot of time to create name recognition and communicate the candidate's positions. Most campaigns begin at least a year before the primary elections, some even earlier. More time means more money is needed to maintain the campaign. In the 2008 campaign, $2.4 billion was spent on the presidential race; over $1 billion of which was spent by the two major candidates. Barack Obama spent $730 million and John McCain spent $333 million. Compare this to the $718 million spent in 2004 and $343 million in 2000. The rising costs of campaigning have caught the attention of many people who are concerned about maintaining our freedom and liberty. The high costs can restrict who can afford to run for office. It can also lead to wealthy citizens and organizations having a disproportionate influence on the elections.

Campaign finance reform. Does money mean influence? Does greater access to money sources translate into unfair advantages? Those are two of the main assumptions behind efforts to reform the campaign process. The Federal Election Campaign Act of 1971 instituted the equal time rule whereby radio and television stations operating under federal licenses had to give equal coverage to the candidates. The Supreme Court struck down several other aspects of the law in 1974. Congress then attempted to amend it throughout the 1970's, with portions of those laws being struck down as well. One element of the legislation that was upheld was making public financing available for qualified presidential candidates during the primary and general elections. These funds come from a unique source. Near the top of the first page of the U.S. Federal Income Tax Form 1040, there is a box that tax filers can check to contribute three dollars to the general election fund. The Federal Election Commission was established in 1975 by Congress to oversee the public funding as well as enforcing the legislation and disclosing campaign finance information.

The concerns regarding influence still remain. Legislation has been submitted to Congress over the past decades that includes calls for increased disclosure of contributors and limits on the amounts that can be contributed. These limits are applied differently to individuals and organizations. Distinctions have been made between giving funds directly to a candidate's campaign and issue-oriented campaigns. These limits added two more phrases to the campaign funding mix: hard money and soft money. Hard money refers to the contributions that are regulated by law. Soft money refers to funds donated to political parties in a way that gets around those regulations. The Bipartisan Campaign Reform Act of 2002, more commonly referred to as the McCain–Feingold Act, sought to correct these abuses. The intricacies of these laws have birthed a variety of funding organizations such as Political Action Committees (PAC's) and Authorized Campaign Committees. The latter is why you hear a line at the end of a campaign commercial stating that the candidate authorized the ad. PAC's are divided into those that support multiple candidates and those that do not. The fact that the word *bipartisan* was included in the 2002 law shows that the problem is recognized by individuals in both parties and across the political spectrum.

Another ruling by a federal court in 2010 spawned Super PAC's, technically known as independent expenditure-only committees. Such organizations may raise unlimited sums of money from corporations, unions, associations, and individuals. The unlimited funds can be used to advocate for or against political candidates, but may not be contributed directly to the political candidate. The Super PAC must report the donations and sources to the Federal Election Commission on a monthly or quarterly basis.

Adding to the difficulty of defining restrictions and limits is the abundance of issue advocacy ads. Sometimes referred to as "electioneering communications," these ads discuss issues that are often split along parties lines. They can indirectly or overtly provide support for the party's candidate. Attempts to regulate these have also been successfully challenged in the courts. In all of the cases, the issue comes down to the public's right to hear and be heard, whether through financial contributions or through the media. Critics of reform legislation argue that in an effort to restrict abuses, the right to free speech is curtailed.

Shaping public opinion. Our representative form of government requires an informed electorate to function properly. Each citizen is obligated to take the responsibility to become informed. That may not be as easy as it sounds. The reason is the difference between information and *public opinion*. An opinion is a belief or conclusion held with confidence. It may or may not be based on accurate information or proof. For example, a person may automatically vote for a candidate simply because he or she belongs to a

A town meeting is a typical campaign stop for presidential candidates.

particular party, whether or not the voter has evaluated the candidate's positions. Another definition says that an opinion is the prevailing view. Voting based simply on who is the most popular or which stance is the most widely-held one undermines the principles on which a republic is established.

The irony is that even though we live at a time in history where information can be shared almost instantly, it is often difficult to find objective, accurate, and complete information. Much effort goes into putting the right spin on a candidate's position, and that presentation can vary depending on the audience. This doesn't mean the candidate is deliberately trying to mislead. But it does help to recognize why candidates seem to flip-flop on the issues so much. It is not uncommon for campaigns to be based on talking points. These are key phrases or buzz words that the candidate wants to emphasize. Ideally, they should summarize the candidate's positions, but often they are designed to be easily remembered rather than give specifics.

One reason why such ambiguous talking points have become so popular is the role of the media in campaigns. In the past, newspapers were the primary source of election information. Now radio, television, and the Internet are the primary sources. These mediums all favor short bits of information commonly referred to as sound bites. These are catch phrases that capture the viewers' attention. They may or may not be the key points. Since only so much coverage is available, reporters can only summarize a candidate's presentation. Inevitably, some material will be cut. Depending on the reporter or editing staff's perspective, what gets cut and what is aired can greatly influence how the material comes across. Comments can be taken out of context so that they mean something quite different. Slanting information on purpose in this way is called *bias*.

An important step in combating bias is to examine the source of the information. Just because something appears in the media does not mean it is true. In a few cases, something can be communicated on purpose that is knowingly false. This is called *disinformation*. It is becoming more prevalent, particularly through the Internet, since anyone can post anything and remain anonymous. Opinions can be shared that have little or no basis in fact. Supporters of such social media point to the right of free speech, paying little attention to the right not to be slandered or libeled. Critics argue that this encourages voters to focus more on public opinion than on accurate information.

In order to evaluate the source of information, you need to identify the underlying point of view of the author. This is known as a *worldview.* A worldview is based on the core values, beliefs, and assumptions about life that a person holds. A worldview answers the "big questions" about life. For example, what is truth and can it be known? In our post-modern culture, the answer to that question for many people is that there are no absolute truths and what is true is relative, based on the situation. To see how worldview can affect the campaign process, consider the history of journalism. In the mid-1900's, journalists were expected to remain as objective as possible when reporting the news. Any hint of personal opinion was edited out. If the news reporter felt strongly about the topic, he or she could write an article for the Op-Ed page (short for Opinion and Editorial page). Opinions were clearly marked as such, and the reader could evaluate the person's opinion based on the supporting evidence that was offered. By the end of the twentieth century, the distinction between objective news reporting and opinion pieces was blurred.

The 1960 elections marked another turning point in campaigns. This was the first time a presidential election had occurred when the majority of households had televisions. The first televised debates pitted the then Vice President Richard Nixon against a relatively unknown senator from Massachusetts, John F. Kennedy. Kennedy was young, handsome, and charismatic. Nixon was not. Political commentators remarked that if the debates were evaluated based on tactics and points made, Nixon won. Yet Kennedy was deemed the overall winner based on public opinion. He had captured the viewers' attention based on presentation, not necessarily content. This impact of the media has colored the campaign process ever since.

Another way the media influence elections is through public opinion polls. This is where an organization pays a research firm to question portions of the public about their voting intentions and views on the issues. In a small town meeting or caucus, it is possible for every person to voice their intentions. It is impossible to question every person in the nation. Instead a sample is taken that is supposed to represent the entire populace. A reputable research firm goes to great lengths to obtain a representative sample that has similar characteristics to the general population. As you may guess, this is very difficult to achieve. The chances of error can be significant. There is a way to estimate this margin of error, and this plus-or-minus-range should be included whenever statistics are reported.

The nature of public opinion is that the more something is reported, the more it influences public opinion. There are now public opinion polls that seek to measure how much public opinion polls impact public opinion. This tendency of the media's reporting to sway voter habits has raised another issue. Should the media project winners before the polls have closed across the nation? In the 1980 presidential election, one network predicted a victory for Ronald Reagan fifteen minutes after the polls closed on the east coast, based on exit polls of only 20,000 people. *Exit polls* question voters about who they voted for as they exit the polling station. It is assumed that the respondents actually voted for the person they reported. It was only 5:15 pm on

the west coast. When voter turnout dropped significantly, many concluded it was because voters felt there was no longer any reason to vote. Since that election, the networks voluntarily adopted the policy of not projecting a winner within a state until all polls have closed for that state. However, in the 2000 presidential election, it was alleged that some media outlets released exit poll results for Florida before the polls closed in the state's panhandle, which falls under a different time zone. Nor does it fix the issue across the different time zones of our country. In some nations such as Great Britain, it is a criminal offense to report polling results before all polls have closed. In still others, the exit polls have been banned altogether.

Rule by public opinion. The founders of our nation went to great lengths to balance the rule of the majority with the rights of the individual. The checks and balances inserted into our government's structure were designed to guard against abuses of power. The founders recognized the dangers and instability of public opinion. It is important for elected representatives to consider the views of their constituents when making policy decisions. After all, voters who have elected them to office can also vote them out of office. But as we have seen, public opinion can be swayed by factors other than accurate information and valid evidence. Public opinion is often driven by emotional responses to events. Immediately after the 9/11 attacks, there were widespread calls for more intensive screening of passengers at airports. Once the procedures were in place and passengers were faced with long delays, public opinion shifted the other way.

Should a congressional representative only consider the views of the constituency when making policy decisions or should the needs of the whole country be considered as well? One example is known as pork-barrel spending. This refers to federal funds given for local projects. Even though these projects,

Political rallies are another way for citizens to express their views and shape public opinion.

such as dams, libraries, and road construction, only benefit a small area, it was assumed that what helps one part of the nation helps the nation as a whole. In practice, however, the projects can be outlandish, obscure, and over-priced for what the local district gets for the money. In many cases, the projects are designed simply to gain the financial support of specific individuals or organizations in the office-holder's district. The funding provision is often tacked onto a totally unrelated piece of legislation in order to force the rest of the representatives to vote for it, thus by-passing the normal evaluation procedures. In 2010, Citizens Against Government Waste identified 9,129 of these projects buried in the twelve appropriation acts. Those projects added $16.5 billion dollars to the budget deficit.

Should the representatives follow the party lines in voting since the party officials helped elect them to office, or should they follow their conscience? Should the president or any other elected official push a policy that goes against the majority of public opinion if he or she believes it is in the best interest of the nation? These are not easy questions to answer. In every case, they assume that the individuals involved respect and honor God, His authority, and His principles. It has been said that we no longer live in a society based on biblical principles. If that is true, these questions become even harder to answer.

Political labels and ideology. While our country favors a two-party system, the two major parties vying for power have changed throughout our history. To complicate matters, the labels attached to the same platform have changed. In other cases, the same word is attached to different platforms. In still other cases, positions on certain issues have shifted from one party to the opposite one. The chart of presidential elections in the appendix shows some of these changing party labels. The two major labels that illustrate opposite ends of the political spectrum are *conservative* (known as right-wing) and *liberal* (known as left-wing). Generally speaking, liberals believe the government should take an increasing role in the lives of the citizens. If this means more regulations, restrictions, services, and taxes to pay for this increased role, then those should be legislated accordingly. While they believe the government needs to be able to protect and defend the nation, they favor less spending for the military and more emphasis on global peace initiatives. They tend to favor higher taxes, especially on the wealthy, rejecting the idea that such taxes hinder economic growth. Conservatives believe that government should have a restricted role in the lives of the citizens. Regulations should be kept to the minimum in order to foster the free enterprise system upon which this nation was built. What services are deemed necessary should be provided by state and local offices or the *private sector* whenever possible. While they believe our nation needs to cooperate with global peace initiatives, they do not favor doing so at the expense of national sovereignty. They also favor more funding on the military to protect our national interests as well as lower taxes on the wealthy to stimulate economic growth. When it comes to social issues, the stances flip. Liberals are more likely to favor less control and invite more openness. Conservatives are more likely to favor more control and protect traditional values.

As with any label, the definitions are not clear cut. Within each label, you can find ultra-conservative conservatives, moderate conservatives, and liberal conservatives. You can find conservative liberals, moderate liberals, and ultra-liberal liberals. Liberals who promote rapid reform on a large scale are known as Progressives. Democrats who hold a liberal stance on government and regulation, yet hold to more conservative views on the social issues are known as Blue Dog Democrats. President George W. Bush promoted the term "compassionate conservatives" in the 2000 and 2004 elections. The phrase described those individuals who favor conservative views of limited government and conservative values on social issues, yet assert the need to provide for those who are less fortunate through some sort of government intervention.

Thomas Jefferson, the primary architect of the Declaration of Independence and a member of the committee who drafted the Constitution, cautioned that "the natural progress of things is for liberty to yield and government to gain ground." Jean Jacques Rousseau, whose writings provided much of the ideological framework for our nation, added the following warning. "Free people, remember this maxim: we may acquire liberty, but it is never recovered if it is once lost." Friedrich A. von Hayek, a noted Austrian economist and political philosopher of the twentieth century, wrote: "Emergencies have always been the pretext on which the safeguards of individual liberty have been eroded." President Ronald Reagan was fond of offering this reminder: "Freedom is never more than one generation away from extinction. We didn't pass it to our children in their bloodstream. It must be fought for, protected, and handed on for them to do the same." President James Madison likewise reminded the American people. "I believe there are more instances of the abridgment of freedom of the people by the gradual and silent encroachments by those in power than by violent and sudden usurpations." Thomas Jefferson's assertion that "democracy demands an educated and informed electorate" means that the issues raised here cannot be ignored. The number of voices raised in warning suggests that the issue can be easily overlooked. Every citizen has the responsibility to be diligent in recognizing and understanding the issues faced by our country.

The use of the ballot

One of the best illustrations of liberty in action is the voting process. To many students in your class, voting may simply mean that your parents go to the polls on election day to mark a piece of paper, punch a hole on a card, or perhaps move some levers on a machine. Actually voting is using one of the most precious freedoms we have in America. It is carrying out one of the greatest responsibilities a citizen can have in our republic.

Requirements for voting are generally set by state law. The national Constitution does say, however, that every state, in setting requirements, must give equal rights to people of all the different races and to women as well as to men.

A few of the other voting requirements made by most states are:
1. Voters must be citizens of the United States.
2. Voters must be legal residents of the precinct or district in which the vote is cast.
3. Voters must be at least eighteen years old, sane, and not in prison. A primary election may require them to declare their party preferences, but such a procedure is never followed in a general election.
4. Voters must register with the clerk of their voting district or precinct several weeks

Unfortunately, voter turnout drops for primaries and off year elections.

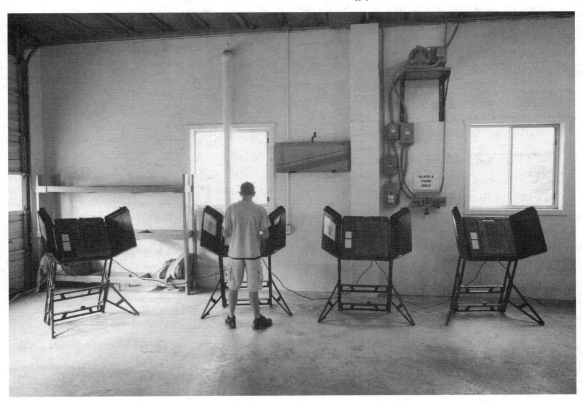

before the election day arrives. This registration book is kept at the polls on election day so the election supervisor may be sure that a voter meets all the requirements. Before being allowed to mark the ballot, voters must sign the registration book. This is done so that a person will not be able to vote twice.

In recent elections, verifying who is eligible to vote and confirming valid ballots have become pivotal issues, and in some cases, may have influenced the winner. In the 2000 election, a problem with "hanging chads," where ballots were not fully punched, went all the way to the Supreme Court. More recently, documented cases of wide-spread voter fraud have been cited. This issue will need to be addressed in order to ensure our freedom of choice is maintained.

Anyone unable to go to the polls on election day may obtain an *absentee ballot* from the local election board. After being marked, the ballot must be put in a sealed envelope and returned to the election officials. They must see that it is counted along with all other votes on election day. Persons in the armed services and citizens visiting or residing in foreign countries may also vote and send ballots to the proper authorities.

Types of elections

Elections of many kinds are held in each community each year. School societies elect school board members. Church congregations elect elders and deacons. Clubs elect their own presidents, vice-presidents, and other officers. Each organization generally requires only one election.

The elections of public officials are, however, divided into two classes—the *primary* and *general elections*. The purpose of the primary election is rather easily understood. If six Republicans and six Democrats all *filed* as candidates for the office of county treasurer, it would be almost impossible for one person to be elected to office with a majority vote on the first ballot. In the primary election the person of each party who receives the most votes is nominated to serve as the candidate of that party in the general election. In the general election the voters must choose their new county treasurer from the two candidates who were nominated by their parties in the primaries.

Between the primary election and the general election the campaign is actively carried on by candidates of both political parties. Telephone poles and vacant buildings are covered with posters and pictures. Debates are carried on in the streets, over the radio, and on television. Citizens everywhere discuss and argue the issues and the qualifications of the candidates. Newspapers give all of the citizens an opportunity to prepare themselves to vote wisely on election day.

When the morning of election day arrives, campaign voices are generally quiet. Voters go to the polls to perform the serious obligation of casting their votes. Flags mark the precinct polls and remind voters that they are enjoying an American liberty. The practice of *electioneering*, where campaign workers try to influence voters as they enter the polls is typically prohibited in most locations, or at least restricted.

The citizen steps up to the table of the election official. The official checks to see that the person is properly registered. The voter then signs the registration book. In some precincts, you may mark a paper ballot in a private booth and drop it into a locked ballot box. Other precincts may use voting machines. Precincts that use the computer punch-card system give the voter the needed card. In a private booth, the voter punches holes to indicate the choices. Such computer cards have done much to speed up the process of tallying the votes.

Within 24 hours, in most cases, the will of the people is known. Whether the same officeholders are retained or new ones elected, the continuation of government has been an orderly process.

Voting is a precious liberty

The right to vote, the use of the ballot, is one of our most precious liberties. We must use it wisely to choose the best leaders for our government. As we use our right to vote, we are under God's controlling providence. The ballots cast by our citizens on election day are used to bring God's appointed people to their positions of leadership. We know this is true because the Bible says, ". . . the Most High is sovereign over the kingdoms of men and gives them to anyone he wishes" (Dan. 4:25). When we use our freedom to vote, we help our nation, under God, provide liberty and justice for all.

Do you remember what you have read?
1. What are the advantages of a secret ballot?
2. What advantage do the voting machine and computer punch-card system have over the paper ballot?
3. What is electioneering and why do you think it is discouraged?
4. Under what conditions would a person use an absentee ballot?
5. What is the difference between a primary and a general election?
6. Suppose you should come to the polls just before closing time and ask to vote. How would the election official know whether or not you had already voted earlier in the day?

For further thought
1. Should foreigners living in the United States be allowed to vote? Why or why not?
2. How does our national voting percentage compare with that of other countries? Draw some conclusions from your comparison. Should we make voting compulsory?
3. Discuss the following topics:
   a. Every voter should be a regular member of a political party.
   b. All qualified persons who fail to vote at any

election should be fined.
   c. Every voter should be able to read and write the English language.
   d. Every voter should be required to show photo identification.
   e. Is voting for a write-in candidate wasting or exercising one's voting responsibility?

Things to do
1. Debate this issue. *Resolved:* That presidential and vice-presidential candidates be selected by means of a national primary election instead of party conventions.
2. Write several headlines suitable for newspaper articles covering issues in current politics—local, state, and national. Have some headlines reflect the position of the "in's" and some of the "out's."
3. Make a scrapbook that follows the development of a national, state, or local election.
4. Have members of the class prepare speeches on the benefits of electing women to office.
5. Conduct a survey in your community asking your parents and other adults the following questions. Tabulate the results on a percentage basis.
   a. In how many of the last four national elections have you voted?
   b. Can you name the defeated presidential candidates in the last four elections?
   c. Can you name the two United States senators from your state and the national representative from your district?
6. Make a report on important minor parties (Populist, Prohibition, etc.) in our nation's history. When were they important and what contributions did they make?
7. Hold a mock political convention nominating candidates for President and Vice-President.
8. Investigate the cost of running for political office. Determine how a candidate raises and spends campaign money. Discuss the problems involved in financing a political campaign. Write a policy statement governing political fund contributions to avoid having big contributors buy special favors from candidates.

9. Make a study of the pre-election political activity carried on by a local officeholder during the weeks prior to election. Have a class committee interview that person or someone who was active in the campaign. Discuss and plan things the class could do to help a candidate they wish to support win a bid for election. Carry out the plans.

Words to study

absentee ballot	general election
bias	incumbent
bipartisan	liberal
conservative	literacy test
constituents	mudslinging
disinformation	primary election
electioneering	private sector
exit polls	public opinion
file	worldview
focus groups	

Preparing for the future

Likely most of the men and women who hold government positions of responsibility and leadership today did not plan to do so when they were younger. Instead they became interested in government service later when the opportunity to do so appeared. If such an opportunity for government service arose later in your life, would you be able and willing to accept its challenge? What can you do now to be ready for such service if God would lead you to such an opportunity later?

1. *Obtain a good education.*
   Study many topics and read widely to build your broad general knowledge. Select courses that deal intensively with history, government, and the problems of society.

2. *Develop self-confidence.*
   Join a debate club, volunteer for leadership in chapel, campaign for student-body offices, give oral reports, and take part in oratorical contests.

3. *Develop an interest in public affairs.*
   Read newspapers and news magazines regularly. Discuss current issues with others. An active interest in public affairs does not come to you full-grown when you are an adult—it must be cultivated and developed while you are growing up.

4. *Maintain a good reputation.*
   Practicing good citizenship as you grow up will help you to be a good citizen as an adult. This is one of the best ways to be sure that you will be ready to serve as a public official when you are an adult.

5. *Observe Christian political leaders.*
   Read about Christians who have served in political office. Talk or write to those now serving to learn how they relate their Christian faith to their work in government.

Unit six For all

I pledge allegiance
to the flag of the United States of America
and to the republic for which it stands,
one nation under God, indivisible,
with liberty and justice for all.

Our nation under God must seek
to provide liberty and justice for
all our people because these people
make up our nation. They are our nation.
Every individual person makes up a small
but important part of it. Each person
has an eternal soul; each is an
image-bearer of God. The inalienable
rights of life, liberty, and the
pursuit of happiness have been given
to all by the Creator of all.

Our citizens do not exist for the good
of our government; no, rather
our government was instituted by God
to provide order and to restrain evil
so that the rights of the individual citizen
might be protected. Our nation
is made up of millions of people
widely different in race, religion,
and cultural background.

In this unit we shall study these people
and how, under God's guiding care,
they came to be citizens
of the United States of America.
We shall also see how an immigrant
can become a citizen today.

But in considering "all" of our citizens,
we must not overlook ourselves.
In the final chapter we shall consider
our own responsibilities as we seek
to keep our pledge of allegiance
to our nation under God.

Chapter 18

A nation of immigrants

Important ideas to look for:
- Immigrants came to the United States for various reasons.
- Immigration to the United States is referred to as "old" and "new."
- Immigrants made a great contribution to American culture.
- Our government no longer limits immigration by a national origins quota system.

People from many lands

We are a nation of immigrants. All the people of our country are either immigrants themselves, or descendants of people who were. (Scientists generally agree that even the American Indian originated on another continent.) The ancestors of some of us arrived in America more than three hundred years ago. The forefathers of others have come to America more recently. The United States is called a "pluralistic society" because people of every nationality have come to make their homes here. Out of the different cultural backgrounds of our immigrant people, our nation has developed and grown.

Large-scale immigration

. . . Give me your tired, your poor,
Your huddled masses yearning to breathe free,
The wretched refuse of your teeming shore.
Send these, the homeless, the tempest-tossed
 to me:
I lift my lamp beside the golden door.
 —From "The New Colossus," by Emma
 Lazarus, inscribed on the base of the
 Statue of Liberty

Many early immigrants came to America in search of religious freedom—the Pilgrims, the Puritans, the Quakers, the Huguenots, and some other groups. Some people came because they wanted greater political freedom than they could find in their European homelands. Others came because the nation in which they lived was filled with political unrest or was often at war. The famine in Ireland brought many immigrants from that country. To all of the poor people of other continents, to people who had been made homeless by the ravages of war, to people who lived in "huddled masses," America was a land of golden opportunity.

The old immigration Although the stream of immigrants had been rather steady since the close of the Revolutionary War, the flow began to increase rapidly after 1840. The Homestead Act, passed in 1862, granted 160 acres of land to anyone who would improve it and live on it for five years. This free land brought many settlers to the central and western parts of our country. The Contract Labor Law, passed by Congress in 1864, permitted American factory owners to hire workers in Europe and bring them to America to work. This system enabled many people to come to America who could not otherwise do so because they could not pay their ship fare. Now the factory owner could buy the ticket and take its cost out of the wages the person would later earn in the American factory. In the years before 1890 most of the immigrants came from the

Free land provided by the Homestead Act attracted many immigrants; often whole settlements would travel westward together.

countries of western and northern Europe. These people found it quite easy to adjust to the living conditions in America. They soon learned the English language; they learned the customs in America quickly. They found it easy to feel at home. The immigrants who came to America before 1890 made up what is known as "the old immigration."

The new immigration After 1890 a noticeable change began to take place in the stream of immigrants that was moving from Europe to America. Instead of a majority of people coming from England, Sweden, Norway, Ireland, Germany, and other northern European countries, the immigrants from the countries of southern and eastern Europe came in the largest numbers. Italians, Slavs, Serbs, Russians, Poles, Jews, Greeks, Rumanians, and many others came to take their place in the nation of immigrants. The years of 1890-1920 are called the period of "the new immigration."

When the people of the old immigration arrived in America, land was cheap or free, and plenty of it was available. Factories needed workers, so it was easy to find a job, and housing was not too crowded. They found it quite easy to learn the language and adopt the customs of the people already in the United States.

This statue in New Mexico is dedicated "To the pioneer mother of America, through whose courage and sacrifice the desert has blossomed, the camp became the home, the blazed trail the thoroughfare."

But when the new immigrants began to arrive, the best land had already been claimed. Most of them had to live in the crowded areas of large cities. The best jobs in the factories had already been taken. Because the members of the new immigration were generally very poor, they did whatever work they could find. Working in the mines and factories, they accepted whatever wages they were offered. Because they were willing to work for very low wages, the newer immigrants were disliked by many workers of the old immigration.

The people from southern and eastern Europe found it more difficult to learn the language used in the United States. Their language sounded strange to the earlier immigrants who were now able to talk English.

Because of this language problem, large groups of immigrants from one country would gather to live in some section of a large city. Here they would continue to speak their own language and use their old-world customs. Nearly every large city had a section where Polish was spoken, a "Little Italy," a "Chinatown," or an immigrant group from some other nation. Each of these ethnic groups has contributed to the culture of our country. Gradually, the people of the new immigration also felt more "at home" in America.

Homelands of our immigrants In 1820 our government began to keep a record of the people who entered the United States. Since that time, people of many nations have entered and become citizens of our country. More than a million immigrants came from each of eleven nations in the 173 years between the beginning of 1820 and the end of 1993 (see chart next page).

During the last two decades, the numbers of people coming from certain homelands has shifted with more individuals coming from Mexico, China, and India. Such shifts are not always apparent when statistics are summarized over long time spans. We should remember that while people are immigrating into the United States, there are others *emigrating*, leaving to become citizens of another country. Still, the numbers leaving are nowhere near the number of immigrants.

Do you remember what you have read?

1. From what countries did people of the "old immigration" come to the United States?
2. Why did people of the "new immigration" have so many more problems when they arrived?
3. List five reasons why early immigrants came to America.
4. What is the difference between an emigrant and an immigrant?

Things to do

1. Make a chart showing the names of your parents, your grandparents, and your great grandparents. Show how many were natural

born citizens of the United States and how many came to our country as immigrants.

2. Have a committee of your class conduct a survey of the teachers and pupils in your school to find out how many were born in a foreign country, how many have one or both parents who were born in a foreign land, and how many have one or more grandparents who were born in a foreign country.

3. Visit an old cemetery or museum in your community to find out the names of the earliest settlers. Discuss ways in which their ethnic background and culture has left its influence in your community life today.

Contributions of immigrants

The immigrants who came to America brought with them their ideas and hopes, their skills and energy, their way of life. As these people settled in the United States, the ideas they brought from the Old World mingled with the ideas of the pioneers and people who were already living in America. Under God's providential care, this mixture of ideas from all groups and nationalities of immigrants gradually produced what we call the "melting pot" of our American culture. Immigrants arriving today still add to American culture.

When our nation was just beginning, it was blessed with varied and abundant natural resources. But it takes people to develop resources. Mining coal and working in the steel mills, plowing the prairie sod and cutting down the forests, mixing concrete for buildings and pounding spikes into the heavy railroad ties—much of this hard, tiring, and often low-paid work needed for the development of our natural resources was done by the people who had recently come to America.

Many foreign-born people brought us their inventive talents. Alexander Graham Bell, who was born in Scotland, is a good example of our many foreign-born inventors. Others, like Andrew Carnegie, also from Scotland, became leaders in the world of business and industry. Charles Steinmetz, born in Poland,

taught us a great deal about electricity. Albert Einstein, a German, helped our nation in the field of science with his research in nuclear physics. In the field of music we find that a majority of our prominent figures were foreign-born: Fritz Kreisler in Austria, Victor Herbert in Ireland, Enrico Caruso in Italy, and Serge Koussevitzky in Russia. Samuel Gompers, born in England, became a labor leader in America. Carl Schurz from Germany became a senator and Secretary of the Interior; he helped to start our civil service program.

To this small list could be added the names of many, many other immigrants who have helped America in the past. More could be added every year as new immigrants enter our country to take up their work beside us. For this nation of immigrants, whether they have been here for many years or have recently arrived, our government seeks to provide liberty and justice, hope and opportunity for all.

Homelands of Legal immigrants 1820 to 2011	
Mexico	7,824,123
Germany	7,222,813
United Kingdom	5,433,850
Italy	5,394,801
Ireland	4,782,924
Canada	4,604,505
Former USSR	4,051,170
Austria	2,672,537
Hungary	2,255,724
Sweden	1,698,352
China	1,686,141
France	1,417,876
Norway	854,898
Greece	763,088
India	721,214
Japan	611,448
Netherlands	401,755
All other countries	23,156.488
Total	**75,553,707**

Attitudes toward immigrants

Not many of us know what it is to leave our friends and relatives in order to start a new home in a strange land. We can hardly realize the problems of moving to a new country where people cannot understand us and where we cannot understand them, where the customs of the people are quite different from those we are used to, where we cannot read the signs, and where the laws are strange to us.

If we are truly thankful to God for the blessings of freedom that He has given to us, we should be happy to share these blessings with others who have recently come to our nation. We must be willing to allow others the same freedoms we wish for ourselves. When we do this we will be following the Golden Rule: "Do unto others as you would have others do unto you." This is one of the first rules of Christian citizenship.

It is strange that some people in our nation distrust or dislike the foreign-born newcomers. Most people in the United States are immigrants or descendants of immigrants. The immigrants who came early surely should not look down on those who arrived later; for, as humorist Will Rogers remarked, "Not everybody was able to catch the first boat."

If an immigrant or any newcomer arrives in your school or in your neighborhood, you have an opportunity to carry out Christ's wish: ". . . I was a stranger and you invited me in . . . whatever you did for one of the least of these brothers of mine, you did for me . . ." (Matt. 25:35,40).

Control of immigration

As the stream of immigrants flowing into America increased in size, many citizens became alarmed. They feared that foreign-born people were entering the United States faster than we could train them in the ways of American citizenship.

Others realized that when immigrants came to America, they were often willing to work for lower wages than the Americans were used to receiving. These lower wages tended to lower the American standard of living. This was particularly true on the West Coast of our country, where Chinese coolie labor was being used in mining and railroad-building. In 1882 the Chinese Exclusion Act became our first immigration law. This act allowed Chinese to enter our country for short visits or for study in our schools, but did not permit them to stay, become citizens, and take jobs.

In 1907 President Theodore Roosevelt made a *gentleman's agreement* with Japan. This was not a written law, but the Japanese immigration was greatly restricted.

By 1924 other laws excluded all Oriental people except for temporary visits. Since World War II, Korean War orphans, Vietnamese refugees, and a few other Asians have entered. A foreigner who wishes to enter the United States to work may not do so if United States laborers are available for such labor and if the employment of *aliens* would adversely affect them.

In addition to the Chinese Exclusion Act of 1882, other laws were added that year to keep beggars and stowaways, and criminals and insane people from entering the United States. In 1885 the Contract Labor Law was repealed so that businessmen could no longer hire people in foreign countries and bring them into the United States to work. People with serious contagious and incurable diseases were excluded in 1891. Another restriction, the literacy test, was added in 1917. This test required an adult to read and write in some language before entering the United States. This same law kept out alcoholics and subversive people who believed in the violent overthrow of our government.

Together, these immigration laws kept out many people who could have freely entered before. These laws also provided that any immigrant not permitted to enter had to be taken back to his homeland by the steamship company.

The quota system In spite of all the restrictions, large numbers of immigrants continued to stream into the United States. Because Congress was worried about the widespread unemployment in the United States in 1921, they passed the Emergency Quota Act. In 1924 the Lodge-Johnson Act made the "quota system" more permanent. This act said that a European country could send only a limited number of immigrants to our country in any one year. The quota of a country was to be 2 percent of the number of people from that country in the United States in 1890. This plan favored the countries of northern and western Europe because immigrants from these countries had come in the largest numbers during the old immigration.

Although the original Lodge-Johnson Act quotas have been changed many times, the quota system is still with us today. The *National Origins Act* of 1929 limited the total number of immigrants to 150,000 per year. This lowered the quotas of most countries even more. This act was more fair to the countries of the new immigration because it changed the date for figuring the quota from 1890 to 1920. In 1952 another change was made when the Oriental Exclusion Policy was repealed and all the countries of Asia and the Far East were also included in the quota system.

Between the years 1929 and 1965 the quota of a country was figured as a percentage of the citizens from that country living in the United States at the time of the 1920 census, but no country had a quota of fewer than 100 immigrants per year. Great Britain had the largest quota 65,721; second was Germany with 25,814; other examples would be Holland, 3136; U.S.S.R., 2697; and, far down the list, Japan, 185, and China, 105.

In the wake of the 1964 Civil Rights Act, Congress set out to reevaluate the nation's immigration policies, trying to balance humanitarian and economic factors as well as making the quota system fairer. They phased out the quota system over several years and allowed immigrants from any one, non-Western Hemisphere country to enter on a "first come, first qualified" basis that still stands today. The law increased the totals from countries outside of the western hemisphere to 170,000 per year and established a maximum of 120,000 for Western Hemisphere nations.

For the first time in America's history, Western Hemisphere immigrants, including Latin Americans and Mexicans, were given a numerical ceiling, and special attention was given to refugees. The Immigration Act of 1965 gave high preference to those individuals with special talents or skills needed in our country. In addition, Western Hemisphere immigrants had to secure a job in the U.S. before they were allowed entry, even though no corresponding penalty was instituted for businesses hiring illegal immigrants. Priority was given to immigrants who had a close family relationship with U.S. citizens or permanent resident aliens. No numerical limits were place on the number of these re-unification visas, reflecting the value placed on the family unit.

While the intent was to make the policies fairer, several unintended consequences caused concern and laid the groundwork for a host of problems that are now being faced today. Many felt the law only substituted discrimination based on national origin with that of job skills, resulting in a "brain drain" on other nations. Removing the national quotas benefited the Asia-Pacific Triangle the most, leading to a significant influx from that region, while prospective Western Hemisphere immigrants now faced a processing backlog. Since the children of resident foreigners born in the U.S. are naturalized citizens, and since the parents of such a U.S. citizen could become beneficiaries, the incentive to immigrate illegally skyrocketed. Many U.S. companies simply turned a blind eye to the labor certification process, preferring to hire illegal aliens who were willing to work for lesser wages. The result was that the job market for Americans was decimated in certain occupations. For immigrants from all countries, the preference provided for family members fueled an unforeseen "chaining" effect: after adult brothers and sisters became citizens, their respective spouses would have preference, which in turn would cause their

The Immigration and Nationality Act was signed into law in 1968; quite appropriately, on the site of the Statue of Liberty.

immediate relatives to gain preference, and so on.

In response, Congress amended the 1965 legislation in 1976 and 1978, removing the hemisphere distinctions and establishing a worldwide policy with a quota of 290,000, including the 20,000 per country limit, but still excluding the immediate family members from that ceiling. Many critics felt that while the unified world policy seemed more equalitarian, it overlooked our nation's traditional ties with certain countries, and fueled further illegal immigration from Mexico.

The accelerated migration of undocumented aliens and the economic woes of the early 1980's led Congress to enact the Immigration Reform and Control Act (IRCA) in 1986. It sought to offer a compromise between competing forces. Certain farming sectors required migratory workers to process the harvest. Others felt the nation bore a responsibility for turning a "blind eye" and allowing so many illegal immigrants to enter, many of whom had set up life here. Calls for widespread amnesty were considered in order. This, in turn, brought concerns that this would only encourage more undocumented migration. So the bill made provisions for stronger enforcement and added penalties for knowingly hiring undocumented workers.

Our nation's inability to control the influx of undocumented migration along the Mexican border took on new significance in the light of the events of 9/11 and the subsequent economic collapse. The immigration issues teetered precariously between concerns for security and globalization. The strain placed on tax-funded social services such as schools, family assistance, and emergency rooms, particularly in states that are suffering budget shortfalls, intensified the debate. Critics countered that the undocumented workers added payroll taxes to the mix, ignoring the fact that most of these weren't listed on the payroll and were paid "under the table." The federal government has done little to address

This old photograph shows how a group of newly-arrived immigrants were examined at Ellis Island.

the burden on the states, except to declare unconstitutional the regulations the states have tried to put into effect to enforce the nation's immigration laws.

In addition to these economic issues, our immigration policies have impacted social, religious, political, and demographic sectors as well. Many in the African-American community feel that the nation has ignored the on-going problem of discrimination as well as the worsening conditions of the inner cities. Poor living conditions for many illegal immigrants have encouraged gang membership. Rival gangs based on different races plague cities and suburbs alike. Children from Hispanic households are less likely to speak English than their non-Hispanic immigrant counterparts, making it difficult to mainstream them into graded classrooms. Health standards also tend to be lower among foreign-born individuals, which have led to a resurgence of diseases that were otherwise rarely encountered in the United States.

Several immigration reform bills were

introduced in Congress in 2005 and 2007 in an attempt to find a bipartisan solution to these problems. Neither bill passed.

Exceptions to the quota system Beyond the quota system, the nation's immigration policies allowed for other considerations. Throughout history Congress has accommodated special situations that arose. After World War II there were many people of war-torn countries who were homeless. They were anxious to come to the United States, but their national quotas were filled. Congress met this emergency by passing the Displaced Persons Act. This act allowed 400,000 of these homeless people to enter our country. This did not mean that our nation had discarded the quota system. These immigrants were figured as a part of their countries' future quotas. Some countries had used up their quotas for the next fifty years. The 1965 law removed this strange problem.

In 1953 Congress passed a law permitting many more refugees from Iron Curtain countries to enter the United States. These people needed to meet the personal characteristics required of all immigrants. They had to be sponsored by a friend or relative in America who would guarantee to arrange for a home and job for the immigrant and his family so that the government would not have to support them.

At the end of the Vietnamese War in 1975, our government made special arrangements to bring about 130,000 refugees into our country. In 1980 Castro allowed thousands of people to leave Cuba. They came by boat to Florida. Similar situations of distress or political oppression have resulted in refugees from areas such as Bangladesh, Ethiopia, and Iran.

Aliens Not all of the people from foreign nations who enter the United States come as immigrants with a desire to make their homes here. Many aliens come into our country as nonimmigrants. Some come as students; others come as tourists, news reporters, or temporary laborers. Each must apply for a specialized visa, depending on the purpose of their stay. While they are here, they are under the authority of our government and must obey our laws. In the past, aliens had to register with the government each January through the U.S. postal service. Yearly registration was dropped in favor of requiring notification of changes of address and certain other specifications. In the post-9/11 era, the USA Patriot Act mandated the development of an entry-exit notification system, with different registration requirements based on certain countries of origin. Elements of that law have been disputed, prompting attempts to drop the requirements either through legislative changes or executive orders.

The Immigration Act of 1965 did away with the country-of-origin quota system, but there are still quotas in place for the different types of visas. Currently each year, only 226,000 immigrants can receive family-based visas; 140,000 can receive employment-based green cards; 55,000 can receive green cards in a lottery; and 90,000 can enter as refugees. A green card is the generic name given to the United States Permanent Resident Card (USCIS Form I-551), formerly the Alien Registration Card. Not surprisingly, it is green in color, and many precautions have been instituted to discourage illegal duplication, in much the same way as the nation's currency. Permanent residents eighteen years of age or older must carry their valid physical green card at all times. Failing to do so carries the possibility of a fine of up to $100 and/or imprisonment for up to 30 days for each offense. The lottery refers to the Diversity Visa program instituted in 1995 as the result of the Immigration Act of 1990. The goal was to diversify the immigrant population by selecting applicants from countries with low rates of immigration during the previous five years. Certain countries that have sent more than 50,000 immigrants in the previous five years are excluded. The lottery specifications do not include refugees or those seeking

Shiu-Chen Chiang, 84, recites the Pledge of Allegiance with over 1,700 other new American citizens after they were sworn in during a ceremony in San Jose on June 19, 1996.

asylum. In 2012, over 14 million applicants applied for the 55,000 available visas.

Evaluation of our immigration system

Is our immigration system pleasing to God? Do we have a right to keep so many people of foreign nations out of our country? If God has blessed us with rich natural resources, should we not be more willing to allow anyone who wishes, to enter our country and share these blessings with us? The answers are especially important since most of the people who ask to enter our land come from countries of hunger, distress, and want.

In addition there is a growing concern about the cost of providing health care for families, and education for children, in states such as Florida and California where large numbers of aliens both legal and illegal are crossing our borders. How can our nation be "under God" if it excludes so many who would like to enter?

To answer these questions, we should begin by remembering that God has ordained many governments in this world. Long ago at the Tower of Babel God caused many languages to exist so that the people would spread over the world and eventually form many nations. To each of the governments that God has ordained, He has given the responsibility of serving as a servant of God for good to the people of that nation. This command makes each government responsible for the general welfare of its **own people**. God does not expect or command the government of India to provide for the general welfare of the people of Switzerland; nor does He expect the government He has ordained in Denmark to provide liberty and justice for the people of the United States.

At the same time we must bear in mind that concern and compassion for others may not stop at a political boundary. To be indifferent to the needs of others wherever they live is as wrong today as it was when Christ condemned those who were concerned only about those of their own kind (Matt. 5:46-48). The government's exercise of authority must weigh the best interests of its own citizens against those of all people throughout the world. We are not only globally connected; all are endowed by the Creator with life.

Genuine concern for others demands that we share with them the opportunities we enjoy; this is the real issue. There are at least two ways to approach the problem. One is to allow people to migrate to a nation where immigrants envision greater opportunities; the United States has long been looked upon as such a land.

Another possibility is to extend to other nations such help as will make their citizens more willing to stay in their native lands and help develop their resources and create new opportunities there. Resources don't just "exist," waiting to be found like a coin on the street. In a sense they "become" as a result of what people do to make them serviceable. Think of what such contrasting nations as mountainous Switzerland and desert-like Israel have done to develop resources and provide for their growing populations. When an immigration problem arose in the city of Geneva in 1550, during the days of John Calvin, no immigration quotas were imposed on refugees, but instead new industries were begun to provide employment.

Examples of the United States assisting other nations are the Marshall Plan to a war-torn Europe following World War II and the Point Four Program, through which aid was extended to other nations as well. In any case the motivation should be a concern and love for others; love finds its expression in different ways at different times and places.

Immigration policies are usually a mixture

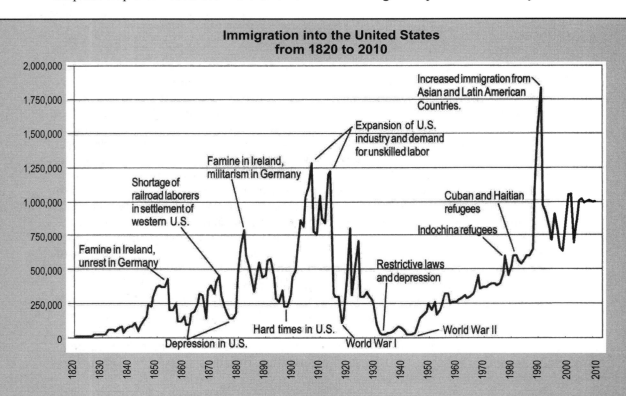

Immigration into the United States from 1820 to 2010

of allowing would-be immigrants to enter and prohibiting them from coming in great numbers. The United States has never had to face the problem of what to do when people leave a nation in swelling numbers. East Germany handled its problem by putting up the Berlin Wall and other fencing to keep its citizens from leaving.

A problem similar to that of immigration from abroad involves migration from one part of the United States to another. Such movement is often from areas with few employment opportunities such as some farming areas, Appalachia, or from cities where factories close and many people lose their jobs.

There are no legal restrictions to prohibit anyone from moving to any other place in the United States. The question is whether it would be better to provide opportunities for the people where they now live rather than to allow them to drift haphazardly into the large metropolitan areas which already have a good share of poverty, unemployment, and overcrowded housing.

Do you remember what you have read?
1. In what ways have immigrants helped our nation?
2. Name five immigrants who have become leaders in America.
3. Why is immigration control necessary?
4. Is a quota system still used to control the rate of immigration to the United States?
5. Who gets preference for immigrating to this country?
6. List five kinds of people who may not enter the United States today.
7. Who are aliens?

8. What two factors or concerns have driven the changes in immigration legislation over the last few decades?

For further thought
1. If a new student enrolled in your class—
   a. What could your class do as a group to make the newcomer feel at home?
   b. What could you do as an individual to make him or her feel welcome?
2. If our country had never restricted immigration, how would it probably be different today?

Things to do
1. Debate the following issue. "*Resolved:* That our immigration laws be changed to allow many more immigrants to enter our country."
2. Then read about the problem of individuals who cross the border illegally from Mexico into the United States. What impact do these illegal immigrants have on the job market? How are states such as California, New Mexico, and Arizona trying to deal with the burden of providing services for such people?
3. Select one person to look up the poem "The New Colossus" by Emma Lazarus and read it to the class.
4. Make a study of the problems that recent Hispanic and Oriental immigrants have had in adjusting to life in the United States.

Words to study
alien
"brain drain"
demographics
gentleman's agreement
National Origins Act
proselyte
quota

Chapter 19

Citizenship in a land of diverse people

Important ideas to look for:
- United States citizenship comes by birth or naturalization.
- The process of naturalization involves several steps.
- Our country is made up of many different groups of people.
- Our government exists for the welfare of all its citizens.

Who is a citizen?

When the Constitution was written in 1789, it said nothing about who was or could become a citizen of our country. Not until 1868, when the Fourteenth Amendment was passed, did we have an official definition of a citizen. This Fourteenth Amendment stated, "All persons **born or naturalized** in the United States, and subject to the **jurisdiction** thereof, are citizens of the United States and of the state wherein they reside." From this amendment we see that citizenship can be obtained in two ways: by birth or by the process of naturalization.

Natural-born citizenship Natural-born citizenship under the jurisdiction of the United States of America is a rich blessing. It is one that God gives even though the person who receives it is unable to appreciate it at the time.

A person born under the jurisdiction of the United States, and therefore a natural-born citizen, is any person born in any one of our fifty states. One is also a natural-born citizen who is born in Puerto Rico, Guam, the Virgin Islands, on any United States ship, or in a United States embassy in a foreign country.

A child who is born in a foreign country is also a natural-born citizen of our country if the parents are United States citizens. In fact, a child is a citizen if only one parent is a citizen of the United States. However, such children must come to live in our country or one of its territories by the time they are twenty-three years old, or else they must live here for five years between their fourteenth and twenty-eighth birthdays. If they do not come to live in some part of our nation during that time, but choose to stay in a foreign country, they lose their citizenship.

Although our lawmakers may not be aware of it, our system of giving citizenship to children born of American parents in foreign nations is parallel to a greater plan for citizenship in God's kingdom. In His plan, children of believing parents are included as citizens of God's kingdom; that is true even if only one of the parents believes in Christ (I Cor. 7:14). However, the children must accept the Lord as personal Savior as soon as they come to years of understanding; when they believe God's promises personally, their citizenship is secure.

Insofar as they follow the basic principles of government for God's kingdom, our human laws are just and good.

Citizenship by naturalization Although

most of our citizens today are natural-born citizens, we still have many who are naturalized. To become a naturalized citizen of our country, an immigrant must follow the orderly plan set up by our government for doing so. When a person becomes a naturalized citizen in a new country, the process is almost the same as when a child is adopted by a new set of parents. Adopted children live in new homes, obey new parents, help in the operation of a new family, and try to get along well with new brothers and sisters. So also newly naturalized citizens take their places in our country among the other citizens. They share in their privileges and do their part in fulfilling their responsibilities.

Collective or group naturalization

Many times in the history of our land, Congress has added to the area of our country. We purchased the Louisiana Territory in 1803, Florida in 1819, and Alaska in 1867. We added Texas in 1845. The people who were living there then were made citizens of the United States by special acts of Congress. The individual persons in these territories did not have to take a literacy test or meet the other personal, physical requirements. Instead they became citizens simply because their land became a part of the United States. By another special act in 1924, Congress gave all Native Americans the full rights of citizenship in our country.

Individual naturalization When a person living in a foreign nation decides to come to the United States and make a home here, he must first of all go to the United States embassy or consul in his own nation. Our ambassador or a member of his staff will check to see if the person who wishes to go to America can meet the personal requirements. That is, he will give the prospective immigrant a literacy test and will check to see that he has no contagious or incurable disease. Our ambassador has the responsibility of checking the record of the person who wants to come to the United States to see that he is not a beggar in his own country, that he is not insane, an alcoholic or a drug *addict*, or affiliated with a known terrorist group. After the immigrant has passed all the personal requirements, he will be evaluated based on the current criteria for issuing visas. However, if the immigration quota is filled for that year, his name will be placed on the waiting list until a new quota is opened.

Being a citizen of the United States provides many rights, but also carries many responsibilities. Thus, the decision to become a U.S. citizen through naturalization is important. In most cases, a person who wants to naturalize must first be a permanent resident. By becoming a U.S. citizen, the individual gains many rights that permanent residents or others do not have, including the right to vote. To be eligible for naturalization, the person must first meet certain requirements set by U.S. law.

The basic requirements are: (1) be 18 years of age or older; (2) be a permanent resident for a certain amount of time (usually 5 years but less for some individuals); (3) be a person of good moral character; (4) have a basic knowledge of U.S. history and government; (5) have a period of continuous residence and physical presence in the United States; and (6) be able to read, write, and speak basic English. There are exceptions to this last rule due to age or permanent physical or mental impairment.

A permanent resident who has been and continues to be married to and living in a marriage relationship with a spouse who is a U.S. citizen may apply for citizenship after three years. Individuals currently serving honorably in the U.S. military, with at least one year of service, may apply while they are in the military or within six months of discharge. Certain spouses of U.S. citizens and those who served in the U.S. military during a past war or are serving currently in combat may be able to file for naturalization even sooner.

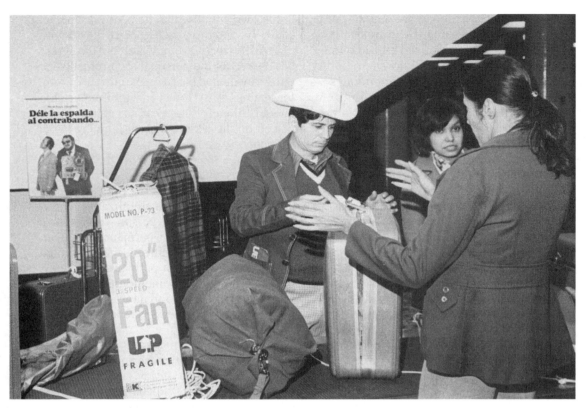

People entering the country must clear their belongings through customs. Immigrants must have their personal requirements rechecked.

Nonresidents. In some ways the process of coming to America has been simplified, and in some ways it has become more complicated. There are over twenty types of non-immigrant visas for people traveling to the United States and staying temporarily. There are many more types of visas for those coming to live permanently. The type of visa is determined by the purpose of the stay and the individual's circumstances.

When a person living in a foreign nation decides to come to the United States and make a home here, he must first apply for an immigrant visa for permanent residence. In general, to be eligible for an immigrant visa, a foreign citizen must be sponsored by a U.S.

citizen relative, a lawful permanent resident of the U.S., or by a prospective employer. The individual must then be awarded an approved petition filed with the U.S. Citizenship and Immigration Services (USCIS). There are different approval processes depending on the individual's immigrant category: immediate relative and family sponsored, employer sponsored, and special immigrants.

Once the immigrant petition has been approved, the individual then begins the preliminary processing for a visa with the U.S. Department of State, National Visa Center, including gathering the necessary documentation. These include an Affidavit of Support, birth certificate, police reports, marriage certificate, photographs, immunization records, and a medical exam and/or information from a physician panel. Once the necessary documents have been confirmed and the corresponding fees have been paid, the applicant will be interviewed at the U.S. Embassy or Consulate General in the current country of residence.

Our government has produced a document entitled, "Welcome to the United States: A Guide for New Immigrants," that is a comprehensive resource containing practical information to help immigrants settle into everyday life in the United States. It also contains basic civics information that introduces newcomers to our system of government. The guide is available in fourteen languages. There is also a similar document entitled, "A Guide to Naturalization," that explains the entire process, step-by-step.

The naturalization process Once a person has become a permanent resident of the U.S. and has met the length of residency and other requirements for naturalization, a Naturalization Eligibility Worksheet must be completed, along with the Application for Naturalization (Form N-400). All forms are available through the government's website. Along with the form, the applicant must submit passport-style photographs, documents, fees, and be fingerprinted at an approved USCIS location. If all the documentation is in order, the applicant will be given an interview appointment. The appointment includes answering questions about the application and the individual's background, as well as taking English and civics tests.

If the individual's application is approved, he or she will receive a date for the naturalization ceremony. At that time, the applicant must return the Permanent Resident Card, answer questions about what he or she has done since the naturalization interview, and take the Oath of Allegiance. It is then that the person receives the U.S. Certificate of Naturalization that has been signed by a federal judge. The new citizen now has all the rights and privileges of a natural-born citizen except that the person may not serve as President or Vice-President of the United States.

The process of becoming a naturalized citizen is a long one. We ask immigrants to live in our country for at least five years (in most cases) before we accept them as citizens. During this waiting period they learn American ways and get used to American liberties and responsibilities. We expect our citizens to vote; therefore, we want citizens who can speak and understand English, and are familiar with the issues, so that they can decide how to vote intelligently. We want them to know what allegiance to our nation requires before we ask them to pledge their loyalty, faithfulness, and obedience.

Losing citizenship

When immigrants take the oath of allegiance they ask God to help them keep that promise. Natural-born citizens also pledge their allegiance to their nation under God. Even though they make the pledge, citizens sometimes are not sincere and fail to keep that promise of allegiance. Then our government may take away their citizenship.

Citizenship may be lost for acts of treason, for attempting to overthrow the government by force, for serving in the army of another nation, for evading the draft in time of war, or for deserting the armed forces. Some persons who are guilty of these crimes are put to death; others are placed in prison; others are *deported* to the country they were loyal to instead of being loyal to the United States.

Losing the privileges of citizenship

Not very many people actually lose their citizenship because of treason or for any of the other reasons we have just mentioned, but very often people lose the privileges of citizenship. One of the privileges of citizenship is the right to vote. This privilege is lost by people who are placed in prison; American citizens in prison are not released on election day so they may go to the polls to vote.

Whenever a person misuses his citizenship privileges, he can expect to lose those privileges. For example, we have the right to assemble peacefully to hold a meeting. But if we hold a meeting that is noisy and disorderly, that disturbs the peace of the city where it is held, we can expect that the law enforcement officers will stop the meeting. As citizens we also have the privilege of freedom of the press and of speech, but if we misuse these rights, we will be guilty of libel and slander. We may not lose our United States citizenship because of this action, but we may lose some of the privileges of citizenship.

Many of the privileges of citizenship are not exercised today because of indifference. Some citizens do not vote on election day because they will not take the time or because they feel that voting is unimportant. That day and that opportunity will never return. The benefits of citizenship can be lost through neglect, just as well as if the citizens were kept away from the polls by an armed guard.

Do you remember what you have read?
1. In what two ways can a person become a citizen?
2. What is collective or group naturalization?
3. What are the basic requirements for a person who wishes to become a naturalized citizen?
4. How can a person lose citizenship?

For further thought
1. A child is born on a United States ship while it is anchored in the harbor of Hong Kong. The child's parents are both Chinese citizens. Is the child a United States citizen?
2. A child is born in Dallas, Texas. Both of his parents are citizens of Mexico. Is the child a citizen of the United States?
3. Why do we ask an immigrant to take an oath of allegiance before we accept him as a citizen?
4. Do you think that natural-born citizens appreciate the advantages of United States citizenship (a) *as much as*, (b) *more than*, (c) *less than* naturalized citizens? Give a reason for your answer.

5. In what ways do the privileges of citizenship often become useless?

Words to study

addict	deport
anarchist	petition of citizenship
customs officer	port of entry
declaration of intention	preliminary hearing

Many groups make up our nation's people

The people of our nation are Americans. As citizens we all pledge allegiance to the same flag. We sing the same national anthem. We promise to be obedient to the same laws. We have many things in common. We honor the office of the President. We pay our taxes according to the same laws. We are willing to help defend our nation from its enemies when this becomes necessary.

In addition to these similarities, groups of citizens and individual citizens differ from one another. They differ in appearance, in the values they hold, and in their lifestyles. Unfortunately, the history of our country shows that the majority has often failed to honor the rights, the beliefs, and feelings of minorities. In an effort to make a minority group conform to the wishes of the majority, the majority has sometimes applied gentle pressure. At other times, the majority has used force to control minorities. This is neither just nor Christian. The real test of a democracy is not how often a majority has its way, but how well liberty and justice are being provided for all citizens.

In 1964, Congress passed the landmark Civil Rights Act that prohibited major forms of discrimination based on race, ethnic group, religion, and gender. It outlawed unequal application of voter registration requirements as well as racial segregation in public schools, at the workplace, and public facilities (such as restaurants and buses).

A Variety of Minorities

If the real meaning of liberty is to allow people to make choices in keeping with their convictions, then the majority should not impose its demands on any minority. Nor should any minority insist on their demands taking precedence over any other minority or the majority.

Unfortunately, the full inalienable rights of life, liberty, and the pursuit of happiness have been denied to many segments of our population, based on race, ethnicity, gender, and religion. To compensate for this, some institutions use a quota system in an effort to force a level of equal representation, however they have defined it. Critics argue that this procedure only continues the practice of discrimination. They point to the government's own admission that quotas were unfair in the immigration policies to support their case.

The 2010 census showed that close to 39 million Black or African-Americans and over 50 million Hispanics live in the United States.

Just twenty years ago those numbers were 32 million Blacks and 26 million Hispanics. This shows how the immigration policies have changed the demographics of our country. The census also showed that there are almost 3 million Native Americans, accounting for just under one percent of our population. This percentage has remained unchanged over the two decades. The percentage of males to females in the population was about even (approximately 50% each).

In addition to these commonly-recognized minorities, our nation's population is comprised of many diverse segments, most of whom have experienced discrimination in some form. For example, the Amish and Hutterites, religious minorities, have been treated as objects of curiosity. They have been limited by laws designed to restrict their chosen way of life.

Our nation's diversity is evident in this classroom. All of our students should be equally prepared to succeed in our society.

Likewise, other hidden forms of discrimination exist that get little attention in the media. Parents who have decided to send their children to a Christian school or to homeschool not only must pay the cost of a Christian education and buy curriculum, they are forced to continue to pay taxes to support the public school system that has denied the rights of Christians to express their faith. In many school systems, a misunderstanding and misapplication of the laws excludes Christianity from even being mentioned, let alone taught, while other religions are studied. The Christian heritage of our nation is increasingly being removed from our history books, as well as the biblical basis for government and the American republic as it was founded. More recently, some Christian organizations have been forced to hire individuals who oppose the organization's doctrines, while Christian business people have been forced to pay benefits for services that go against their beliefs.

Many of the government and court buildings across America—including the lampposts outside the U.S. Supreme Court—display a sculpture of Lady Justice holding a balance and blindfolded. The balance stands for the principle of equal justice under the law for all U.S. citizens. The blindfold means that no physical, social, financial, or demographic characteristics should influence treatment under the law. Every American should apply this same standard to our treatment of others and the decisions we make. It is a biblical standard based on how the Creator views such distinctions (see 1 Corinthians 12:13 and Galatians 3:28).

Part of the duty of Christian citizens is to work for the greater justice in one's nation. Whether or not you or some member of your family will benefit from the changes is not the important issue. Rather it is showing love for one's neighbor. Guarding liberty and working for the well-being of all people in our nation is one way of doing so.

Psalm 82 calls us to defend "the weak and fatherless" and "maintain the rights of the poor and oppressed." It is sad that this concern for justice and the value of human life have not been more evident in American history.

There is nothing new about people abusing one another. Ecclesiastes 5 reminds us that ". . . if you see the poor oppressed . . . and justice and rights denied, do not be surprised at such things . . ." The day will come when all wrongs will be made right. In the meantime, as we pray, "Thy kingdom come . . . ," we are to live and work as members of it.

Occupational groups About 45 percent of our nation's people are employed in the standard occupations of business life. These people are not the very young or the very old; most are between the ages of eighteen and sixty-five. They are the wage earners of our country. With God's blessings, it is their work that keeps our factories running, our farms producing food, our businesses operating.

Each group has its own special problems and special needs. All of these groups look to our government for liberty and justice.

Age groups As our government seeks to provide liberty and justice for all, it must be aware of the different age groups of our people. Our population can be divided into age groups as shown in the chart.

Although the millions of citizens of our country who are under five years old are not quite ready to vote, our government must provide for their welfare. This is done

Composition of the U.S. by age group
(based on the 2010 Census)

Under 5 years old	6.5%
Between 5 and 19 years old	17.2%
Between 20 and 65 years old	61.0%
Over 65 years old	15.3%

through laws that protect their health and provide for them when their parents are unable to do so.

One of the chief requirements for the five to seventeen age group is a good education. People between the ages of eighteen and sixty-five are concerned with the completion of a college education and the opportunity to work and earn a living. Those over sixty-five have the special problem of paying their bills after their earning power has nearly ended. These population groups make up our nation. Our government must seek the welfare of all. It must try to give each person the opportunity for the "pursuit of happiness."

Groups with special problems One of the duties of government is to provide for the needs of its citizens when they are unable to provide for themselves.

Blind people have special problems. Although we cannot fully understand what a world of darkness is like, we can realize that blind people need the help of others. There are 1.3 million legally blind people in our country today. Our government must also help them in their "pursuit of happiness."

To help these people, many of our state governments have set up special schools where seeing-eye dogs are trained for them. The dogs must learn to stop at steps and curbs where blind people might stumble. They must be taught to go around low-hanging branches of trees, or other objects, and to avoid other dangerous situations. After a blind person becomes accustomed to a dog, he or she can go through traffic, into trains, into elevators, and almost anywhere that people with sight can go.

Schools for blind people teach the Braille system of reading and writing. This system gets its name from Louis Braille, a blind Frenchman who first figured out how it could be used. Raised dots spell out words that a blind person can read with the fingertips. Writing is done with a sharp-pointed instrument. Today many blind persons are taught to type on a Braille computer. Sometimes blind teachers are hired to work in these schools because they are better able to understand the problems of the blind student.

When a blind person requests books from a library for the blind, the government pays the postage on the books. A few magazines, such as *Reader's Digest*, publish Braille editions. The American Bible Society also helps blind persons. The society has already distributed tens of thousands of copies of the Bible in Braille.

Many people in the United States are physically challenged. Some of these persons were born this way while others developed disabilities over time or through accidents and sickness. Diseases such as rickets, tuberculosis, and polio have also caused permanent disabilities for many people. These people often need special care and accommodations in order to function in society. In 1990, Congress passed the Americans with Disabilities Act. The main purpose of this civil rights legislation was to prohibit discrimination based on disability. It also modified healthcare policies and mandated changes to federal, state, and municipal facilities to give equal access to persons with disabilities.

Millions of people in our nation—about one person in every five—suffer from some degree of hearing loss. Many of these people are not aware of the fact that their hearing ability is below normal. Others are not able to fully enjoy music or hear everything someone says to them. Yet most of these people are quite able to go about their daily work.

However, there are thousands of people who are totally deaf. They have difficulty talking with their families and friends. Although they are unable to perform many types of work, they are not as disabled as blind people are. Many of the occupations that are closed to blind people are still open to those who are deaf.

In their efforts to help the deaf, our state

A child learns Braille with the aid of a teacher. Advances in technology have enhanced communication options for the blind.

governments have started special schools where lip-reading and sign language are taught. Children who are born deaf have an especially difficult time learning to talk because they have never heard the sounds of letters and words. They are taught to feel for the sound vibrations on their teacher's throat and are shown how to hold their lips and tongue to make these same vibrations.

Trade schools are very effective in training deaf people to earn a living. Occupations that require manual skills such as dressmaking or working in a bakery are easily learned by deaf persons. Many others choose computer programming or other more highly skilled trades. A high percentage of students who graduate from schools for the deaf are able to find jobs and earn a living.

Our government not only helps those who have been disabled by accidents, it also does all it can to prevent accidents from happening. Laws for safety on the road and at work are useful only when the citizens observe them. Every citizen must participate in the prevention of accidents by obeying all laws for safety.

The mentally challenged also need special care. Many who are unable to care for themselves are provided for in hospitals and other institutions. Special schools work with others who are able to learn simple tasks. People who are mentally ill are cared for by doctors who have been especially trained to help them. Each year thousands of mentally ill persons are restored to health through clinics and hospitals operated for this purpose. Mental health is a great blessing. Our nation, under God, must also seek to help that special group of people in our population who need care or treatment for mental illness.

Liberty and justice are **for all**. In our study of the people of America, we have learned that our people are similar in many ways. They pledge allegiance to the same flag; they are faithful, loyal, and obedient to the same nation. Yet Americans are also quite different in many ways. Each group has its own characteristics and desires. Every individual within each of these groups has individual needs and opinions, abilities and skills.

Guarding the right of each individual to life, liberty, and the pursuit of happiness, regardless of the group the person belongs to, is one of the basic duties of our government.

Do you remember what you have read?
Complete the following sentences.
1. Two ways in which all Americans are alike are _____ and _____ .
2. Two ways in which all Americans are different are _____ and _____ .
3. One problem faced by racial minorities in America is _____ .
4. Only 45 percent of Americans are wage earners. The other 55 percent are not wage earners because _____ .
5. Seeing-eye dogs are helpful because _____
6. Blindness is a more serious handicap than deafness because _____ .

For further thought
1. Statistics show that many cases of blindness could have been prevented. What can we do to safeguard our eyes?
2. What attitudes should a person have toward the mentally ill or mentally challenged?

3. How have minority groups been discriminated against in the following areas: education, housing, lodging, restaurants, job opportunities?
4. Is it possible for a Christian to justify racial segregation?
5. About 20 percent of Americans belong to rather small Protestant denominations. Name as many of these denominations as you can.

Things to do
1. Make a study of the problems of Native-Americans as a minority group in the United States. Discuss ways in which past wrongs could be corrected and similar problems could be avoided in the future.
2. Topics for Special Reports
   a. Braille system of reading and writing
   b. Schools for the training of seeing-eye dogs
   c. Activities carried on in schools for the deaf
   d. Artificial limbs

Research projects
1. If special education classes or other programs for assisting physically challenged children or adults are provided in your community, have a committee from your class make a visit to the rooms or obtain information from the directors. Ask the committee to report their findings to the class.

2. Most states have schools and institutions for the blind, deaf, and mentally ill. Make a report on these special schools and institutions which are located in your state.
3. Research the latest statistics of the U.S. Census Bureau or look in *The World Almanac* to obtain the latest statistics of race, religion, occupation, and age. In your report compare the figures with those of the previous census.
4. The percentage of people in our nation who are over 65 years old is increasing. What provision has been made for the care of the aged in your community? Discuss the obligation of children to care for their aged parents.
5. Interview a few naturalized citizens and write a report based on their answers to the following questions:
   a. Why did they decide to come to the United States?
   b. What steps were taken to emigrate?
   c. What problems did they face on arrival?
   d. What steps had to be completed in the process of naturalization?
   e. What has their citizenship meant to them?
6. Study the life of Dr. Martin Luther King, Jr. and report to the class on his contribution to the development of racial integration and equal rights for African-Americans.

Chapter 20

I pledge
and
I practice

Important ideas to look for:
- A pledge of allegiance requires loyalty, obedience, and faithfulness.
- Faithfulness in loyalty and obedience is a strong test of Christian citizenship.
- Good citizenship requires that people care about themselves and their places in the community.
- A responsible citizen is an informed citizen.

A pledge is a promise

"I pledge allegiance to the flag of the United States of America and to the Republic for which it stands, one nation under God, indivisible, with liberty and justice for all."

The Pledge of Allegiance is a promise, a genuine promise, one that you must think about seriously as you place your right hand over your heart, a promise that must be kept even though it requires extra effort.

When you first learned the words of the pledge, they probably meant very little to you. Perhaps you smiled because a child in your first-grade class did not know which hand to use or where his heart was. You probably recited the pledge in a meaningless monotone as if you were reciting some poem that you had to memorize, even though you didn't understand what the poet was trying to say.

Today, however, you are more aware of what allegiance is, for you are just completing a study of government. You have reviewed the historical background of our nation. You have learned much about how laws are made and which government officials are to carry out these laws. You know which powers Congress

has and which it does not have. You know about justice courts and courts of appeal. Your study has given you a knowledge of the structure and functions of government.

Knowing all this is important, but it is just a beginning. Knowledge alone does not make a good citizen. Correct and reasonably complete information is necessary to make wise decisions. But it is useful only when we decide for or against an issue.

Making wise decisions or choices is one of the most important steps in Christian citizenship. Choosing must follow knowing, but our choices or decisions must be guided by the Bible.

A decision must next be put into action. You may know all about something going on in your community and conclude that it is wrong, but until you begin to act to change it, the knowledge and the decision are useless.

Keeping our pledge of allegiance

Allegiance demands loyalty Being loyal means that we place allegiance to our nation above allegiance to all other nations. If we are called upon to defend our country against her enemies, we must be ready and willing to do so.

Romans 13:7 says, "Pay all of them their dues, taxes to whom taxes are due, revenue to whom revenue is due, respect to whom respect is due, honor to whom honor is due." When we are loyal to our country, we are willing to pay the "taxes" required of us in support of our country.

Respect and honor also deal with the loyalty that we must show to those whom God has placed over us as our governing authorities. They include parents, teachers, and ministers as well as the officials of the civil government. Respecting and honoring authority is a part of being loyal.

Loyalty includes the use of our franchise. Voting wisely is one way of showing our loyalty. When we pledge allegiance, we promise to do our part in the selection of government officials and the enactment of wise laws that are in harmony with God's law. People who are not interested enough in the welfare of their country to vote in an election are not keeping the solemn promise to be loyal.

Someday we may be summoned to serve on a jury. Willingness to do so is one way of showing that we believe in liberty and justice for all. This is another way of keeping our pledge of allegiance. It would be impossible to control crime and defend the innocent if loyal citizens did not serve as truthful witnesses and fair jurors.

We are not the only persons who pledge allegiance to our nation. When we keep our

When we pledge allegiance, we express respect, honor, and loyalty to our country. Some youth organizations still foster citizenship skills as part of their programs, however, reciting our Pledge of Allegiance is now often neglected in our society.

National Voter Turnout in Presidential Elections: 1960-2008

Year	Voting-Age Population	Voter Registration	Voter Turnout	% Turnout of Voting-Age Population
1960	109,159,000	64,833,096	68,838,204	63.1%
1964	114,090,000	73,715,818	70,644,592	61.9%
1968	120,328,186	81,658,180	73,211,875	60.8%
1972	140,776,000	97,328,541	77,718,554	55.2%
1976	152,309,190	105,037,986	81,555,789	53.6%
1980	164,597,000	113,043,734	86,515,221	52.6%
1984	174,466,000	124,150,614	92,652,680	53.1%
1988	182,778,000	126,379,628	91,594,693	50.1%
1992	189,529,000	133,821,178	104,405,155	55.1%
1996	196,511,000	146,211,960	96,456,345	49.1%
2000	205,815,000	156,421,311	105,586,274	51.3%
2004	221,256,931	174,800,000	122,294,978	55.3%

promise to be loyal, faithful, and obedient, we do so in the presence of others. This means that good citizenship demands cooperation. When we work with our fellow citizens to solve the problems of our community, we are also keeping our pledge of allegiance.

Think for a moment of our life at school or at home. Everyone is needed to keep the school yard clean and neat. Everyone needs to help so that walls are not disfigured and desks marred. We already realize that it takes only a few poor citizens to make restrooms messy and coatrooms disorderly. Just a few disloyal members can destroy the reputation of an entire class group or school. Every member of a group needs to cooperate—cooperation for the welfare of all is the mark of a promise that is being kept.

Allegiance demands obedience There is an old saying, "If you learn to be obedient, you have come a long way on the path that God would have you go." When we learn to be properly obedient, we have come a long way on the path of keeping our pledge of allegiance. Romans 13 commands us to ". . . submit . . . to the governing authorities. . . ." It is impossible to have an orderly nation unless there is enforcement of and obedience to law.

We call our nation a Christian nation not because all of our citizens love and serve God, but because its standards of right and wrong are traditionally based upon the teaching of the Christian faith. For example, all of the laws for the protection of property are based upon the commandment, "You shall not steal" (Exod. 20:15). As citizens we pledge our obedience to these laws. We keep our promise by never taking anything that does not belong to us, and by caring for that which has been entrusted to us, such as our books and desks in school.

Civil laws which guard the relationships of people toward one another are based on God's moral law: "Love your neighbor as yourself . . ." (Mark 12:31). Traffic laws protect the lives of neighbors; slander laws protect their reputations.

Obeying the law is an important part of keeping our pledge of allegiance. Yet there cannot possibly be enough laws to cover all the actions of every citizen. Leaders of organized crime study our laws very carefully. Then they commit crimes in a way that keeps them just out of the law's reach.

When our government punishes those who disobey the law, it is simply carrying out the task that God has given it to do. Parents, teachers, and officials of the church and state all have this same responsibility to exercise their authority.

Sometimes the laws themselves are a problem for the Christian citizen. There are laws which permit legalized gambling, abortion-on-demand, easy divorces, or a quick bankruptcy under certain conditions to avoid the payment of a debt. Because a deed is not legally wrong does not mean that it is morally and spiritually right. Christian citizenship demands not only that we obey the laws of our nation, but that we work tirelessly to remove improper laws.

To be obedient, a person needs to exercise self-control. By controlling ourselves, we often avoid the need for control by others. Self-control is keeping our pledge because we are ". . . subject, not only because of possible punishment, but also because of conscience . . ." (Rom. 13:5).

Allegiance demands faithfulness Being loyal and obedient is one thing—being faithfully loyal and obedient is something else. We all know people who turn their loyalty and obedience on and off like a kitchen faucet. Perhaps they are loyal in front of others to impress them. Others are obedient to authority only when that authority is present. Such part-time allegiance is not enough. **Faithfulness is simply continuous loyalty and obedience.** Here is one of the greatest weaknesses of Christian citizens. We are usually sincere in

our loyalty and obedience—when we think of it. We are not constantly concerned about faithful or continuous loyalty and obedience.

An early pledge

The pledge that we make from time to time today is often taken lightly because we do not feel the weight of the promise that so easily falls from our lips. But one early pledge made by our American forefathers was not taken lightly.

In Congress, July 4,1776
The unanimous declaration
of the thirteen united States of America,
When in the course of human events,
it becomes necessary for one people
to dissolve the political bands which
have connected them with another, and
to assume among the powers of the earth,
the separate and equal station to which
the laws of nature and of nature's God
entitle them, a decent respect to the opinions
of mankind requires that they should
declare the causes which impel them
to the separation.
We hold these truths to be self-evident,
that all men are created equal,
that they are endowed by their Creator
with certain inalienable rights,
that among these are life, liberty
and the pursuit of happiness . . .

We have studied the first part of the Declaration of Independence quite carefully. We know that it declared the thirteen colonies to be free from England. We have read so often the three inalienable rights which it lists that we know them from memory.

But we must also take a careful look at the last paragraph. It contains a pledge of allegiance. This pledge expresses a strong faith in God's providing care. It also contains a promise. The men who signed the Declaration of Independence pledged all that they had for the cause of freedom—their lives; their fortunes, or possessions; and their sacred honor, or good reputations.

> . . . And for the support of this declaration, with a firm reliance on the protection of divine Providence, we mutually pledge to each other our lives, our fortunes and our sacred honor.

This pledge was soon put to a very severe test. The years that followed were filled with the bitter and bloody Revolutionary War. During this time it was not easy for the fifty-six men who had signed the Declaration of Independence to keep their pledge. Many hardships seemed to make it impossible for them to keep their promise. In spite of all these obstacles and in spite of all it cost them, they remained true to their word.

Nor can we expect that the task of keeping our pledge of allegiance will always be easy. In fact, we, too, may find that it is often very difficult to be loyal, obedient, and faithful. To do so will require our utmost efforts.

Loyalty to country and to self

We have studied a great deal about our government and the responsibility that we have toward it. We have learned many ways to keep our pledge to our nation. We must remember that we are a part of that nation.

The second portion of the law of God tells us to love our neighbors as we love ourselves. When we love ourselves too much, we become selfish. But, nevertheless, we do have a great responsibility to care for ourselves because we are made in the image of God. Caring for ourselves is a part of good citizenship.

Know yourself To be good citizens, we should realize that we have sinful natures, that if we follow our own natural desires, we will be led to disobedience. Paul said, "For what I do is not the good I want to do; no, the evil I do not want to do—this I keep doing" (Rom. 7:19). If we know ourselves

as sinners, inclined to do evil, we will watch our conduct. We will seek to control our bad tempers; we will be on guard against poor citizenship in our lives.

Know your interests and abilities Knowing these things will help us to choose our life's work in a field where we will be able to use our abilities in the most effective way to God's glory. Here we will have a feeling of achievement; we will be happy and at the same time we will contribute the most to our nation.

Protect your health To be able to keep our pledge of allegiance, we need healthy bodies and minds. A person who continually needs the care of others cannot do a great deal to help the nation. When we observe the rules of health—cleanliness, good food, temperance, enough rest and sleep, exercise, and fresh air—we are making it possible to keep our promise of loyalty, faithfulness, and obedience.

Find your work If our country were filled with lazy citizens who expected the government to support them because they were unwilling to choose jobs and work at them, our nation would soon fall. As good citizens, we need to be industrious and punctual. This means that we must put our work, our duties, our businesses before pleasure. It means also that we must keep at our work steadily until it is finished. We have the privilege of selecting our life's work, but we also have the task of being diligent in the work we have chosen.

Be a good steward of "your property" "Your property" is an expression that must fit within the Biblical truth, "The earth is the Lord's and everything in it . . . " (Ps. 24:1). When we think of the possessions with which God has blessed us, we must realize that we are stewards responsible to God for their use. We may not use our possessions to harm others, nor may we use them simply to satisfy our own selfish needs. Instead, our possessions should serve as a means for good citizenship both in God's kingdom and in our nation.

Be a wise consumer Each day we use some of the natural resources of our land to sustain our lives, to clothe ourselves, and to heat our homes. When we go to a store or market, we should be careful in the selection of the things we buy. We should ask ourselves these questions:

"Do I need this article?"
"Can I afford it?"
"Will it fill the purpose for which I am buying it?"

Wise consumers make dependable citizens; they do not waste or misuse our natural resources. Do you recall the story of Jesus feeding the five thousand? After the meal, the disciples were told to gather the fragments: "Let nothing be wasted" (John 6:12). Wasting the resources God has given to us is still displeasing to Him, for He does not change (see Malachi 3:6).

Be courteous "Politeness is to do and say the kindest thing in the kindest way." Kindness to others is a mark of good citizenship. We have many opportunities every day to be courteous to others. At home with our parents, brothers, and sisters, with our classmates and teachers at school, with all those about us, we have the opportunity to be helpful, cheerful, and sympathetic. As we are courteous to others, we are keeping our pledge of allegiance by helping others in their pursuit of happiness.

When we help others to find happiness, we come the closest to finding it ourselves.

Practice fair play When our school team goes to play in an athletic contest with another school, the team represents the school. We want them to play fairly, according to the rules of the game. They should respect the

In sports, in personal life, in business, and in public affairs, practicing good sportsmanship is practicing good citizenship.

ruling of the game officials without becoming angry. But the cheering section, the spectators, represent the school in much the same way. They need to display a good spirit by cheering a team even when it is losing; they should applaud for a good play or fairness and respect shown by a member of the opposing team as well as by one of their own players. Spectators as well as players need to accept the ruling of the referee without question or booing. A game won by unfair play is, in a larger sense, a game that is truly lost.

But good sportsmanship goes further than just the way we feel about winning or losing a game. It is necessary for a healthy outlook on life in a republic such as ours. In our two-party political system, only one candidate can win an election. Our business system is based upon competition among companies. Good sportsmanship will help us to be better, happier citizens if we know how to win without being filled with pride, to lose without being filled with defeat, and to play fairly in all our efforts.

Use leisure time wisely People today have more leisure time than those who lived a few generations ago. Time-saving machines, shorter working hours, and improved methods of transportation have all helped to make this possible. Keeping our pledge of allegiance, however, is a full-time responsibility. It does not apply only to our on-the-job time. Wise use of our leisure time is becoming increasingly important for good, consistent citizenship. The temptation to be unfaithful in our loyalty and obedience is often greatest during our leisure time. Idleness often leads people to gossip and mischief. Idle people may even turn to crime.

> In works of labour, or of skill,
>   I would be busy too;
> For Satan finds some mischief still
>   For idle hands to do.
>   —Isaac Watts

To make wise use of our leisure time, we should select worthwhile activities that will bring us happiness and bring joy to others. Many hobbies are very enjoyable, such as outdoor projects and music. We should remember to select hobbies that are suited to our own abilities and interests. Above all, the activities that occupy our leisure time should help us to serve God while they promote good citizenship.

Keep yourself informed To be good citizens, we need to be informed citizens. Newspapers and news magazines carry articles and stories about each day's most important events. Radio and television news broadcasts often bring on-the-scene reports from the place and at the very time that some important event is taking place. Being well-informed takes both time and effort.

If you are well-informed on many different topics, you will be able to talk easily and intelligently with others. Such information will keep your conversation from being dull and meaningless. Your knowledge will help to give you confidence in yourself. It will make you more at ease in public; it will help you to make and keep friends.

As you gather information and talk of current affairs with others, you must be very alert for propaganda. Many news articles or broadcasts present only one side of an issue. Sometimes certain facts are left out of a story while others are made to seem much more important than they actually are. You need to evaluate the information you read and hear. You need to compare different viewpoints about an issue and make your own decisions and choices, using the teachings of the Bible as your guide.

Because it is impossible to be completely informed about everything, you should spend more time gathering accurate information about the really important rather than the unimportant issues. Information, however, is not enough. A person can be highly educated and well-informed and yet be a relatively inactive citizen. Accurate information and wise decisions must lead to well planned

A good leisure-time activity is one that will enrich your life and the lives of others. It will serve God and promote good citizenship. Above, a group of Huron Valley, Michigan school children proudly stand in front of a home they helped restore last Christmas in April. (See page 157 for more information.)
Christmas in April U.S.A. takes place on the last Saturday in April in 600 cities across all 50 States.

actions—all three are necessary for good citizenship.

Be courageous It takes courage to stand for what we believe is right and true. We have already learned that it is wrong to go with a crowd to do evil. But to leave a group and stand on one's own feet as an individual is often very difficult.

God has promised that He will bless the nation that honors Him. Although our pledge states that our nation is under God, we must have courage to overcome the evils that are found in our land. Often it would be much easier to go with others and do as they do even though we know we should not. Under such conditions keeping our pledge of allegiance takes much courage.

Do you remember what you have read?

Complete the following sentences.

1. A pledge is _____.
2. Allegiance means_____ .
3. I can be loyal to my country by _____.
4. We call our nation a Christian nation because _____
5. Self-control is important because_____ .
6. To use our leisure time properly we should _____ .
7. A person can become well-informed about world affairs by_____ .
8. Courage is often necessary for good citizenship because _____
9. How can you tell if a person . . .
   . . . practices fair play?
   . . . is a good steward of the possessions God has given?
   . . . is a wise consumer?
10. List several ways in which citizenship could be improved . . .
   . . . in and about your school.
   . . . in your community.

Research project

Select an editorial or article from a recent issue of a newspaper or magazine. Try to point out the bias of the author in politics, in religion, in social or racial issues.

A PERSONAL PLEDGE

The "Pledge of Allegiance to the Flag" as it was written by Francis Bellamy was first recited on October 12, 1892, at services marking the 400th anniversary of Columbus' discovery of America. Since that date it has been repeated by millions of citizens of many different generations. Sometimes it has been repeated with much feeling, for example, when a group of immigrants received their United States citizenship. During those years of our history when our nation was at war, the allegiance of the citizens living in those times was tested in many ways. We have the privilege of living in the twenty-first century. The future will provide many opportunities to work for liberty and justice. Our country, our citizenship, our flag all have special meaning for us. To give a personal meaning to your allegiance, write a pledge of your own to express your feelings toward your flag and your country.

Conclusion

God ordains governments on the earth. These governments are always under God's watchful, loving care. They are always subject to the justice of His law. He has established them to provide good services for the people of the land, for they are servants of God for good. He has also given them authority to punish evildoers as they bear the sword. It is to our government under God that we pledge our allegiance.

God is sovereign. He is Lord of lords, and King of kings. His Word commands, "Everyone must submit himself to the governing authorities." We are instructed to "give to Caesar what is Caesar's . . . " (Luke 20:25).

God demands that we obey the governments that He has established. But He also calls us to a higher allegiance when He says, "Give . . . to God what is God's." Jesus has told us to seek first the kingdom of heaven. As Christians, we have a dual citizenship. Our citizenship in the Kingdom of God requires our greatest loyalty. It must be the motive for our desire to be good citizens of our country.

You are now completing this course of study about government. We hope you have enjoyed learning about the various offices and agencies that make up the structure of government.

You have had a glimpse of government in action, for you have seen how our nation's

Above: Three Korean girls pledge their allegiance during their naturalization ceremony. Below: A 5-year-old Vietnamese boy becomes an American citizen.

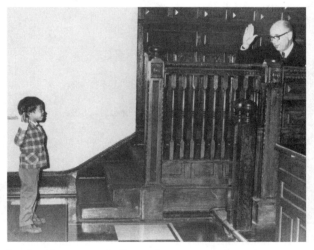

leaders have created new laws, amendments and political organizations to solve new problems and meet new challenges.

Now the future challenges you to make wise decisions as you put your knowledge to work:

Will you grow into a person of integrity in public and private life, a person others can depend upon?

Will you grow in awareness of opportunities to be of service to others, to your city, state, and nation, and of the need to be as well informed as possible?

Will you become a person who knows that one's highest allegiance is to the King of kings? Therefore will you support or oppose laws and other issues in keeping with justice and righteousness, the kind that "exalts a nation?"

The following words are inscribed on the Department of Justice Building in Washington, D.C.: "Justice in the life and conduct of the state is possible only as first it resides in the hearts and souls of the citizens." Good citizenship begins within us. It begins with a desire and determination to keep our pledge of allegiance.

A pledge is a promise. Promises of any kind can be kept only with the strength that we receive from the Lord. With our pledge, we would do well to add a silent prayer to God for the ability needed to keep our promise.

Each time we pray the Lord's Prayer, we say, ". . . Thy will be done on earth as it is done in heaven." Doing God's will on earth is the task of our lawmakers, our judges, our government officials, and every member of our nation. This is the standard for truly Christian citizenship. We know not what the future holds, but we know who holds the future. In the years that lie ahead, may we always recognize that our nation is **under God.**

Text of the

Declaration of Independence *

In Congress, July 4,1776. The unanimous Declaration of the thirteen united States of America.

When in the Course of human events it becomes necessary for one people to dissolve the political bands which have connected them with another, and to assume among the powers of the earth, the separate and equal station to which the Laws of Nature and of Nature's God entitle them, a decent respect to the opinions of mankind requires that they should declare the causes which impel them to the separation.—We hold these truths to be self-evident, that all men are created equal, that they are endowed by their Creator with certain unalienable Rights, that among these are Life, Liberty and the pursuit of Happiness.—That to secure these rights, Governments are instituted among Men, deriving their just powers from the consent of the governed,—That whenever any Form of Government becomes destructive of these ends, it is the Right of the People to alter or to abolish it, and to institute new Government, laying its foundation on such principles and organizing its powers in such form, as to

them shall seem most likely to effect their Safety and Happiness. Prudence, indeed, will dictate that Governments long established should not be changed for light and transient causes; and accordingly all experience hath shewn, that mankind are more disposed to suffer, while evils are sufferable, than to right themselves by abolishing the forms to which they are accustomed. But when a long train of abuses and usurpations, pursuing invariably the same Object evinces a design to reduce them under absolute Despotism, it is their right, it is their duty, to throw off such Government, and to provide new Guards for their future security.—Such has been the patient sufferance of these Colonies; and such is now the necessity which constrains them to alter their former Systems of Government. The history of the present King of Great Britain is a history of repeated injuries and usurpations,

---

*This text follows exactly the spelling and punctuation of the original document.

all having in direct object the establishment of an absolute Tyranny over these States. To prove this, let Facts be submitted to a candid world.— He has refused his Assent to Laws, the most wholesome and necessary for the public good.— He has forbidden his Governors to pass Laws of immediate and pressing importance, unless suspended in their operation till his Assent should be obtained; and when so suspended, he has utterly neglected to attend to them.— He has refused to pass other Laws for the accommodation of large districts of people, unless those people would relinquish the right of Representation in the Legislature, a right inestimable to them and formidable to tyrants only.— He has called together legislative bodies at places unusual, uncomfortable, and distant from the depository of their public Records, for the sole purpose of fatiguing them into compliance with his measures.— He has dissolved Representative Houses repeatedly, for opposing with manly firmness his invasions on the rights of the people.— He has refused for a long time, after such dissolutions, to cause others to be elected; whereby the Legislative powers, incapable of Annihilation, have returned to the People at large for their exercise; the State remaining in the mean time exposed to all the dangers of invasion from without, and convulsions within.— He has endeavoured to prevent the population of these States; for that purpose obstructing the Laws for Naturalization of Foreigners; refusing to pass others to encourage their migrations hither, and raising the conditions of new Appropriations of Lands.— He has obstructed the Administration of Justice, by refusing his Assent to Laws for establishing Judiciary powers — He has made Judges dependent on his Will alone, for the tenure of their offices, and the amount and payment of their salaries — He has erected a multitude of New Offices, and sent hither swarms of Officers to harass our people, and eat out their substance.— He has kept among us, in times of peace, Standing Armies without the Consent of our legislatures — He has

affected to render the Military independent of and superior to the Civil Power.— He has combined with others to subject us to a jurisdiction foreign to our constitution, and unacknowledged by our laws; giving his Assent to their Acts of pretended Legislation:— For quartering large bodies of armed troops among us:— For protecting them, by a mock Trial, from punishment for any Murders which they should commit on the Inhabitants of these States:— For cutting off our Trade with all parts of the world:— For imposing Taxes on us without our Consent:— For depriving us in many cases, of the benefits of Trial by Jury:— For transporting us beyond Seas to be tried for pretended offences:— For abolishing the free System of English Laws in a neighboring Province, establishing therein an Arbitrary government, and enlarging its Boundaries so as to render it at once an example and fit instrument for introducing the same absolute rule into these Colonies:— For taking away our Charters, abolishing our most valuable Laws, and altering fundamentally the Forms of our Governments:— For suspending our own Legislatures and declaring themselves invested with power to legislate for us in all cases whatsoever.— He has abdicated Government here, by declaring us out of his Protection and waging War against us. — He has plundered our seas, ravaged our Coasts, burnt our towns, and destroyed the lives of our people.— He is at this time transporting large Armies of foreign Mercenaries to compleat the works of death, desolation and tyranny, already begun with circumstances of Cruelty & perfidy scarcely paralleled in the most barbarous ages, and totally unworthy the Head of a civilized nation.— He has constrained our fellow Citizens taken Captive on the high Seas to bear Arms against their Country, to become the executioners of their friends and Brethren, or to fall themselves by their Hands.— He has excited domestic insurrections amongst us, and has endeavoured to bring on the inhabitants of our frontiers, the merciless Indian Savages, whose known rule of warfare, is an undistinguished destruction of all ages, sexes and conditions. In every stage of these Oppressions We have Petitioned for Redress in the most humble terms: Our repeated Petitions have been answered only by repeated injury. A Prince, whose character is thus marked by every act which may define a Tyrant, is unfit to be the ruler of a free people. Nor have We been wanting in attentions to our Brittish brethren. We have warned them from time to time of attempts by their legislature to extend an unwarrantable jurisdiction over us. We have reminded them of the circumstances of our emigration and settlement here. We have appealed to their native justice and magnanimity, and we have conjured them by the ties of our common kindred to disavow these usurpations, which would inevitably interrupt our connections and correspondence. They too have been deaf to the voice of justice and of consanguinity. We must, therefore, acquiesce in the necessity, which denounces our Separation, and hold them, as we hold the rest of mankind, Enemies in War, in Peace Friends.—

WE, THEREFORE, the Representatives of the united States of America, in General Congress, Assembled, appealing to the Supreme Judge of the world for the rectitude of our intentions, do, in the Name, and by Authority of the good People of these Colonies, solemnly publish and declare, That these United Colonies are, and of Right ought to be FREE and INDEPENDENT STATES; that they are Absolved from all Allegiance to the British Crown, and that all political connection between them and the State of Great Britain, is and ought to be totally dissolved; and that as Free and Independent States, they have full Power to levy War, conclude Peace, contract Alliances, establish Commerce, and to do all other Acts and Things which Independent States may of right do.—And for the support of this Declaration, with a firm reliance on the protection of divine Providence, we mutually pledge to each other our Lives, our Fortunes and our sacred Honor.

Those who signed the declaration were:

Georgia:
Button Gwinnett
Lyman Hall
George Walton

North Carolina:
William Hooper
Joseph Hewes
John Penn

South Carolina:
Edward Rutledge
Thomas Heyward, Jr.
Thomas Lynch, Jr.
Arthur Middleton

Maryland:
Samuel Chase
William Paca
Thomas Stone
Charles Carroll
    of Carollton

Virginia:
George Wythe
Richard Henry Lee
Thomas Jefferson
Benjamin Harrison
Thomas Nelson, Jr.
Francis Lightfoot Lee
Carter Braxton

Pennsylvania:
Robert Morris
Benjamin Rush
Benjamin Franklin
John Morton
George Clymer
James Smith
George Taylor
James Wilson
George Ross

Delaware:
Caesar Rodney
George Read
Thomas McKean

New York:
William Floyd
Philip Livingston
Francis Lewis
Lewis Morris

New Jersey:
Richard Stockton
John Witherspoon
Francis Hopkinson
John Hart
Abraham Clark

New Hampshire:
Josiah Bartlett
William Whipple
Matthew Thornton

Massachusetts:
John Hancock
Samuel Adams
John Adams
Robert Treat Paine
Elbridge Gerry

Rhode Island:
Stephen Hopkins
William Ellery

Connecticut:
Roger Sherman
Samuel Huntington
William Williams
Oliver Wolcott

List of Presidents and Vice Presidents - 1788 to 1892

Election Year	Years Served	President	Vice President	Party
1788/1792	1789-1797	George Washington	John Adams	none
1796	1797-1801	John Adams	Thomas Jefferson	Federalist
1800	1801-1809	Thomas Jefferson	Aaron Burr	Democratic-Republican
1804			George Clinton	Democratic-Republican
1808	1809-1817	James Madison	George Clinton	Democratic-Republican
1812			Elbridge Gerry	Democratic-Republican
1816/1820	1817-1825	James Monroe	Daniel D. Tompkins	Democratic-Republican
1824	1825-1829	John Quincy Adams	John C. Calhoun	Democratic-Republican
1828	1829-1837	Andrew Jackson	John C. Calhoun	Democrat
1832			Martin Van Buren	Democrat
1836	1837-1841	Martin Van Buren	Richard M. Johnson	Democrat
1840	1841	William Harrison	John Tyler	Whig
	1841-1845	John Tyler	none	Whig
1844	1845-1849	James Polk	George Dallas	Democrat
1848	1849-1850	Zachary Taylor	Millard Fillmore	Whig
	1850-1853	Millard Fillmore	none	Whig
1852	1853-1857	Franklin Pierce	William King	Democrat
1856	1857-1861	James Buchanan	John C. Breckinridge	Democrat
1860	1861-1865	Abraham Lincoln	Hannibal Hamlin	Republican
1864			Andrew Johnson	Republican
	1865-1869	Andrew Johnson	none	Union
1868	1869-1877	Ulysses S. Grant	Schuyler Colfax	Republican
1872			Henry Wilson	Republican
1876	1877-1881	Rutherford B. Hayes	William Wheeler	Republican
1880	1881	James Garfield	Chester Arthur	Republican
	1881-1885	Chester Arthur	none	Republican
1884	1885-1889	Grover Cleveland	Thomas Hendricks	Democrat
1888	1889-1893	Benjamin Harrison	Levi P. Morton	Republican
1892	1893-1897	Grover Cleveland	Adlai Stevenson	Democrat

List of Presidents and Vice Presidents - 1896 to 2008

Election Year	Years Served	President	Vice President	Party
1896	1897-1901	William McKinley	Garret Hobart	Republican
			Theodore Roosevent	Republican
1900	1901-1909	Theodore Roosevent	none	Republican
1904			Charles Fairbanks	Republican
1908	1909-1913	William Howard Taft	James Sherman	Republican
1912/1916	1913-1921	Woodrow Wilson	Thomas R. Marshall	Democrat
1920	1921-1923	Warren Harding	Calvin Coolidge	Republican
	1923-1929	Calvin Coolidge	none	Republican
1924			Charles Dawes	Republican
1928	1929-1933	Herbert Hoover	Charles Curtis	Republican
1932	1933-1945	Franklin D. Roosevelt	John Nance Garner	Democrat
1936			Henry Wallace	Democrat
1940			Harry S. Truman	Democrat
1944	1945-1953	Harry S. Truman	none	Democrat
1948			Alben Barkley	Democrat
1952/1956	1953-1961	Dwight D. Eisenhower	Richard Nixon	Republican
1960	1961-1963	John F. Kennedy	Lyndon B. Johnson	Democrat
	1963-1969	Lyndon B. Johnson	none	Democrat
1964			Hubert Humphrey	Democrat
1968	1969-1974	Richard Nixon	Spiro Agnew	Republican
			Gerald Ford	Republican
1972	1974-1977	Gerald Ford	none	Republican
			Nelson Rockefeller	Republican
1976	1977-1981	Jimmy Carter	Walter Mondale	Democrat
1980/1984	1981-1989	Ronald Reagan	George Bush	Republican
1988	1989-1993	George Bush	Dan Quayle	Republican
1992/1996	1993-2001	Bill Clinton	Al Gore	Democrat
2000/2004	2001-2009	George W. Bush	Dick Cheney	Republican
2008	2009-?	Barack Obama	Joe Biden	Democrat

The Star-Spangled Banner

1. Oh,   say! can you see,   by the dawn's ear - ly   light,
2. On the shore, dim - ly   seen through the mists of the   deep,
3. Oh,   thus be it ever when   free men shall stand

What so   proud - ly we hailed at the   twi - light's last gleam - ing,
Where the   foe's haugh - ty   host in dread si - lence re - pos - es,
Be -   tween their loved homes and the   war's des - o - la - tion!

Whose broad stripes and bright stars, through the   per - i - lous   fight,
What is   that which the breeze, o'er the   tow - er - ing   steep,
Blest with   vic - t'ry and peace, may the   heav'n-res - cued   land

O'er the   ram - parts we watched were so gal - lant - ly stream - ing?
As it   fit - ful - ly   blows, half con - ceals, half dis - clos - es?
Praise the Pow'r that hath made and pre - served us a   na - tion!

And the rock-ets' red glare, the bombs burst-ing in air, Gave
Now it catch-es the gleam of the morn-ing's first beam, In full
Then con-quer we must, when our cause it is just, And

proof through the night that our flag was still there. Oh,
glo - ry re - flected now shines on the stream. 'Tis the
this be our motto: "In God is our trust." And the

say, does that Star - Span - gled Ban - ner yet wave
Star - Span - gled Ban - ner, oh, long may it wave
Star - Span - gled Ban - ner in tri - umph shall wave

O'er the land of the free and the home of the brave?
O'er the land of the free and the home of the brave!
O'er the land of the free and the home of the brave.

Index

Housing and Urban Development, Department of, 192

Immigration, 184, 218-229
    Act of 1965, 223
    Act of 1990, 226
    attitudes toward, 222
    contributions of, 221
    control of, 222-226
    evaluation of, 227-229
    homelands, 220, 221 (chart)
    laws, 102, 184
    "new," 219-220
    "old," 218-219
    quota system, 223-227
    reasons for, 218, 228 (chart)
    Reform and Control Act of 1986, 224
    Service, 184, 232-233
    sources of, 220, 221 (table)
Immunity, political, 70
Impeachment, 61-64, 97
Incorporated communities, 159
Indians, *See Native Americans.*
Indictment, 116, 173
Initiative, 145
Inquest, 156
Interior, Department of, 91, 186
Internal Revenue Service, *127*, 181-182
Intolerable Acts, 33

Jackson, Andrew, *71*, 94, 195, 254
Jefferson, Thomas, 36, 86, 94, 132, 254
Jeopardy, double, 116-118
John (King), 22-24
Johnson, Andrew, *64*, 254
Johnson, Lyndon B., *89*, *93*, 134, 223, 224, 255
Joint Chiefs of Staff, 183
Judges, 100
Judicial branch, 57
    federal, 93-94, 98-104, 116-117
    jurisdiction, 100-102
    local, 101 (chart), 116-119, 171-174
    state, 42, 101 (chart), 116-119, 147-148
Judicial review, 102
Junkets, 69
Justice, 170-178
    balance with liberty, 176
    definition of, 170-171
    Department of, 183-185
    of the peace, 159, 171
    provided for, 171

Kennedy, John F., *89*, 108, 115, 134, 255
Kennedy, Robert F., 115

Key, Francis Scott, *xv-xvi*
King, Martin Luther, Jr., 115

Labor
    Department of, 189-190
    organizations, 67, 142
    Statistics, Bureau of, 189
Laissez-faire, concept of, 12
"Lame duck," 130
Land Management, Bureau of, 186
Land Ordinance of 1785, 157
Large state plan, 47
Law, due process of, 117, 123
Law enforcement, 10, 11, 42
    county, 152 (chart), 153-156, 154 (chart)
    federal, 96-97, 184-185
    local, 42, 159, 162-164 (charts)
    state, 147
Laws, 57-58
    enactment of, 71-74
    ex post facto, 82-83
"League of Friendship," 32
Lee, Richard Henry, 35-36
Legislative bills, 68-69, 71-74
Legislative branch, 57
    county, 154
    federal, 47-48, 59-84, 95-96, 110, 124-131, 176
    local, 157, 162-164
    state, 42, 143-146
Legislatures
    federal, 47-48, 59-64, 95-96, 124-128, 130
    Idaho, *143*
    state, 143-46
    types of, 47-48
Leisure time, 246
Letters of marque and reprisal, 78-79, 83
Libel, 114
Liberty, 170-171, 178, 198
    balance with justice, 176
    definition of, 170
    provided for, 171
Lincoln, Abraham, 125, 179, 254
Liquor
    industry, 142
    prohibition of, 128-29
    repeal of prohibition, 131-32
Literacy, 15, 126-127, 213, 223, 231
Livingston, Robert, 36
Lobbying, 67
Local government, 153-168
    cities, 159-165, *166-67*, 172
    in the colonies, 29-30
    incorporated communities, 159, 171-172